Dust

∾

CAROLYN STEEDMAN

Manchester University Press

Copyright © Carolyn Steedman 2001

The right of Carolyn Steedman to be identified as the author of this work
has been asserted by her in accordance with the Copyright, Designs and
Patents Act 1988.

Published by Manchester University Press
Oxford Road, Manchester M13 9NR, UK
and Room 400, 175 Fifth Avenue, New York, NY 10010, USA
www.manchesteruniversitypress.co.uk

Distributed exclusively in the USA by
Palgrave, 175 Fifth Avenue, New York NY 10010, USA

Distributed exclusively in Canada by
UBC Press, University of British Columbia, 2029 West Mall,
Vancouver, BC, Canada V6T 1Z2

British Library Cataloguing-in-Publication Data
A catalogue record for this book is available from the British Library

Library of Congress Cataloging-in-Publication Data
A catalog record for this book is available from the Library of Congress

ISBN-10: 0 7190 6015 X

ISBN-13: 978 0 7190 6015 1

First published 2001 by Manchester University Press

First digital, on-demand edition produced by Lightning Source 2006

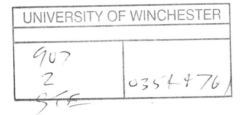

Contents

	Acknowledgements	*page* vii
	Preface	ix
1	In the archon's house	1
2	'Something she called a fever': Michelet, Derrida and dust	17
3	The magistrates	38
4	The space of memory: in an archive	66
5	To Middlemarch: without benefit of archive	89
6	What a rag rug means	112
7	About ends: on how the end is different from an ending	142
8	The story of the dust	157
	Bibliography	171
	Index	192

So with the house empty and the doors locked and the mattresses rolled round, those stray airs, advance guards of great armies, blustered in, brushed bare boards, nibbled and fanned, met nothing in bedroom or drawing-room that wholly resisted them but only hangings that flapped, wood that creaked, the bare legs of tables, saucepans and china already furred, tarnished, cracked. What people had shed and left – a pair of shoes, a shooting cap, some faded skirts and coats in wardrobes – these alone kept the human shape and the emptiness indicated how once they were filled and animated; how once hands were busy with hooks and buttons; how once the looking glass had held a face; had held a world hallowed out in which a figure turned, a hand flashed, the door opened, in came children, rushing and tumbling; and went out again. (Virginia Woolf, *To the Lighthouse*, Harmondsworth, Penguin, [1929] 1975, 147.)

Acknowledgements

Here is a reworking and rewriting of several published articles and unpublished papers. A version of Chapter 7 'About Ends: On How the End is Different from an Ending' appeared in *History of the Human Sciences*, 9: 4 (November 1996), 99–114. Chapter 4, 'The Space of Memory: in an Archive', appeared in pretty much the form in which it is included here, in the same journal: 11:4 (1998), 65–83. The Editor of *History of the Human Sciences*, the late Irving Velody was the progenitor of both these, and I dedicate this book to his memory. 'What a Rag Rug Means' was written for Inga Bryden and Janet Floyd's edited collection *Domestic Space. Reading the Nineteenth-century Interior* (Manchester, Manchester University Press, 1999), 18–39. Another version appeared in the *Journal of Material Culture*, 3:3 (1998), 259–81. Parts of Chapter 3 appeared as 'Enforced Narratives. Stories of Another Self', in Tess Cosslett, Celia Lury and Penny Summerfield (eds), *Feminism and Autobiography. Texts, Theories, Methods* (London, Routledge, 2000), pp. 25–39. Portions of 'In the Archon's House' and 'Something She Called a Fever' appeared in the *American Historical Review*, 106:4 (2001). A version of Chapter 5 appeared in the *Michigan Quarterly Review*, 40:3 (2001), both of them (this and that) the result of a salutory experience, of reworking a lecture for a University of Michigan audience that had not, in any of its parts, just driven along the A45, had not seen the cheery hoarding announcing the Middlemarch

Business Park, and thus did not have a ready key for reading George Eliot's novel against the Warwick Plot.

The University of Michigan (this time around, the Advanced Study Centre) showed me an extraordinary generosity (which I fear I have grown used to) in September 2000, when I did most of the work of turning these pieces into a book. The generosity included the work of Laura Cunniff, who by just going out and finding things I had mislaid, made new pathways through this material. I hope she recognises her contribution to bookmaking out of bricolage. I had already talked often and long to my readers of drafts of this book, in particular to those who read the material that ended up in *The American Historical Review*. I owe a good deal to the efforts of John Bowen, Charlotte Brunsden, Colin Jones, Bertrand Taithe, James Vernon, and to three anonymous reviewers for the *AHR*. They will notice however, that through its several transmutations, I took to ignoring those who urged on me a more respectful attitude towards Derrida, and to following those who said it made them laugh, on the grounds (that are later explained) that nothing should ever stop anyone doing a Hester Thrale. New readers may care to be warned that although Derrida's speculations on 'Archive Fever' (Mal d'archive) open this book – the translation of his 'mal' as 'fever' is its necessary device – it neither promises nor delivers an engagement with his thought.

The idea for a book came from Bertrand Taithe, one of the editors of the series 'Encounters' that is here launched by it. We both thought that when welded together, these pieces would make an argument for the Archive and the recent 'turn to the archive' in the human sciences. But – the familiar acknowledgement of the historian who sets out to find what isn't actually there – that's not what this turns out to be. It is – as the Preface discusses – about the practice and writing of history, in the modern period.

Preface

So it turned out not to be about the archival turn. It is about dust. Dust is the immutable, obdurate set of beliefs about the material world, past and present, inherited from the nineteenth century, with which modern history-writing attempts to grapple; Dust is also the narrative principle of that writing; and Dust is the joke.

The Archive in which Dust is found and with which this book also deals, is a particular kind of archive, instituted by state (or quasi-state) organisations since the late eighteenth century, in England and France. These are the archives used by social and cultural historians like myself, and a small and parochial example of a longer and larger collection of the documents of world history, by churches and temples, schools and colleges, monarchs, princes and other kinds of absolutist ruler, and departments of government, within and without Europe, long before the eighteenth century. In a proper and expanded definition of 'archive' this system of recording (listing, in particular), storage and retrieval, is an aspect of the history of written language, and the politics of that history.[1] The modern, public (French and English) archives discussed here were inaugurated simultaneously with a right of public access to their holdings, so while they have been a reference point for political, economic and social history writing from the nineteenth century onwards, non-historians have probably always been the majority of their users.

But the religious and state archives of Europe and North America and their more local records of government and administration were (and still are) evoked in order to describe what it is a historian does and what it is she writes out of that activity, whenever the historical profession is presented to outsiders or to its apprentices. Students are told about the many types and varieties of repository and record office, and the fragmentary, incomplete material they contain; they are told about 'the cult of archive' among certain historians and those sad creatures who fetishise them; they are warned about the seductions of the archive, the 'entrancing stories' that they contain, which do the work of the seducer. They are sternly told that an entrancing story is a quite different thing from the historical analysis that deploys it.[2] In short, they listen to the kind of professional self-presentation that has been common in northern Europe since the mid-nineteenth century; modern students of the discipline are introduced to the idea of an engagement with documentary evidence, collected together in a particular kind of place, as a foundational and paradigmatic activity of historians.[3]

This is done despite the obvious fact that many modern historians simply never use the kind of archives that are the focus of this book and that provide the majority of its examples. There are historians of the ancient world (many ancient worlds), archaeologists, those who work exclusively with printed sources, historians of art and artefacts, oral historians, and many forced by geographical distance and penury (institutional and personal) to rely on microfilm copies of documents, who have never set foot in a départementale or national archive, nor a county or public record office. These many historians (perhaps the majority of actually existing historians, if we take historians end to end and measure their collectivity by the yard) have never taken part in the activity that has been figured as archetypal since academic, professional, 'scientific' history inaugurated itself a century and a half ago, and which provides the persistent image of this book: of a figure solemnly hunched over a list of names, compiled a long time ago for a purpose quite different from the historian's, he or she in determined pursuit of one of the lost ones.[4] This is an odd way of being in the world, and a type of activity that has given rise to a particular form of writing, whose practitioners believe to be about what *is not* as much as what has been found; a form of writing which celebrates the constraints on it, constraints which – so it is said – are made by the documents themselves: what they forbid you to write, the permissions they offer.

All of this is to say that there are many kinds of historian, who do not undertake the kind of social history that is the focus of this book, and who may wish to exclaim in protest at the use of 'we': 'speak for yourself!' (Which is what I have done.)

Notes

1 'All their [the Aztecs'] achievements were doomed to oblivion by the Spanish conquest … For good measure they burned their victim's entire archives, so that all that has come down to us is three Maya manuscripts and some fifteen Aztec texts.' Henri-Jean Martin, *The History and the Power of Writing* (Chicago, Chicago University Press, [1994] 1998), p. 26. Throughout the notes to all chapters, [1994] is the date of original publication, 1998 the edition being cited.

2 Ludmilla Jordanova, *History in Practice* (London, Arnold, 2000), pp. 186–9.

3 Richard Evans, *In Defence of History* (London, Granta, 1997) for a recent example.

4 Jacques Rancière, *The Names of History. On the Poetics of Knowledge* (Minneapolis, University of Minnesota Press, [1992] 1994).

In the archon's house

IN THE SUMMER of 1994, Jacques Derrida presented a paper to a London conference convened to discuss the topic of 'Memory: The Question of Archives'. He delivered the English-language version of *Mal d'archive: une impression freudienne* on a major occasion of what many came to call (after him, and after this conference) 'archivisation'.[1] In the opening stretches of 'Archive Fever' (the title in English translation), Derrida presented his audience with the image of the *arkhe*, as a place where things begin, where power originates, its workings inextricably bound up with the authority of beginnings and starting points. The *arkhe* figured in a brief account of the Greek city state, as Derrida pointed to its official documents, stored in the *arkheion*, the superior magistrate's residence. There, the magistrate, the *archon* himself, exercised the power of those documents of procedure and precedence, in his right to interpret them, for the operation of a system of law.

In Derrida's description, the *arkhe* – the archive – appears to represent the *now* of whatever kind of power is being exercised, anywhere, in any place or time. It represents a principle that in Derrida's words, is 'in the order of commencement as well as in the order of commandment' (9). The fever, or sickness of the archive is to do with its very establishment, which is at one and the same time, the establishment of state power and authority.[2] And then there is the feverish desire – a kind of sickness unto death – that

Derrida indicated, *for* the archive: the fever not so much to enter it and use it, as to *have* it, or just for it to be there, in the first place.

For those historians who heard or read 'Archive Fever', it raised the puzzling question of what on earth an archive was doing there (in the first place) at the beginning of a long description of another text (someone else's text, not Derrida's) that dealt, as he too would at length, with the topics of Sigmund Freud and psycho-analysis. There was a further puzzlement (or more accurately, a bemusement feigned to mask a kind of *artisant* irritation) among those who knew the 'archival turn' to be well underway by 1994, with Derrida merely (though compellingly) providing a theoretical perspective on the institution of archives, the practices of reading and writing attendant on them, and the systems of regulation and coercion they have (sometimes) underlined.[3] Moreover, Michel Foucault had raised the 'question of the archive' as early as the 1960s. In *The Archeology of Knowledge* the archive does not so much stand in for the idea of what can and cannot be said, but rather *is* 'the system that establishes statements as events and things'.[4] Antoinette Burton reminds us that it was also in the 1960s that Foucault described the magical qualities of archives, their ability to function as 'a reflection that shows us quite simply, and in shadow, what all those in the foreground are looking at', the way in which the archive restores 'as if by magic, what is lacking in every gaze'.[5] In the image of the *arkhe* presented to the audience in the Freud House on that day in June 1994, some may also have seen the surfacing, or coming into focus, of an intermittent dialogue between Foucault and Derrida on these very topics: the archive as a way of seeing, or a way of knowing; the archive as a symbol or form of power.[6]

Some listeners and readers of 'Archive Fever' – sad fetishists and social historians in particular – were aware of a new politics of the archive in which Derrida's account was bound to find its place. In the 1990s battle between the ancients and the post-moderns –

between the old social history and the new cultural history – social historians had turned their attention to the archive, claimed it as their very own place, in which they were more at home than any other kind of historian. Burton suggests that taking it into their protective custody in this way, making it the very symbol of their authenticity, they downplayed or even denied what she has called 'the shifting fortunes' of the discipline[7]

For the main part Derrida's 'Archive Fever' is not about archives at all, but is rather a sustained contemplation of a work of history, of Yosef HayimYerushalmi's *Freud's Moses. Judaism Terminable and Interminable* (1991). As a historian of Sephardic Jewry with a strong interest in questions of memory, Yerushalmi came, by way of his participation in a psycho-analytic study group on anti-semitism, to reading Freud's *Moses and Monotheism.* In its pages, Yerushalmi encountered Freud as a historian, or at least (in Freud's own formulation) someone who had produced a 'historical novel', or a kind of historical story, in order to understand the period of baroque anti-semitism through which he was living.

Derrida had long seen in Freudian psycho-analysis a desire to recover moments of inception, beginnings and origins which – in a deluded way – we think might be some kind of truth, and in 'Archive Fever', desire for the archive is presented as part of the desire to find, or locate, or possess that moment of origin, as the beginning of things. Yerushalmi's book, concerned as it is with the traces and marks of Judaism on psycho-analysis (and indeed, with Judaism as its origin, or progenitor), is vehicle for further examination of this theme. Yerushalmi's is a speculative account of Freud's writing of *Moses and Monotheism,* though not half as speculative as is the text itself, which is famously based on no historical evidence whatsoever. Yerushalmi on the other hand, had a fairly complete account of the process of its composition, from correspondence about it, from a hitherto unnoted draft (obtained with astonishing ease from the Freud Archive at the Library of Congress) and from the context within which Freud wrote, retrieved from newspaper files and a more general socio-political history of the rise of Nazism in central Europe. Yerushalmi's overall purpose in the book is to get Freud to admit that psycho-analysis is a Jewish science: the final chapter takes the form of a monologue, addressed directly to the dead author.[8] The 'impression' of Derrida's subtitle is the imprint of Judaism and 'the Jewish science' on Yerushalmi, and indeed on Derrida himself. But the signs and traces that Freud dealt in, and the particular mark that is circumcision, constitute a kind of archive that Derrida seemed to believe most historians would not be interested in.

The *archon* and his *arkheion* allowed Derrida some commonplace speculation about the future of the archive, as the register, ledger and letter are replaced by e-mail and the computer file.[9] They also prompted some pertinent discussion of the politics of various kinds of modern repository (anyone who had read Yerushalmi's book might have been reminded of the furore of the 1980s over notorious restrictions of access to the Freud Archive).[10] Many kinds of repository were strapped together here, in the portmanteau term 'the archive', as Derrida considered their limits and limitations, their denials and secrets. Indeed, the *arkhe* appeared to lose much of its connection to the idea of a place where official documents are stored for administrative reference, and became a metaphor capacious enough to encompass the whole of modern information technology, its storage, retrieval and communication. These opening sections of 'Archive Fever' are the one that have been most taken up and commented on, in the English-speaking world, since 1994.[11] Ann Laura Stoler notes the figurative status of 'the Archive' in cultural theory which, by employing Derrida's observations on that June afternoon in 1994, has forged a powerful metaphor for the processes of collecting traces of the past, and for the forgetting of them.[12] This book repeats a strange move, which is to concentrate on what Derrida did not say, on that which was not the focus of his attention. 'The history of the archive is a history of loss' says Antoinette Burton, but in this case there has been a move into some place beyond, or outwith loss: a very great assiduity of attention to looking for and finding what wasn't there, in Derrida's text.[13]

The setting in which Derrida delivered the very first 'Archive Fever' explains to some extent what on earth an archive was doing there, as the prolegomenon to a discussion of psycho-analysis, and a return to the questions he first raised about it, in the late 1960s.[14] In a substantial family house in Maresfield Gardens, in the Freuds' home in exile, Derrida looks up from the word-processed text from which he read (he makes much in 'Archive Fever', of the 'little portable Macintosh on which I have begun to write' [22]) and says:

> It is thus … that archives take place … This place where they dwell permanently, marks this institutional passage from the private to the public … It is what is happening, right here, when a house, the Freuds' last house, becomes a museum: the passage from one institution to another. (10)

The immediacy of that archive – an archive in process, taking place at that moment – seems to have forced a beginning to a conference presentation and a book, at the same time as it reiterated arguments that Derrida had been making for thirty years, about the Western obsession with finding beginnings, starting places, and origins.[15] 'Archive Fever' explores the relationship between memory and writing (in its widest meaning, of recording and making marks), and Freud's own attempts to find adequate metaphors for representing memory. Derrida sees in Freud's writing the very desire that *is* Archive Fever: the desire to recover moments of inception: to find and possess all sorts of beginnings.

∿ 5

The etymology of Derrida's opening passages is given to us with the accompanying and paradoxical assertion about words ('archive', 'arkhe', 'arkheion', 'archon') as origins: 'Let us not begin at the beginning,' he says, 'nor even at the archive. But rather at the word "archive".' What 'archive' may be doing there *at all* then, is the work of meditating, on starting places, on beginnings, the search for which, because it is impossible, Derrida names as a sickness, a movement towards death. Moreover, he reiterated here, to want to make an archive in the first place, is to want to *repeat*, and one of Freud's clearest lessons was that the compulsion to repeat is the drive towards death.[16] And the puzzling etymological prolegomenon may also be seen as one more example of the textual techniques exercised in Derrida's philosophy. The binary oppositions that underpin Western metaphysics can be made to shift, by inflating a concept so that it joins up with its supposed opposite, thereby demonstrating that – there is no opposition at all. This is a procedure seen at work most clearly in Derrida's attention to the topic of writing. By insisting that 'writing' includes all signs, traces, mnemonic devices, inscriptions and marks – by thus interrogating the word 'writing' in order to release it from the empirical understanding that is held in place by the usual opposition between 'speech' and 'writing' we are – perhaps – led to understand that it *includes* its opposite, 'speech', and that the distinction between the two (and all sorts of distinction) may be thought right through, all the way to the other side.[17] 'Archive' is thus inflated to mean – if not quite Everything – then at least, all the ways and means of state power; Power itself, perhaps, rather than those quietly folded and filed documents that we think provide the mere and incomplete records of some of its inaugural moments.

We are often told to note the rhetorical structure of Derrida's writing, as being at least as important as its argument; but the structure of 'Archive Fever' is odd indeed. In a quite calculated way, it refuses to begin its discussion of beginnings (or not-beginnings), for all the world as if it were a primer offering instruction in the principle of deferral. We have (in the English-language version) something untitled, which is an introduction (three pages). Then there is an 'Exergue', which occupies eight pages.[18] He comments on it, on his own use of 'a proven convention' that 'plays with citation' and that gives both order and orders to what follows. 'What is at issue here', he says 'starting with the exergue, is the violence of the archive itself, *as archive,* as *archival violence*'.(12) In fact, there are three *exergues,* numbered and laid out as separate sections. Then there is a Preamble (three pages), a Foreword (twenty-six pages), Theses (three of them, occupying seven pages in total), and finally, a Postscript (two pages). There is and always will be, it seems, trouble in getting started and finished.

The Foreword carries the main argument, about Freud's Jewishness, and the contribution of Jewish though to the idea of the archive, via psycho-analysis. The archive is a record of the past, at the same time as it points to the future. The grammatical tense of the archive is thus the future perfect, 'when it will have been'. Perhaps, says Derrida, Freud's contribution to any theory of the archive is that there isn't one: that no storehouse, especially not the psycho-analytic archive of the human psyche, holds the records of an original experience, to which we may return. Yet psycho-analysis has been responsible for some of this trouble with archives, for it wants to *get back*: it manifests a desire for origins, to find the place where things started, before the regime of repetition and representation was inaugurated.

In the French book-version of 'Archive Fever' there is also inserted a loose-leaf notice that is three pages long, headed 'Prière d'insérer' (in my library copy it is placed behind the title page and before an explanatory note about the Freud Museum conference). This makes much clearer than can be done in English the questions of social evil with which Derrida intended to deal in the body of the text. Here (the French *mal* does not mince its meaning) there are both archives (selected and collected rememberings and forgettings) *and* also the political disasters of the late twentieth century, which are named as archives of *evil*:

> Les désastres qui marquent cette fin de millénaire, ce sont aussi des *archives du mal*: dissimulées ou détruites, interdites, détournées, 'refoulées'. Leur traitement est à la fois massif et raffiné au cours de guerres civiles ou internationales, de manipulations privées ou secrètes.[19]

Derrida broods on revisionist histories that have been written out of these 'archives du mal' (a shadow of a suggestion here, then, that it is not archives *at all* that he has in his sights, but rather, what gets written out of archives: formal, academic history); but he broods as well on never giving up on the hope of getting proof of the past, even though documentary evidence may be locked away and suppressed. He emphasises again the institution of archives as the expression of state power. And he appears to urge a distinction between actual archives (official places for the reception of records, with systems of storage, organisation, cataloguing) and what we all too frequently reduce them to: memory, the desire for origins, 'la recherche du temps perdu'. 'Prière d'insérer' also makes plainer the relationship between psycho-analysis and archival practice that is explored in the main text. Psycho-analysis ought to revolutionise archival questions, dealing as it does with the repression *and* reading of records, and because of the privileged place it is supposed to give to all marks and traces made on the body and the mind (though there is the distinct suggestion here that it does nothing of the sort). Above all, this brief insertion makes it clear that in *Mal d'archive* Derrida will deal not only with a feverish – sick – search for origins, not only with archives of evil, but with 'le mal radical', with evil itself. The two intertwined threads of argument to follow in the main body of the text, about psycho-analysis and Yerushalmi's questioning of Freud's Jewishness, underpin a history of the twentieth century that is indeed, a history of horror. To say the very least, if you read in English, without the insert and with the restricted, monovalent, archaic – and, because archaic, faintly comic – 'fever' of the English translation, rather than with 'mal' (trouble, misfortune, pain, hurt, sickness, wrong, sin, badness, malice, evil …) you will read rather differently from a reader of the French version.[20]

Many English-speaking readers – this one, too – have assumed that 'Archive Fever' has something to do with archives (rather than with psycho-analysis, or memory, or finding things); and even when the reaction has been more philosophical, Derrida has been addressed through his *archon* and the *arkheion*.[21] But commentators have found remarkably little to say about record offices, libraries and repositories, and have been brought face to face with the *ordinariness*, the unremarkable nature of archives, and the everyday disappointments that historians know they will find there. There is a surprise in some of these reactions, at encountering something far less portentous, difficult and meaningful than Derrida's archive would seem to promise.[22]

As might be expected of an experience that is an important professional rite of passage, no one historian's archive is ever like another's (let alone like Jacques Derrida's). Each account of his or her experience within them will always produce counter narratives, of different kinds of discomfort. The English translation of *Mal d'archive* makes Archive Fever an aspect of origins fever; the fever described in Chapter 2 is one that might actually be contracted in the dust of an archive. And this actual fever (Archive Fever Proper) will turn out to be only one more item in the litany of complaints that historians have drawn up, in the deeply *uncomfortable* quest for original sources that the new practice of 'scientific' history inaugurated, in the middle of the nineteenth century, and which is till the dominant idea of practice among modern, professional, Western historians.[23] Bonnie Smith has described these moans and groans: 'the indignities' endured by Eugène Burnouf, for example, when searching out English manuscript sources in the 1830s; the 'sleepless nights … hard beds, "sad collections of meat and vegetables cooked in water"', horrible food, people wearing horrible clothes, desperate social encounters with fellow historians who live in the provincial towns where records are kept, their sad and dispirited wives. (As the gender of history and historical practice has changed, and women have set out on their own campaigns to release '"those many princesses, possibly beautiful"', which are the languishing records awaiting their rescuer, we must add to this list of the social terrors involved in archive work, the sad and dispirited husbands of provincial historians.)[24] Any one else's archive can always make the historian expostulate: 'Archive Fever indeed! *I* can tell you *all about* the archive.'

In a parody (but not *quite* a parody) of empirical doggedness, we shall cling to the coat-tails of one figure of Derrida, one image, *one literal meaning* of 'fever' (which wasn't even a word that was there to start with), and find not only a different kind of sickness, but also the magistrate who is actually present in his text, though wrongly named. There is always a pleasure as a reader in finding something that the writer did not know was there (or that he has hidden, deep in its crevices and cracks); and in this case, there is a particular pleasure in wilfully asserting of a text so intimately connected by its authorship to the practice of deconstruction, that there *is* something there, *at all*, in the first place. Indeed, in one view, the practice of history in its modern mode is just one long exercise of the deep satisfaction of *finding things*.[25]

The joke – the form of the joke – structures what follows here. There is the calculated naivety involved in the literal interpretation of a trope, in the insistence on finding both the Archive and the

Fever in 'Archive Fever': of missing the point, in order to make another one. The point is to raise a laugh, not only at the presumption involved in doing any such thing, but also, at the end, to raise serious doubts about whether the medical condition of 'archive fever', so carefully pathologised in the following pages, has ever been experienced by anyone, especially by she who claims it. I want to laugh at my pretensions (indeed, so that I may cut the ground from under the feet of those who bring that charge), and to make others laugh. That laughter would be no criticism of Derrida (part of the point is to miss his), but rather an acknowledgement of what he showed in *Mal d'archive*: that if we find nothing, we will find nothing in a place; and then, that an absence is not *nothing*, but is rather the space left by what has gone: how the emptiness indicates how once it was filled and animated. Although 'Archive Fever' may have nothing at all to do with archives and the attendant practices of history, Derrida showed us a *place* in *Mal d'archive*, a building, with an inside and outside, which is often a house (occasionally a home). He suggested that in an archive we are under some kind of house arrest. These points are made – this taxonomy of the archive develops – out of the longings and seductions with which Derrida does deal, under different titles, using different names.

In one of his more cheerful discussions, Freud described the benignity of humour, and the comfort and support it offers us in the vicissitudes of life.[26] Much earlier, in the more renowned 'Jokes and their Relationship to the Unconscious', he had made plain the very great pleasures made available by *seeing* the absurdity of the world's dislocations: the charming unexpectedness of knowing oneself part of the effect produced, when time and event miss a beat, stumble; and then the restoration of their timing.[27] When Hayden White discussed nineteenth-century history writing in its comic mode, he did not attribute to Leopold von Ranke, for example, the ability to provoke an 'intensity of pleasure', that found 'vent in hearty laughter'.[28] Rather, by making reference to the literary form of the comic, he drew attention to the resolution that Ranke achieved in his depiction of events: his achievement of harmonious endings. In Freud's account, humour is a kinder thing than the joke. He speculated that it might indeed be the super-ego speaking, offering kindly words of comfort to the intimidated ego, in the language of a good and protective parent: 'Look! Here is the world, which seems so dangerous. It is nothing but a game for children – just worth making a jest about!' But if Derrida's *Mal d'archive* provokes that more serious thing, which is a joke, it is because the shade of the history writing that haunts its pages is – really – no laughing matter. In this light then, if there is laughter, it will be some kind of homage, or at the very least, a recognition, of what it is that has been revealed.

Notes

1 Page references in the text above are to the English-language version of *Mal d'archive* published in the journal *Diacritics*. Jacques Derrida, 'Archive Fever. A Freudian Impression', *Diacritics*, 25:2 (1995), 9–63. Written (word-processed) in French in May 1994 (every version mentioned below is most precise about the dates of composition and indeed, the machine on which it was composed), this English-language version translated by Eric Prenowitz then appeared in book form a year later: Jacques Derrida, *Archive Fever. A Freudian Impression* (Chicago, Chicago University Press, 1996). The French version appeared in 1995: *Mal d'archive: une impression freudienne* (Paris, Editions Galilée, 1995). All of these appear to have had their origin in the piece written for the June conference, which was organised by the Société International d'Histoire de la Psychiatrie et de la Psychoanalyse and the Freud Museum. At that point, the paper was called 'The Concept of the Archive: A Freudian Impression'.

2 That the inauguration of modern national archives is intimately bound up with the development of European nation states has long

been recognised. See Jacques Le Goff, *History and Memory* (New York, Columbia University Press, [1977] 1992), 87–9. Carolyn Steedman, 'The Space of Memory: In an Archive', *History of the Human Sciences*, 11:4 (1998), 65–83. The colonial archive has been much scrutinised as a source of imperial power. See for example, Christopher Bayley, *Empire and Information: Intelligence Gathering and Social Communication in India, 1780–1870* (Cambridge, Cambridge University Press, 1996); Nicholas Dirks, 'Colonial Histories and Native Informants: Biography of an Archive', in N. Dirks (ed.), *Colonialism and Culture* (Ann Arbor, University of Michigan Press, 1992), pp. 279–313. Indrani Chatterjee, 'Testing the Local Against the Colonial Archive', *History Workshop*, 44 (1997), 215–24.

3 Arlette Farge, *Le Goût de l'archive* (Paris, Editions du Seuil, 1989); Sonia Combe, *Archives Interdites. Les Peurs françaises face à l'histoire contemporaine* (Paris, Albin Michel, 1994); Roberto Gonzalez Enchevarria, *Myth and Archive. A Theory of Latin American Narrative* (Cambridge, Cambridge University Press, 1994); Richard Thomas, *The Imperial Archive. Knowledge and the Fantasy of Empire* (London Verso, 1990); Natalie Davis, *Fiction in the Archives. Pardon Tales and their Tellers in Sixteenth-century France* (Oxford, Polity, 1987).

4 Michel Foucault, *The Archeology of Knowledge* (London, Tavistock, [1969] 1972), pp. 79–131; James D. Faubion, *Michel Foucault. Aesthetics, Method and Epistemology. Essential Works of Foucault 1954–1984, 2* (New York, The New Press, 1998), pp. 289–90, 309–10.

5 Antoinette Burton, 'Thinking Beyond the Boundaries: Empire, Feminism and the Domains of History', *Social History* 26:1 (2001), 60–71. Michel Foucault, *The Order of Things. An Archeology of the Human Sciences* (New York, Vintage, [1966] 1973), p. 15.

6 Jacques Derrida, '"To Do Justice to Freud": The History of Madness in the Age of Psychoanalysis', in Arnold I. Davidson (ed.), *Foucault and His Interlocutors* (Chicago, University of Chicago Press, 1997), 57–96.

7 Burton, 'Thinking Beyond', pp. 66–7.

8 Yosef Hayim Yerushalmi, *Freud's Moses. Judaism Terminable and Interminable* (New York, Yale University Press, 1991). For the draft of *Moses and Monotheism* see pp. 3, 16–17, 101–3. For surprise at ease of access to this archive, see J.M. Masson, *The Assault on Truth. Freud's*

Suppression of the Seduction Theory (Harmondsworth, Penguin, 1985); and Janet Malcolm, *In the Freud Archives* (London, Macmillan, [1983] 1997), esp. pp. 19–21, 27–35.

9 For other such speculation, see Terry Cook, 'Electronic Records, Paper Minds: The Revolution in Information Management and Archives in the Post-custodial and Post-modernist Era', *Archives and Manuscripts*, 22:2 (1994), 300–29. See also Leonard Lawlor, 'Memory Becomes Electra', *Review of Politics*, 60:4 (1998), 796–8.

10 Janet Malcolm gives a summary account of this affair in *In the Freud Archives* and in the 'Postscript', which she wrote for the 1997 edition; see n. 8 above.

11 See 'Special Issue. The Archive', *History of the Human Sciences*, 11:4 (1998), and 'Special Issue. The Archive Part 2', *History of the Human Sciences*, 12:2 (1999).

12 Ann Laura Stoler, 'Colonial Archives and the Arts of Governance'. Paper presented to the 'Archives and Social Memory' Seminar, Institute of Advanced Studies, University of Michigan, September 2000. Leonard Lawlor discusses the 'fever to save ... and a fever to destroy', in Lawlor, 'Memory', p. 796.

13 Burton, 'Thinking Beyond', p. 66.

14 Jacques Derrida, 'Freud and the Scene of Writing', in *Writing and Difference*, trans. Alan Bass (London, Routledge & Kegan Paul, [1967] 1978), pp. 196–281. Jacques Derrida, *The Post Card: From Socrates to Freud and Beyond*, trans. Alan Bass (Chicago, University of Chicago Press, [1980] 1987). See Herman Rapaport, 'Archive Trauma', *Diacritics*, 28:4 (1998), 68–71, where we are asked to 'consider *The Post Card* [as] ... the displaced main act of *Archive Fever*'.

15 For origins fever, see Jacques Derrida, *Grammatology*, trans. Gayatri Chakravorty Spivak (Baltimore and London, Johns Hopkins University Press, [1967] 1976).

16 Expressed at many points during Freud's writing career, the clearest statement of the argument is to be found in 'Beyond the Pleasure Principle', *Standard Edition of the Complete Psychological Works of Sigmund Freud*, 18 (London, Hogarth Press, [1920] 1950), pp. 3–64.

17 Derrida, *Grammatology*, pp. 101–64 and passim.

18 The exergue is more common in French academic writing than in English, its literal meaning being the tiny space on a coin, below the

principal device, which is used either for the engraver's initials, or for the date. But in its scholarly use in France it connotes the *hors d'oeuvre*, rather than something that is integrated into the whole design, as are the initials or a date on a coin.

19 'The disasters which mark the end of the millennium, are also *archives of evil*: hidden or destroyed, forbidden, misappropriated, "repressed." Their usage is at once clumsy and refined, during civil or international wars, during private or secret intrigues.'

20 And with yet more difference if you read as a British speaker of English, for whom fever is something you have only after medical pronouncement, probably after being hospitalised (though babies can have a fever, domestically recognised by their parents). 'Running a temperature' is used to mean the everyday American–English 'fever', where the word is not comic and not archaic. In employing 'mal', Derrida bypassed the conventional term for describing a passion for the past. See Le Baron de Barante, *Etudes Historiques et Biographiques* (Paris, Didier, 4 vols, 1857), 2, p. 215, where he discusses 'cette fièvre historique, qui n'a pas encore produit ses effets' (this historical fever, which has not yet produced its effects).

21 See Christina Howells, *Derrida. Deconstruction from Phenomenology to Ethics* (Cambridge, Polity Press, 1999), pp. 112–16.

22 Few have been as plain-speaking as Tom Osborne is, in 'The Ordinariness of the Archive', *History of the Human Sciences*, 12:2 (1999), 51–64. See the other contributions to this issue of *History of the Human Sciences*, and also 11:4 (1998). Her publishers promoted Arlette Farge's extraordinary *Le Goût de l'archive* as an invitation to follow her 'dans son plaisir *quasi quotidienne* (italics mine) "d'aller aux archives"'. (In her almost daily pleasure "of going to the archives".)

23 Bonnie Smith, *The Gender of History. Men, Women and Historical Practice* (Cambridge, MA, Harvard University Press, 1998), pp. 118, 120–1.

24 Smith, *The Gender of History*, 118.

25 Christina Crosby, *The Ends of History. Victorians and 'The Woman Question'* (London and New York, Routledge, 1991), pp. 69–109.

26 Sigmund Freud, 'Humour', *Standard Edition of the Complete Psychological Works of Sigmund Freud*, 21 (London, Hogarth Press [1927] 1961), pp. 159–66.

27 Sigmund Freud, 'Jokes and their Relationship to the Unconscious', *Standard Edition of the Complete Psychological Works of Sigmund Freud*, 8 (London, Hogarth Press, [1905] 1960). See especially 'Jokes and the Species of the Comic', 181–236.

28 Hayden White, *Metahistory. The Historical Imagination in Nineteenth-century Europe* (Baltimore and London, Johns Hopkins University Press, 1973), pp. 163–90. Sigmund Freud, 'Humour', p. 166.

∼ 2

'Something she called a fever':
Michelet, Derrida and dust

I breathed in their dust.
(Jules Michelet, *Oeuvres Complètes*, IV)

ARCHIVE FEVER, INDEED? I can tell you *all about* Archive Fever!

Actually, quite apart from anything written by Derrida, or anything reflected on by his critics, Archive Fever comes on at night, long after the archive has shut for the day. Typically, the fever – more accurately, the precursor fever – starts in the early hours of the morning, in the bed of a cheap hotel, where the historian cannot get to sleep. You cannot get to sleep because you lie so narrowly, in an attempt to avoid contact with anything that isn't shielded by sheets and pillowcase. The first sign then, is an excessive attention to the bed, an irresistible anxiety about the hundreds who have slept there before you, leaving their dust and debris in the fibres of the blankets, greasing the surface of the heavy, slippery counterpane. The dust of others, and of other times, fills the room, settles on the carpet, marks out the sticky passage from bed to bathroom.

This symptom – worrying about the bed – is a screen anxiety. What keeps you awake, the sizing and starch in the thin sheets dissolving as you turn again and again within their confines, is actually the archive, and its myriads of the dead, who all day long, have pressed their concerns upon you. You think: these people have left me *the lot*: each washboard and doormat purchased; saucepans, soup tureens, mirrors, newspapers, ounces of cinnamon and dozens of lemons; each ha'penny handed to a poor child, the minute agreement about how long it shall take a servant to get to keep the greatcoat you provide him with at the hiring; clothes pegs, fat hog meat, the exact expenditure on spirits in a year; the price of papering a room, as you turn, in the spring of 1802, from tenant farmer with limewashed walls, into gentleman with gentleman's residence. Everything. Not a purchase made, not a thing acquired that is not noted and recorded. You think: I could get to hate these people; and then: I can never do these people justice; and finally: I shall never *get it done.*

For the fever – the feverlet, the precursor fever – usually starts at the end of the penultimate day in the record office. Either you must leave tomorrow (train times, journeys planned, a life elsewhere) or the record office will shut for the weekend. And it's expensive being in the archive, as your credit card clocks up the price of the room, the restaurant meals. Leaving is the only way to stop spending. You know you *will not finish*, that there will be something left unread, unnoted, untranscribed. You are not anxious about the Great Unfinished, knowledge of which is the very condition of your being there in the first place, and of the grubby trade you set out in, years ago. You know perfectly well that the infinite heaps of *things* they recorded, the notes and traces that these people left behind, constitute practically nothing at all. There is the great, brown, slow-moving strandless river of Everything, and then there is its tiny flotsam that has ended up in the record office you are at work in.[1] Your craft is to conjure a social system from a nutmeg grater, and your competence in that was established long ago. Your anxiety is more precise, and more prosaic. It's about PT S2/1/1, which only arrived from the stacks that afternoon, which is enormous, and which you will never get through tomorrow.

And then, just as dawn comes, and the birds start to sing, you plunge like a stone into a narrow sleep, waking two or three hours later to find yourself wringing with sweat, the sheets soaked, any protection they afforded quite gone. The Fever – the precursor fever – has broken. But in severe cases, with Archive Fever proper, that is not the end, at all. A grey exhausted day in the record office (you don't finish), a long journey home, a strange dislocation from all the faces, stations, connections, delays, diversions, road-works you feel you must endure (that you add to the long list of historians' hyperbolic complaints stretching back to the century before last) – all these are in retrospect the mere signals of the terrible headache that will wake you at two o'clock in the morning, in your own bed, the pain pressing down like a cap that fits to your skull and the back of your eyes, the extreme sensitivity to light and distortion of sound, the limbs that can only be moved by extraordinary effort, and the high temperature. Archive Fever Proper lasts between sixteen and twenty-four hours, sometimes longer (with an aftermath of weeks rather than days). You think, in the delirium: it was their dust that I breathed in.

∾

The field of occupational (or industrial) disease emerged in its modern mode in Britain during the early part of the nineteenth century. The physicians and apothecaries attached to the textile-district infirmaries whose work it largely was, were of professional necessity interested in the diseases arising from relatively new industrial processes and the factory system. Nevertheless, in acknowledging their seventeenth- and eighteenth-century predecessors they continued to work within a framework that had long been established, of dangerous and malignant trades, especially in hide, skin and leather processing and in the paper-making industries. Moreover, attention to the environmental hazards to workers' health produced by newer nineteenth-century industrial processes served to elaborate an eighteenth-century attention to atmospheric conditions as a cause of disease.[2]

Medical investigations of the early nineteenth century drew very marked attention to dust, and to its effect on hand and factory workers. The largest section of Charles Thackrah's well-known investigation of the early 1830s, into 'the agents which produce disease and shorten the duration of life' across the trades and professions, was devoted to workers 'whose employments produce a dust or vapour decidedly injurious'.[3] He concentrated in particular on paper-makers, who were 'unable to bear the dust which arises from cutting the rags', and dressers of certain types of coloured decorative leather, who needed to pare or grind the finished skins.[4] In the Forbes *et al. Cyclopaedia of Practical Medicine* of 1833, a new category was defined, 'The Diseases of Artisans'. Among the many debilities suffered by hand workers discussed here were those produced by 'the mechanical irritation of moleculae, or fine powders', either in a reaction on the skin of the worker (the fellmongerer's and tanner's carbuncle was an example of ancient provenance), or in some form of pulmonary or respiratory ailment.[5] The particular hazards of cotton dust, in the processing of fibre for spinning and weaving, and in the rag trades in general (in paper making until wood pulp largely replaced rags, and in the flock and shoddy used in upholstery and bedding) continued to be investigated until well into this century, and indeed, byssinosis was not recognised in the USA as an occupational disease of cotton workers until the 1960s.[6] The maladies attendant on the skin processing and allied trades were much commented on. After woollen manufacture, leather-working was the most important eighteenth-century industry, both in terms of the number of workers employed and its output.[7] In the UK the category of trades which were considered dangerous from the dusts they produced was widened during the course of the nineteenth century. By its end, bronzing in the printing process, flax and linen milling, cotton and clothing manufacture, brass finishing and ivory and pearl button-making were among the dusty occupations subject to regulation.[8]

Medical attention continued to be framed and categorised by the dust question. At the top of Leonard Parry's 1900 list of the risks and dangers of various occupations were those 'accompanied by the generation and scattering of abnormal quantities of dust'.[9] Discussing occupations 'from the social, hygienic and medical points of view' in 1916, Thomas Oliver urged his readers to remember 'that the greatest enemy of a worker in any trade is dust', and that 'dust is something more than merely particles of an organic or inorganic nature. Usually the particles which rise with the air are surrounded by a watery envelope and clinging to this moist covering there may be micro-organisms.'[10] As the defensive action of trades unions moved from questions of working hours and physically injurious labour to incorporate conditions of labour and health hazards, the question of dust and its inhalation remained a focus, well into the twentieth century.[11]

Long before the (Trades Union Congress) TUC opened its file on 'Dust – Rag Flock', investigators in the yet-unnamed field of industrial medicine had categorised an occupational malaise that was to enjoy only a short period of interest and discussion. 'The diseases of literary men' sat uneasily under Forbes's 1833 heading 'Diseases of Artisans', but nevertheless, that is where he placed them. Very briefly, for perhaps thirty years or so, between about 1820 and 1850, a range of occupational hazards was understood to be attendant on the activity of scholarship. They originated, said Forbes 'from want of exercise, very frequently from breathing the same atmosphere too long, from the curved position of the body, and from too ardent exercise of the brain'.[12] 'Brain fever' might be the result of this mental activity, and was no mere figure of speech.

It described the two forms of meningitis that had been patholo-gised by the 1830s: inflammation of the membranes of the brain (meningitis proper) and of the substance of the brain (cerebritis).[13]

Charles Thackrah divided 'professional men' and the diseases of their occupations into three types: persons whose mental applica-tion was alternated with exercise in the fresh air; those who took no exercise at all; and those who lived and worked 'in a bad atmos-phere, maintain one position for most of the day, take little exercise and are frequently under the excitement of ambition.'[14] 'Brain-fever' or some form of meninginal disturbance was a hazard of this way of working:

> The brain becomes disturbed. Congestion first occurs and to this succeeds an increased or irregular action of the arteries. A highly excitable state of the nervous system is not infrequently produced. Chronic inflammation of the membranes of the brain, ramollisse-ment of its substance, or other organic change becomes established; and the man dies, becomes epileptic or insane, or falls into that imbecility of mind, which renders him an object of pity to the world, and of deep affliction to his connections.[15]

Medical men like Forbes and Thackrah were able to provide physi-ological and psychological causes of the fevers of scholarship (lack of exercise, bad air, and its 'passions', which were excitement and ambition). By the time that a bacteriological explanation for their fevers was available, 'the literary man' as a victim of occupational disease had disappeared as a category. Lacking bacteriological understanding of the dust that preoccupied them, early investiga-tors did not consider the book, the very stuff of the scholar's life, as a potential cause of his fever. And yet the book and its components (leather binding, various glues and adhesives, paper and its edging, and decreasingly, parchments and vellums of various types) con-centrated in one object many of the industrial hazards and diseases that were mapped out in the course of the century.

The hazards of leather working had been known and recorded in the ancient world. Right through the process, from fellmongering (the initial removal of flesh, fat and hair from the animal skins) to the paring and finishing of the cured and tanned skins, workers were known to be liable to anthrax. In medical dictionaries and treatises of the eighteenth century, 'anthrax' meant 'anthracia', 'anthracosis' or 'carbunculus', that is, what came in the late nineteenth century to be defined as the external or cutaceous form of anthrax. Leather workers and medical commentators also knew that the processes of fellmongering, washing, limerubbing, scraping, further washing, chemical curing, stretching, drying and dressing all gave rise to dust, which was inhaled. Descriptions of leather-working in the bookbinding trades also show that the amount of hand-paring, shaving and scraping involved in the process (and productive of dust) remained remarkably consistent across two centuries.[16] In parchment-making, skins were subjected to the same processes as was leather apart from tanning; these, too, changed very little between medieval and modern times.[17] Indeed, the modern treatment of parchment and vellum is almost identical with very old European practices.[18] Parchment-making (essentially, parchment is untanned leather) possibly gave rise to more dust, as it involved the splitting of sheep skins (the vellum process used calfskin, which was not usually split). The many dangers of the paper trade have already been indicated. The nineteenth century saw the proliferation of a vast literature on the airborne hazards of paper-making, which declined towards the end of the century as woodpulp replaced rags as the main component.[19] Charles Thackrah also commented on the disabilities that arose from letter-press printing, 'the constant application of the eye to minute objects, which gradually [enfeebled] these organs', and on the head and stomach aches of which printers complained.[20] By mentioning 'the putrid serum of sheep's blood' which bookbinders and pocket-book-makers used as 'a cement', Thackrah produced the most striking and potent image of the book as a locus of a whole range of industrial diseases.[21] This stinking glue was probably one among several of the transmitters of the Archive Fever (Proper) discussed here.

The bacillus of anthrax was the first specific micro-organism discovered, when in 1850 Pierre Rayner and Casimir Davaine observed *petits batonnets* in the blood of sheep who had died from the disease. When Louis Pasteur published his work on lactic-acid fermentation, Davaine recognised that the little infusoria were not blood crystals but, rather, living organisms.[22] Robert Koch cultivated the bacillus, infected sheep from his cultivation and described its life-cycle in 1876.[23] Considerable investigative energy of the 1880s went into showing that the disease in animals and human beings was identical; that the *bacillus anthracis* was responsible for the disease in all hosts; that the skins, hairs and wool of the animal dying of what was still, in the 1870s, sometimes called 'cattle plague' or 'splenetic fever' retained the infecting organism, which found access to the body of the worker in various ways.[24] Internal and external anthrax were clearly demarcated, provided with nosologies and with miserable prognoses: 'the worker may be perfectly well when he goes to business; he may in a short time become giddy, restless and exhausted; he feels very ill, goes home, becomes feverish … in bad cases, in from twenty four hours to four days the patient dies unconscious.'[25] As a delegate of the National Society of Woolcombers pointed out to the TUC in 1929, 'It is a disease that does not hang on very long. You get it one day and you may be dead the next.'[26]

In Britain, Anthrax was first scheduled as a notifiable disease in 1892.[27] The number of cases rose in the following decades, despite regulation, with workers, trades unionists and medical commentators all ascribing the increase to an upsurge in imports of foreign hides and wools.[28] The disease remained a profound danger to workers in the woollen and allied trades, and in all forms of leather and skin working, until after the Second World War, though a Ministry of Labour Committee of Inquiry into the disease reported that all British cases of internal anthrax up to 1959 had been of the pulmonary variety.[29]

By the 1920s it was common knowledge among workers in wool, hides and hair that it was the anthrax spore that constituted the greatest danger. If an animal dies of anthrax and is immediately destroyed without opening the carcass, or removing the skin, there is probably no risk. However, once the bacillus comes into contact with air, it forms resistant spores.[30] Any wool, fleece or skin touched by infected blood will contain these spores; fleeces and hides when dried are the source of a dust which, containing the spores, may come into contact with skin abrasions, or may be inhaled.[31] It was also common knowledge that the spores were 'very difficult to kill'.[32] A report commissioned by the British leather sellers' trade association in 1911 collated existing work on anthrax and pointed out that in many ways, leather-working provided the optimum conditions for the development of spores; that 'none of the "cures" at present used to preserve hides destroy the Anthrax infection', that the temperature that might destroy the spores was utterly destructive of the hides, and that it was entirely possible that finished leather retained and conveyed the infection.[33] Certainly, the anthrax spore could come through the whole leather-making process unscathed, though 'the question as to whether finished leather can retain and convey the infection' had to remain unsettled, for while cases had occurred 'in men who have only handled leather, and it has been proved that the spore can pass uninjured through all the chemical solutions used in tanning, the possibility of the leather itself having become contaminated by contact with other goods can hardly ever be excluded'.[34]

In the same period as the indestructibility and fatality of the anthrax spore came to be understood, archivists and book restorers started to define a type of leather deterioration, particularly in 'modern' leathers, those of the post-1880 era, when the book binding and finishing trades began to use imported vegetable-cured leather in great quantities.[35] 'Red powdering', 'red decay' and 'red rot' continue to be described in the literature of book conservation.[36] 'Red rot' is as well known among historians as it is among archivists. A crumbling of leather in the form of an orangey-red powdering, it is said to be found particularly in East India leather, prepared with tannin of bark, wood or fruits. It seems then, that dust is more likely to arise from the disintegrating bindings of ledgers, registers and volumes bound at the end of the nineteenth century, than from older material preserved in the archives. But there is a second type of red decay known to conservationists, a hardening and embrittling (rather than powdering) of bindings, which occurs most often in leathers prepared before about 1830. This also gives rise to dust in handling.[37] It seems, from the considerable literature on this topic, that the causes of leather rot must be found in the type of tanning agent or agents used (and these have been numerous) making the finished skin more or less vulnerable to atmospheric conditions.[38] Parchment, which is essentially untanned leather, does not suffer from this kind of deterioration.

∿

So in 1833, when the young Jules Michelet described his very first days in the archives, those 'catacombs of manuscripts' that had made up the Archives Nationales in Paris a decade before, and wrote of the historian restoring its 'papers and parchments' to the light of day by breathing in their dust,[39] this was not the figure of speech that he intended, but a literal description of a physiological process. He had recently read Giambattista Vico's (1668–1744) *Principi di una Scienza Nuova*, and with its lessons about human agency in mind he addressed the nameless dead who had made the world of civil society, saying to them 'Softly my dear friends, let us proceed in order if you please ... as I breathed their dust, I saw them rise up. They rose from the sepulchre ... as in the Last Judgement of Michelangelo or in the Dance of Death. This frenzied dance ... I have tried to reproduce in [my] work.'[40] In a quite extraordinary (and much scrutinised) passage, it is the historian's act of inhalation that gives life: 'these papers and parchments, so long deserted, desired no better than to be restored to the light of day.'[41] It remains completely uncertain – it *must* remain uncertain; that is its *point* – who or what rises up in this moment. It cannot be determined whether it is the manuscripts or the dead, or both who come to life, and take shape and form. But we can be clearer than Michelet could be, about exactly what it was that he breathed in: the dust of the workers who made the papers and parchments; the dust of the animals who provided the skins for their leather bindings. He inhaled the by-product of all the filthy trades that have, by circuitous routes, deposited their end-products in the archives. And we are forced to consider whether it was not life that he breathed into 'the souls who had suffered so long ago and who were smothered now in the past', but death, that he took into himself, with each lungful of dust.

However, Roland Barthes thought that a quite different process of incorporation was at work, that Michelet actually *ate* history, and that it was eating it that made him ill. The first section of *Michelet par lui-même* ([1954] 1968) was called 'Michelet Mangeur d'Histoire'. Barthes described Michelet's terrible headaches ('la maladie de Michelet, c'est la migraine'), the way in which everything gave him migraine, how his body became his own creation, a kind of steady-state system, a symbiosis between the historian and History, which was ingested in the manner of the Host. This ingested History was also Death: 'Michelet reçoit l'Histoire comme aliment, mais en retour, il lui abandonne sa vie: non seulement son travail et sa santé, mais même: sa mort' [Michelet receives History as food and nourishment, but in return, he gives up his life to it: not only his labour and his health, but even his death.')[42] I suggest that this process did actually take place, not just by analogy with 'le thème christologique' – indeed, Christian theme – that Barthes pursues here (he made much as well, of Michelet's frequent reference to drinking the black blood of the dead), but in the biological realm, as physiological process.

For we must seriously consider, as Jules Michelet was not able to, the archive as a harbourer of the anthrax infection. We must take note of the significant number of cases of anthrax meningitis reported between 1920 and 1950, when it became clear for the first time that the bacillus anthricis could cause, or result in, meningitis, though indeed, its incidence was infrequent.[43] In its modern nosology, meningitis bears strict comparison with the brain fever described nearly two centuries ago, as attendant on the sedentary, airless and fevered scholarly life, spent in close proximity to leather bound books and documents.

We may thus begin to provide the aetiology of Archive Fever Proper; and on a parochial and personal note, suggest that in England at least, the Public Record Office is by far the most likely site for contraction of it. Many of the PRO classmarks consist of dust and dirt and decaying matter put into bundles in the 1780s, and then into boxes 150 years later. In the County Record Offices where, though the stacks may be hundreds of yards long, there are in fact far fewer records stored, documents have nearly always been dusted and cleaned some time since their acquisition. (But that is not strictly point, for the red rot comes off on your hands from the spine of the ledger, the dust still rises as you open the bundle.) Moreover, atmospheric conditions in the Public Record Office, being at the optimum for the preservation of paper and parchment, are rather cold for human beings. You sit all day long, reading in the particular manner of the trade, to save time and money, and in the sure knowledge that out of the thousand lines of handwriting you decipher, you will perhaps use one or two ('the constant application of the eyes to minute objects …'). You scarcely move, partly to conserve body heat, but mainly because *you want to finish*, and not to have to come back, because the PRO is so *far away*, so difficult to get to. That is the immediate ambition that excites you: to leave; though there exist of course the wider passions, of *finding it* (whatever it is you are searching for), and writing the article or book, writing history.[44] All of this must be taken into account, as productive of Archive Fever. But so must the thousands of historians be considered, who like Jules Michelet, have breathed in lungfuls of dust and woken that night or the next, with the unmistakable headache, 'the heavy and often stupefying pain'.[45] We should certainly remember, that in 1947 (the last time the topic was seriously considered in the medical literature) that the incidence of meningeal involvement in anthrax infection was considered to be only 5 per cent.[46] But taking all of this into account, that's what my money is on. We are talking epidemiology here, not metaphor: meningitis due to, or as a complication of anthrax: Real Archive Fever, or Archive Fever Proper: a new entry for the medical dictionaries.

∾

In 1779, Fanny Burney was taken ill when she was staying with her friend, Hester Thrale. (Her *then* friend. This friendship disintegrated some years later, when the widow of the brewing magnate married an Italian – and a mere music master to boot – and became Mrs Piozzi. Many were lost at this time.) Burney was obviously a demanding invalid, or at least, Mrs Thrale found her so: 'Fanny Burney has kept her Room here in my house seven Days with a Fever, or something she called a Fever', wrote her exasperated hostess, in one of the six blank quarto volumes that her husband had given her:

> I gave her every Medicine, and every Slop with my own hand; took away her dirty Cups, Spoons &c moved her Tables, in short was Doctor & Nurse & Maid – for I did not like the Servants should have additional Trouble lest they should hate her for't and now – with the Gratitude of a Wit, She tells me that the *World thinks better of me* for my Civilities to her.
>
> It does! does it?[47]

The cleverness of this entry is utterly charming: the confident move of the pen from the penultimate line to the last, *making* meaning with the space it leaves behind; that exclamation mark, and the bold use of an exclamation and a question mark within one utterance; the insistence that you hear a tone of voice in words that were not, in fact, spoken aloud at all. Now Hester Thrale was, in all manner of ways, a very difficult number indeed, and she is scarcely good evidence for a case that will be put later, of the historian as reader of what is never intended for his or her eyes. Hester Thrale did not write for *me*, but she certainly imagined someone something *like* me reading her private diary, especially her academic readers, for among all its other uses, *Thraliana* was used as a source for her own philological work. She often reflected on what posterity would make of her writing:

> but say the Critics a Violin is not an Instrument for *Ladies* to manage, very likely! I remember when they said the same Thing of a Pen.
>
> I wonder if my Executors will burn the Thraliana! [48]

And she so admired some of her aperçus and turns of phrase that she recycled them in her letters (like the Fanny Burney story). She wrote highly crafted, controlled and managed accounts of her self, directed at future audiences. This was not the aspect of her voluminous writings that fixed my gaze. Rather, it is that question asked in some place between speech and writing – that voiced scepticism, that irony – about someone else's *supposed* fever, so that a joke may be sustained, by casting doubt on anyone who ever claims to have suffered one. In the hallucinatory aftermath of your own Archive Fever, a delicious idea is provoked, of pursuing its origins – of finding out *where it came from* – through Derrida's text, indeed; so that you might end up exclaiming to him: 'It does! does it?' – 'Archive Fever, indeed? *I* can tell you *all about* Archive Fever!'

Notes

1 See Maurice Mandelbaum, *Philosophy, History and the Sciences. Selected Critical Essays* (Baltimore and London, Johns Hopkins University Press, 1984), pp. 97–111, not for his criticism of deconstructive readings of history (which will be discussed below), but for p. 101 and p. 103 and the compelling image of the stream or river in describing what it is historians work on.

2 Jacqueline Karnell Corn, *Response to Occupational Health Hazards. A Historical Perspective* (New York, Van Nostrand Reinhold, 1992); Donald Hunter, *The Diseases of Occupations* (London, English Universities Press, 1955); A. Meiklejohn, *The Life, Work and Times of Charles Turner Thackrah, Surgeon and Apothecary of Leeds (1795–1833)* (Edinburgh and London, E. & S. Livingstone, 1957). The seventeenth-century authority on occupational disease most frequently referred to in the nineteenth century was Bernardino Ramazzini. His *De morbis artificum* (1703) was first done into English in 1705: *A Treatise of the Diseases of Tradesmen* (London, Andrew Bell, 1705). See also Wilmer C. Wright, *De morbis artificum diatriba. Diseases of Workers. The Latin Text of 1713, revised, with translation and notes by Wilmer Cave Wright* (Chicago, University of Chicago Press, 1940). For eighteenth-century 'environmentalist' medicine, and its connection to later miasmic and contagion theories, see James C. Riley, *The Eighteenth-century Campaign to Avoid Disease* (New York, St. Martin's Press, 1987), pp. 13–19, and passim.

3 Charles Turner Thackrah, *The Efects of Arts, Trades and Professions, and of Civic States and Habits of Living, on Health and Longevity: with*

Suggestions for the Removal of the Agents which Produce Disease and Shorten the Duration of Life, 2nd edn (London, Longman, 1832), pp. 63–119.

4 Thackrah, *Effects of Arts*, pp. 66, 70. It was not this genre of investigative literature that Karl Marx used in order to itemise dust as one of the many hazardous conditions of workers' life under capitalism, but rather the reports of parliamentary commissioners of inquiry and public health officials who undertook their investigations with work like Thackrah's as a guide. See Karl Marx, *Capital* (Harmondsworth, Penguin, [1867] 1976), 1, pp. 492–639.

5 John Forbes, Alexander Tweedie and John Conolly, *The Cyclopaedia of Practical Medicine*, 3 vols (London, Sherwood, 1833),1, pp. 149–60; p. 156.

6 Leonard A. Parry, *The Risks and Dangers of Various Occupations and their Prevention* (London, Scott, Greenwood, 1900), pp. 34–5. George M. Kober and William C. Hanson, *Diseases of Occupation and Vocational Hygiene* (London, William Heinemann, [1916] 1918), pp. 666–9. University of Warwick, Modern Records Centre, Records of the TUC, Mss 292/144.3/3; 144.312; D107, 'Dust – Rag Flock, 1937–1947'. Barbara Harrison, *Not Only the 'Dangerous Trades': Women's Work and Health in Britain, 1880–1914* (London, Taylor & Francis, 1996), pp. 58–9; Corn, *Response to Occupational Health*, 147–76 for byssinosis and the recognition of industrial hazard in the USA. See also Christopher C. Sellars, *Hazards of the Job. From Industrial Disease to Environmental Health Science* (Chapel Hill and London, University of North Carolina Press, 1997), and for the truly modern hazards of work, see Catherine Casey, *Work, Self and Society. After Industrialism* (London and New York, Routledge, 1995).

7 Maxine Berg, *The Ag of Manufactures, 1700–1820* (London, Fontana, 1985), pp. 26, 28, 38–9.

8 Harrison, *'Not Only the Dangerous Trades'*, pp. 58–9, 76. Sir Thomas Oliver, *Occupations. From the Social, Hygienic and Medical Points of View* (Cambridge, Cambridge University Press, 1916), 71–84.

9 Parry, *The Risks and Dangers*, pp. 1–42.

10 Oliver, *Occupations*, pp. 59, 71–2.

11 University of Warwick, Modern Records Centre, Records of the TUC, Mss 292/144.3/3; 144.312; D107 'Dust – Rag Flock, 1937–1947'; and

Mss 292/144/211/6, 'Anthrax, 1924–1947'.

12 Forbes *et al.*, *The Cyclopaedia*, p. 159. These works of the 1820s and 1830s nowhere mention S.A.A. Tissot's *De la Santé des gens de lettres* (1766), though his work was translated into English and his perceptions seem omnipresent in the 1820s and 1830s. Samuel Auguste Tissot, *De la Santé des gens de lettres* (Lausanne, Francois Graiset, [1766] 1768). S.A. Tissot, *An Essay on Diseases Incidental to Literary and Sedentary Persons. With Proper Rules for Preventing their fatal Consequences and Instructions for their Care* (London, Edward and Charles Dilly, 1768). S.A. Tissot, *A Treatise on the Diseases Incident to Literary and Sedentary Persons. Transcribed from the last French Edition. With Notes, by a Physician* (London and Edinburgh, A. Donaldson, 1771). Tissot nowhere mentioned scholarship as an occupation that ran the hazard of dust, or miasma; he made no reference to the headache. He attributed most of the scholar's ill to *sitting down*, and not taking exercise.

13 Forbes *et al.*, *The Cyclopaedia*, pp. 281–312, 'Brain, Inflammation of'.

14 Thackrah, *The Effects of Arts*, pp. 173–92. For the ill-health of historians, see Bonnie Smith, *The Gender of History. Men, Women and Historical Practice* (Cambridge, MA, Harvard University Press), p. 120–1. In the 1920s the British Association of Women Clerks focused a century of complaint about writers' cramp among clerical workers, in their attempts to have it scheduled as an industrial sickness with no limit of compensation. But theirs were arguments about the physical effect of minutely repeated movements of hand and arm; the comparison was with telegraphists (telegraphists' cramp was a scheduled industrial disease for which benefit might be claimed indefinitely under the National Insurance legislation of 1911) and with comptometers. It was only in the first half of the nineteenth century that scholarship and literary occupations had attached to them a specific disease of the brain.

15 Thackrah, *The Effects of Arts*, pp. 184–5.

16 David McBride, *Some Account of a New Method of Tanning* (Dublin, Boulter Grierson, 1769). The Dublin Society, *The Art of Tanning and Currying Leather; With an Account of all the Different Processes Made Use of in Europe and Asia for Dying Leather Red and Yellow* (London, J. Nourse, 1774). James Revell, *A Complete Guide to the Ornamental Leather Work* (London, privately printed, 1853). Alexander Watt, *The*

Art of Leather Manufacture, being a Practical Handbook (London, Crosby Lockwood, 1885). H.C. Standage, *The Leather Worker's Manual, being a compendium of practical recipes and working formulae for curriers, bootmakers, leather dressers &c* (London, Scott, Greenwood, 1900). Society for the Encouragement of Arts, Manufactures and Commerce, *Report of the Committee on Leather for Bookbinding. With Four Appendices* (London, William Trounce, 1911). Constant Ponder, *Report to the Worshipful Company of Leathersellers on the Incidence of Anthrax Amongst those engaged in Hide, Skin and Leather Industries* (London, Worshipful Company of Leathersellers, 1911).

17 R. Reed, *Ancient Skins, Parchments and Leathers* (London and New York, Seminar Press, 1972), pp. 46–85. Ronald Reed, *The Nature and Making of Parchment* (Leeds, Elmete Press, 1975).

18 Dard Hunter, *Papermaking. The History and Technique of an Ancient Craft*, 2nd edn (London, Pleiades Books, 1956).

19 Donald Hunter, *The Diseases of Occupations* (London, English Universities Press, 1955), p. 546 suggests that the change took place in the 1890s; but see below, pp. 130–1.

20 Thackrah, *The Effects of Arts*, pp. 42–3.

21 Ibid., p. 45.

22 Jean Théorides, *Un grand médicin et biologiste. Casimir-Joseph Davaine (1812–1882). (Analecta medico-historica* [4]) (Oxford, Pergamon Press, 1968), pp. 72–123, 124–5.

23 W.F. Bynum and Roy Porter, *Companion Encyclopaedia of the History of Medicine*, 2 vols (London, Routledge, 1993), 1, pp. 113–14. Kenneth F. Kiple, *The Cambridge World History of Human Disease* (Cambridge, Cambridge University Press, 1993), pp. 582–4, 'Anthrax'.

24 Parry, *The Risks and Dangers*, pp. 147–54.

25 Ibid., p. 149; Hunter, *The Diseases*, pp. 627–39.

26 University of Warwick, Modern Records Centre, Records of the TUC, Mss 292/144/211/6, 'Anthrax, 1924–1947'. This is a note from Trades Union Congress, *Report*, 1929, pp. 116–18.

27 Harrison, *'Not Only the Dangerous Trades'*, p. 76.

28 University of Warwick, Modern Records Centre, Records of the TUC, Mss 292/144/211/6. 'Anthrax, 1924–1947'. See in this file a letter dated 20 May 1925 from Ben Tillett at the Transport and General Workers' Union, with his opinion that anthrax cases had risen since the end

of the First World War owing to the import of foreign hides, especially those of the Mediterranean goat, and of Indian wool. He enclosed a Memorandum on investigation into anthrax incidence at the International Labour Office, 1924, including the Minority Report of its Anthrax Committee. See E.C. Snow (Manager of the United Tanners' Federation), *Leather, Hides, Skins and Tanning Materials*, Resources of the Empire Series (London, Ernest Benn, 1924), pp. 71–2 for this committee.

29 The Factory Department of the Home Office issued an illustrated 'Precautionary Card for Workers' in 1930, telling them what symptoms of anthrax to look out for: 'Take this card with you and show it to the Doctor.' University of Warwick, Modern Records Centre, Records of the TUC, Mss 292/144/211/6. 'Anthrax, 1924–1947'. Ministry of Labour, *Report of the Committee of Inquiry on Anthrax* (London, HMSO, 1959).

30 Hunter, *The Diseases*, pp. 627–39.

31 Philip Brachman, 'Inhalation Anthrax', *Annals of the New York Academy of Science*, 353 (1980), 83–93, for a history of attention to internal anthrax, by this date 'primarily only of historical interest'.

32 Kober and Hanson, *Diseases of Occupation*, p. 159.

33 Ponder, *Report*, pp. 17, 44, 65.

34 Ponder, *Report*, pp. 65–6.

35 Society for the Encouragement of Arts, Manufactures and Commerce, *Report*, p. 12. H.J. Plender Leith, *The Preservation of Leather Bookbindings* (London, Trustees of the British Museum, [1946] 1967).

36 K.J. Adcock, *Leather. From the Raw Material to the Finished Product* (London, Pitman, nd [1924]), p. 107. Matthew T. Roberts and Don Etherington, *Bookbinding and the Conservation of Books* (Washington, Library of Congress, 1982), p. 214. European Commission, Environment Leather Project, *Deterioration of Vegetable Tanned Leather*, Protection and Conservation of the European Cultural Heritage, Research Report, 6 (Copenhagen, 1997). Bernard C. Middleton, *The Restoration of Leather Bindings*, 3rd edn (British Library, Oak Knoll Press, 1998), p. 36.

37 Roberts and Etherington, *Bookbinding*, p. 214.

38 Ibid., p. 214.

39 'Et à mesure que je soufflais sur leur poussière, je les voyais se soulever.'

Jules Michelet, 'Préface de l'Histoire de France' [1869]; and 'Examen en des Remainments du texte de 1833 par Robert Casanova', *Oeuvres Complètes, Tome IV*, (Paris, Flammarion, 1974), pp. 613–14, 727.

40 Michelet, *Préface*, 613. See below, pp. 103–4 for Vico and his nineteenth-century readers. Giambattista Vico, *The New Science of Giambattista Vico*, trans. Thomas Goddard Bergin and Max Harold Fisch (New York, Doubleday, [1744] 1961).

41 This passage has been discussed by Edmund Wilson, *To the Finland Station, A Study in the Writing and Acting of History* (New York, Doubleday, [1940] 1953), p. 8, by Roland Barthes, *Michelet par lui-même* (Paris, Seuil, [1954] 1968), pp. 89–92 and by Hayden White, *Metahistory*, pp. 149–62.

42 Barthes, *Michelet*, p. 19. See Andy Stafford, 'Barthes and Michelet: Biography and History', *Nottingham French Studies*, 36:1 (1997), 14–23. As noted by Stafford, see Chantal Thomas on *Michelet par lui-même* as 'quelquechose comme le coeur secret de son (Barthes's) oeuvre'. Chantal Thomas, 'Barthes et Michelet. Homologie de travail, parallèle d'affection', *La Règle du jeu*, 15 (1995) 73–84.

43 Hunter, *The Diseases of Occupations*, p. 638. Robert H. Shanahan, Joseph R. Griffin and Alfred P. von Anersburg, 'Anthrax Meningitis. Report of a Case of Internal Anthrax with Recovery', *American Journal of Chemical Pathology*, 17 (1947), 719–22. H. Gross and H. Plate, 'Milzbrandbacillen-Meningistis' ('Meningitis due to Anthrax Bacilli'), *Klinische Wochenschrift*, 19 (5 October 1940), 1036–7. Michel Deniker, Jean Patel and Bernard Jamain, 'Meningite au Cours du Charbon' ('Meningitis as a Complication of Anthrax'), *La Presse médicale*, 46 (13 April 1938), 575–6. R. Bruynoghe and M. Ronse, 'Une Infection méningée par un bacille Anthracoide' ('Meninginal Infection due to Anthracoid Bacillus'), *Comptes rendus des séances de la Societée de biologie*, 125 (1937), 395–7. Hamant, Drouet, P. Chalnot and J. Simonin, 'Hyperacute Meningitis in Anthrax', *Bulletins et mémoires de la Société médicale des hôpitaux de Paris*, 49 (23 January 1933), 14–15. G.R. McCowen and H. B. Parker, 'Anthrax Meningitis', *Journal of the Royal Navy Medical Service*, 18 (October 1932), 278–80. W. K. Dunscombe, 'Meningitis due to B. anthracis', *British Medical Journal* (30 January 1932), 190. A. Aguiah, 'Meningitis caused by Anthrax in Boy of 11', *Bulletin de la Société de pédiatrie de Paris*, 26 (May 1928), 285–91.

44 Tissot may not have mentioned dust, fever or headache in *De la Santé des gens de lettres* (see n. 12 above), but he was eloquent on the passions of scholars: 'ils sont comme les amants qui s'emportent quand on ose leur dire que l'objet de leur passion a des défauts'. (They are like impassioned lovers when one dares to suggest to them that the object of their passion has faults) Tissot, *De la Santé*, p. 122.

45 Forbes *et al.*, *The Cyclopaedia*, 1, 282–3.

46 Shanahan *et al.*, 'Anthrax Meningitis', 721.

47 Katharine C. Balderston (ed.) *Thraliana. The Diary of Mrs Hester Lynch Thrale (Later Mrs Piozzi) 1776–1809*, 2 vols (Oxford, Clarendon Press, 1951), 1, p. 413, entry for 1 December 1779.

48 Ibid., 2, p. 748.

↝ 3

The magistrates

ACCORDING TO BENEDICT ANDERSON, Jules Michelet went in to the archive in order to enact a particular kind of national imagining. The dead and forgotten people he exhumed 'were by no means a random assemblage of forgotten, anonymous dead. They were those whose sacrifices, throughout History, made possible the rupture of 1789 and the self conscious appearance of the French nation.'[1] Anderson is brilliant – and brilliantly funny – on the way in which, after Michelet, 'the silence of the dead was no obstacle to the exhumation of their deepest desires', and how historians found themselves able speak on behalf of the dead, and to interpret the words and the acts they themselves had not understood – 'qu'ils n'ont pas compris'.[2] Anderson's comments make it very clear that the resurrectionist historian creates the past that he purports to restore, in Michelet's case attributing feelings beliefs and desires that he acknowledged were not actually experienced by those he restored to life.

It was not exactly Jules Michelet the historian, nor indeed the Historian, who performed this act of restoration (though it was indeed, precisely, fixed on a day, a date, a lived time, that the young lycéen entered the portals of the National Archives and breathed in the dust of the dead). It was in fact a Magistrate, also called History, who did the work of resurrection:

Oui, chaque mort laisse un petit bien, sa mémoire, et demand qu'on la soigne. Pour celui qui n'a pas d'amis, il faut que le magistrat y supplée. Car la loi, la justice est plus sûre que toutes nos tendresses oublieuses, nos larmes si vites séchées. Cette magistrature, c'est l'Histoire. Et les morts sont, pour dire comme le Doit romain, ces *miserabiles personae* dont le magistrat se préoccupe. Jamais dans ma carrière je n'ai pas perdu de vue ce devoir de l'historien.[3]

(Yes, every one who dies leaves behind a little something, his memory, and demands that we care for it. For those who have no friends, the magistrate must provide that care. For the law, or justice, is more certain than all our tender forgetfulness, our tears so swiftly dried. This magistracy, is History. And the dead are, to use the language of Roman law, those *miserabiles personae* with whom the magistrate must preoccupy himself. Never in my career, have I lost sight of that duty of the historian.)

Is this a reason for the *archon* and the *arkhe being there, at all*, in Derrida's text? Not by reference to the legal system of the Greek city state at all, but somehow, by some means, to Michelet's awesome, yet touching image of 1872–74, of History (or the Historian, or both) charged with the care and protection of the forgotten poor and the forgotten dead? To support this claim, the historian wants to investigate Derrida's educational history, track him through the Algerian lycées he attended, paying full attention to the anti-Jewish legislation then in force, particularly between 1940 and 1943, and the fate of history and history-teaching under Vichy. We might then expect to find a continuation of inter-war uses of a conservative history used to depose the centrality of 1789 and Republicanism in French political culture; but we would almost certainly not find anyone reading Michelet while attending a lycée.[4] By 1939, Michelet's work – when it was remembered – was the province of the primary school and teacher education.[5] Michelet's work on Joan of Arc (originally published in 1841, as part of his unfinished history of the French people) was used by the Right, but not, it seems, during

Vichy.[6] Quite apart from the very likely failure of any attempt to find Derrida reading Michelet and thus about his Magistrate, we would also have to dismiss our search as a tiny, pathetic example of the Western nostalgia – fever, sometimes – for origins, points of beginning, foundations.

But – foundations fever or not – Michelet's Magistrate (or something very like him) *is* there, in 'Archive Fever'. And perhaps we should find unsurprising the presence of this particular figure, for we have learned from Derrida himself that texts (texts of philosophy form the majority of his examples) contain what *apparently* isn't there at all; that they pull against their overt meaning, in the unregarded details, in chains of metaphors, in the footnotes; on all the wilder shores of signification that are signalled by punctuation marks; by absences, spaces, lacunae, all working against their overt propositions.

We could proceed in order this way, reading 'Archive Fever' for another – the other – Magistrate. But it is the *archon*, his house, his justice room, his law books, that open 'Archive Fever', and the problem is that *he is the wrong magistrate*. The *archon* operated a system of law in a slave society, and had a quite different function from Michelet's magistrate. The *archon* dealt with slaves, the majority of local populations, only as aspects of their owners' property and personality.[7] But the Magistrate Michelet names as History, was in different ways, in England and France of the modern period, specifically charged with the care and management of the poor, and with the mediation of social and class relations, and on these grounds, perhaps even Michelet's Magistrate is the wrong one. The 1789 Revolution in France recodified and reorganised the complex judicial system of the Ancien Régime, during which the jurisdiction of a whole complex of different law codes and courts had been eroded by the centralising tendencies of monarchical government.[8] However, the judicial revolution of the early 1790s and the Napoleonic criminal codes of 1808 and 1810 still followed the broad procedural outlines of the Grand Ordinance Criminelle of 1670.[9] The same system for judicial investigation and decision thus held sway before and after the Revolution. It was a forensic and non-confrontational system, by way of marked contrast with England's system of common law. The judge who heard evidence was obliged to act an inquisitoral rather than a prosecutorial role.[10] He operated a system in which privacy of investigation and the written word predominated;[11] in which, in criminal cases, prosecuting council were not permitted to question the defendant and witnesses were questioned alone (and certainly not in the presence of other witnesses). In this way, 'judicial confrontations [resembled] philosophical inquiry by disputation, by the scholastic method'.[12] Privacy, isolation of witnesses from each other, and the forensic method governed the lower courts as well as the justice that was dispensed in the grand regional *parlements*. However, for a wide range of offences committed by the poor, there was no appeal to the *parlement* from seigneurial and manorial courts. It was *les gens sans aveu* (vagrants) in particular, who had no recourse to the higher justice of the *parlements*.[13] The domain in which the *miserabiles personae* were taken note of by the law, was when magistrates in the *parlements* administered and regulated the food supply.[14] Parlementary magistrates certainly raised a chorus of protest against the erosion of their management of the provincial grain trade in the second half of the eighteenth century, though most historians understand this outcry as a fear of disorder rather than as a protective impulse towards the poor, and attribute their protests to a belief that all questions of provision and dearth were in the end, to do with public order.[15] They did not make their protests out of a general obligation to provision the masses, and they were not charged by law with direct oversight of the *menu peuple*, as were English magistrates under the Poor Laws.

These distinctions between two types of Magistrate (what we may call Possible Magistrates) were well understood at the turn of the nineteenth century. Commenting on them in the post-Napoleonic era, Eugène Buret noted that

> En Angleterre, c'est the gouvernement de la société lui-même, c'est la legislation qui nous révèlent depuis deux siècles l'existence de la misère. A partir du fameux acte 43 d'Elisabeth … il s'ecoule pas une seule année sans que la loi n'intervienne pour régler le condition des pauvres.[16]

He went onto describe how 'il n'en est pas de même en France'. France had police regulations governing beggars and vagabonds, but nothing dealing with with 'la misère innocente'; in France the ordinary poor were left to their own devices, or to charity.[17]

Michelet evoked Roman Law in describing the duties and activities of his magistracy, and thus might be thought to make the post-Napoleonic French justice system the ground work of his allegory. But the same broad assumptions of the magistrate's task guided theory and practice under England's system of common law. Statute law ('law positive', in eighteenth-century language) gave the care and protection of the majority of the populace to the justices of the peace, under the Poor Law (this is to leave quite out of the reckoning the question of how nasty, demeaning and actually unjust the treatment may have been, in any particular case). English legal theory of the eighteenth century was quite strongly 'Roman' in implication and interpretation, and the most noted legal commentator of them all, William Blackstone, understood the relationship between master and servant, between subordinates and those who ruled over them, to be the first of the 'great relations' of private life that the law was interested in, and that on which all other forms of personal relationship, subject to law (the married relation, and between parent and child) were based.[18] The English justice of the peace was formally obliged to mediate these relationships, within the social and familial hierarchies of civil society. Operating a legal system with chattel-slavery law, Derrida's *archon* did not – could not – do anything like this.

Could not do anything like the justice of the peace Philip Ward of Stoke Doyle in Northamptonshire, who some time in April 1751 heard a complaint from a Mr Sambrook, watchmaker of Oundle, whose apprentice had assaulted him. A servant or apprentice who did such a thing was liable to one year's imprisonment and additional corporal punishment, but the legislation specified that two justices must sit together to pass sentence in this way.[19] Doyle had already issued a warrant (he could do that on his sole authority) when it occurred to him 'upon second thoughts that I as a single justice can neither punish him upon s.21 of 5 Eliz. c.4 nor upon s.4 of 20 Geo.2 c.19'.[20] He recorded in his notebook his solution to the limits the law placed upon his actions. Calling the arrested apprentice into the justice room at Stoke Doyle House, and 'concealing my want of power I had the words of the Statute read over to him and he immediately desir'd he might be admitted [*sic*] to ask his Masters pardon upon promising never to offend more and so was forgiven'.[21]

Between 1772 and 1810, the Nottinghamshire justice Sir Gervase Clifton recorded several cases of domestic dispute brought before him by maidservants and masters. He had no legal right nor obligation to intervene in these circumstances, and after hearing the parties out, nothing at all ensued. In 1785 for example, Sarah Cumberland, hired servant to Henry Page, a husbandman of Staunton-upon-the Wold, came to his house to complain that

> on Wednesday morning last past as soon as she came from Milking he asked her why she left two dishes and a pan unwashed for [*sic*] and that she told him she had forgot them and that the other wench might get up and wash them whilst she went a milking but he did

not hear her; but asked her what she said she would not tell him upon which he pulled her ears and Kicked her Backside and otherwise Ill used her.

The complaint went absolutely nowhere. The Staunton constable appears not to have been asked to do anything; no summons, no further entry from Sir Gervase, no journey up to the county Quarter Sessions. The most that is clear, is that both Sarah Cumberland and Sir Gervase thought that it was his duty to listen to such a story and complaint, though the law gave him no right of jurisdiction over domestic servants.[22]

The magistrate who is *really* in Derrida's text, exercises a power he doesn't always actually have, that has already always been inaugurated somewhere else; he files away not only official documents (though in these cases, the warrants, the hundreds of recognisances, depositions, examinations that passed under the hand of justices of the peace, and must have passed through Ward's and Clifton's justice rooms, are actually lost) but also in these personal notebooks that they, like many country magistrates, kept to remind themselves of what they had done, as well as what the law said they couldn't do. Complaints about their jurisdiction were many, from very different political perspectives. The irascible anonymous author of *Reflections on the Relative Situations of Master and Servant, Historically and Politically Considered* was enraged at the restrictions on magistrates' activities, the way in which they could not move without information upon oath and depositions in writing, in other words, without procedure.[23] In the 1790s Thomas Gisborne pondered the same question of domiciliation of authority as Derrida was to do, pointing out that the magistrate's jurisdiction was 'extremely extensive and comprises a multitude of persons and cases'. He thought of the men and women brought before the justice of the peace, who were 'almost universally his inferiors; and commonly in the lowest ranks of society'. He pointed out that

> the principal share of his business is transacted in his own house, before few spectators, and those in general indigent and illiterate. Hence he [the magistrate] is liable to become dictatorial, browbeating, consequential, and ill-humoured, domineering in his inclinations, dogmatical in his opinions and arbitrary in his decisions.[24]

The magistrate regulated conduct alone, in his house or in his sessions (he gathered with other justices in petty sessions, and the larger gatherings of Quarter Sessions); he dealt with 'a large number of offences without specific victims and others that involved a failure to abide by some form of local obligation'.[25] This is the reason for the numberless stories of the poor that have end up in the Archive. The nameless apprentice watchmaker of Oundle and Sarah Cumberland of Staunton suggest that the archive that is the real Archive in 'Archive Fever' is not and never has been the repository of official documents alone. And nothing starts in the Archive, nothing, ever at all, though things certainly end up there. You find nothing in the Archive but stories caught half way through: the middle of things; discontinuities.

The Magistrate listened then, to the stories of the *miserabiles personae* with whose care he was charged. A modern autobiographical canon may still be made up of the writings of elite men and women, but in England at least, from the seventeenth century onwards, the emerging administrative state demanded that it was in fact the poor who told their story, in vast proportion to their vast numbers. The major source for Keith Snell's monumental and elegiac account of working-class experience and its expression in rural England between 1660 and 1900 is extant settlement examinations, the many thousands of them that have ended up in county record offices.[26] Under legislation of 1661, magistrates were required to inquire into the origins of those who might become applicants for poor relief. Determining place of settlement, that is, the parish responsible for relief of distress, involved applicants – or potential applicants – in telling a life-story, and having it recorded. Hundreds of thousands of men and women told where they were born, when they were put to work, where they had worked, and crucially, for how long they had worked in any one place, for working consistently in one parish and receiving wages for a calendar year carried one of the most important entitlements to settlement ... 'Samuel Holyday born in Draycott in the parish of Bourton ... lived with his parents until 12 years old'

> then went to Service and Lived in Several places until about ten years ago he was hired to Gabriel Cattern of Harborough near Rugby ... for a year and Served his Said Master the said year Residency in the said parish of Harborough the said term of one year & received his wages.[27]

A century and a half of this kind of formulaic self-narration preceded Mary Manton's examination in the parish of Astley, Warwickshire, in the autumn of 1815:

> Mary Manton says that about September 1813 Mrs Beadman of Market Bosworth in the County of Leicester hired the said Mary Manton to serve her for £7.7.0 but no Time mentioned but when said Mary Manton Came to her Service she hasked her Mistress whether she was hired for 51 week or for 12 months but the Mistress Made answer and Said that was according to her behaviour but about 9 weeks after Christmas 1814 she had some fierce words with his [sic] Mistress whome paid her wages and Left and when [sic] to her Father's house for 1 night only which next Morning Returned to fetch her Cloths. She agreed with her Mistress to Serve her Time out and Rcd. her whole Wages, which she did at this Michaelmas 1814.[28]

The most common narrative extracted from women of the labouring poor, after the one framed by work, was the story of seduction and betrayal. Bastardy examinations, again conducted before justices of the peace, were demanded for the same administrative purposes, for an illegitimate child was a potential drain on parish resources. To extract the name of a putative father and charge him with maintenance, or to return an expectant mother to her true place of settlement offered a clear saving against local rates. Elizabeth Wells, examined in Nottinghamshire by Gervase Clifton in late 1809, was a parish apprentice, that is, a poor child apprenticed out by her home parish, and the legal question here was not who the father of her child might be, but rather, whether or not her home parish or her master had the right to discharge her from her indentures before her time was up:

> The Examination of Eliz. Wells ... Who says she was born in the parish of Ruddington in the County of Nottinghamshire of Parents legally settled there That when she was about nine Years old she was put out parish Apprentice to John Wilkinson of Ruddington Farmer until she was twenty one Years or marriage she was to have her Victuals drink & Cloaths she says she staid there about four years and she getting too big for an under servant her master told her she might go to the Statutes[29] and get hired ... accordingly [she] was hired to George Blount ... Husbandman for one year she staid there two whole years and received her two years wages ... That in ... June 1809 she went over to Ruddington to ... inquire wether she was out of her time under her Parish Indentures to John Wilkinson he ... said she did not belong there and that he had burnt the Indentures. She says she was then hired to John Butler of Clifton ... She was hired for this Year but proving to be with Child of a Bastard child he cannot keep her any longer She is now in her twentieth year and is at present with Mr Butler.[30]

You can certainly hear the legally required questions that structure these autobiographies. Like the haunting self-narratives Henry Mayhew presented his readers with in the mid-nineteenth century, they are written accounts produced by questioning, but from which, in transcription, the interlocutor has been removed.

By these means, multitudes of labouring men and women surveyed a life from a fixed standpoint, told it in chronological sequence, gave an account of what it was that brought them to this place, this circumstance now, telling the familiar tale for the justice's clerk (who was so very used to the formula that Mary Manton becomes a 'he' by boredom of the pen) to transcribe. Apart from not being written down by the person who lived the life, these brief narratives fulfil the criteria for autobiographical narration.[31] And some were written down by the liver of the life presented for scrutiny. The eighteenth-century philanthropic organisation often demanded a story in exchange for its dole. The mid-century London Society for the Encouragement of Honest and Industrious Servants determined that none should join nor have entitlement to a handout unless they gave their account *in writing*: 'Every person applying must deliver in a Petition, a Narrative of Information, containing an Account of his or her Service' – 'with whom, when, where, how long, in what quality.'[32]

These enforced narratives – we have them in *medias res* – were told before all manner of judge. Even the Lord Chief Justice had to hear them. During his term of office (1756–88), Lord Mansfield often lambasted 'the litigious zeal of public bodies' so eager in his view, to see every disputed settlement case 'travel through every stage which the law allow[ed]', all the way from the initial settlement examination by two magistrates, through the county quarter sessions – perhaps through two meetings of the court of quarter sessions, if the disputing parishes were in two different counties – all the way up to London and the Court of the King's Bench, for the judges' opinion. As one of Lord Mansfield's biographers remarks, in disputes like these, where parishes and their ratepayers were responsible for the relief and maintenance of the poor, the collective resources of a county often led them to defy 'the salutory menace of costs', that is, to ignore the considerable outlay of county funds involved in briefing an attorney for a dispute between two quarter sessions, and the even greater expense involved in preparing a case for the higher courts. Mansfield routinely condemned this litigation; indeed the poor laws which provoked it were 'a disgrace to the country'. They were 'a dropsey … swollen to monstrous proportions', commented Cecil Fifoot, by 'the invitation offered to each parish to cast its burden upon its neighbours'.[33] The behaviour of litigious parishes was notorious. Eugène Buret wrote in shocked suprise of English research which showed that a dispute 'entre deux paroisses à l'occasion d'un seul indigent a souvent coûté plus d'argent qu'il n'en avait fallu pour assister tous les pauvres des deux paroisses'.[34]

Mansfield routinely criticised the Poor Laws, but was not as viciously funny about them as Richard Burn (1709–85) shows that it was possible to be. Vicar of Orton in Westmoreland, JP for Westmorland and Cumberland, and author of the best-selling and extraordinarily long-running *Justice of the Peace and Parish Officer* (1st edn, 1756), his was an outrage born of familiarity and fury, as he recorded the activities of overseers of the poor in far north-western villages:

> in practice, the office of an overseer of the poor seems to be understood to be this: To keep an extraordinary look-out, to prevent persons coming to inhabit without certificates, and to fly to the justices to remove them … to warn [all inhabitants], if they will hire *servants*, to hire them half yearly, or by the month, or by the week, or by the day, rather than by any way that shall give them a settlement; or if they do hire them for a year, to endeavour to pick a quarrel with them before the year's end, and so to get rid of them: To maintain their poor as cheap as they possibly can … to hang over them *in terrorem* if they shall complain to the justices for want of maintenance … To move heaven and earth if any dispute happens about a settlement; and in that particular, to invert the general rule, and stick at no expense.[35]

Mansfield's condemnation of the operation of the settlement laws was not borne of this kind of experience, though magistrates in their sessions sometimes cited it approvingly, as if it were.[36]

There were no reporters regularly at work in any of the trial courts before the end of the eighteenth century. However, notes made by an individual judge like Mansfield could become 'the predominant source for the statement of facts in the printed reports of cases heard by the full Court of the King's Bench', and from these we may estimate how many disputed settlement cases, forwarded by litigation-happy courts of quarter sessions, passed before the Lord Chief Justice and his colleagues.[37] Joseph Burchell's *Arrangement and Digest of the Law in Cases Adjudged in the King's Bench and Common Pleas*, which covered the years 1756 to 1794, reported on more than a hundred disputed settlement cases. More than a third of them involved questions of hiring and service, or entitlement to settlement by service. Other means of gaining a settlement (by birth, apprenticeship, marriage, office, certificate, office, purchase and rating) did not give rise to anything like as much litigation.[38] Francis Const's 1793 revision of Bott's standard *Decisions of the King's Bench Upon the Laws Relating to the Poor*, devoted the most space to the question of 'Settlement by Hiring and Service', in that 'late and most active period' in the making of 'law positive' (statute law) and legal judgement, that is, in the 1770s and 1780s.[39]

The women whose stories Mansfield thus received in written form were a sub-category of that larger group of poor, whose entitlement to settlement by service was a matter of dispute between two local authorities, and whose case, contested by county quarter sessions, were finally (or actually, rather rapidly) shot off to London and the Court of the King's Bench, in the final attempt to rid a parish of a claimant for poor relief. The women whose settlement was in dispute raise more interesting questions than do the men in similar situations, because there were more of them, and because women, viewed from the perspective of legal process, raised the most perplexing questions about settlement, and the rights it conferred on its recipient. It was women servants (in the second half of the century, these were domestic servants for the main part) who forced questions about settlement as a form of possession, or property.[40] Their cases refocus the questions of labour, value, and the ownership of labour: of property in one's person and in one's labour (and an important question here, of property in one's story). They offered unmarked and unnoticed contributions to debates in legal and political theory, about service, self-possession, and self-ownership. And their stories force, much as they did for the Lord Chief Justice, the comparison between slavery and servitude, and the legal consequences of inhabiting one or other condition.

In 1785 Mansfield heard the case of Charlotte Howe, slave and servant of Thames Ditton in Surrey, though not directly, and not from the narrative produced by question and answer before the bar, but rather from the tale compiled by several hands (clerk to the justices, overseers of the poor, Thames Ditton attorney, members of the Courts of Quarter sessions for Surrey and Middlesex). Indeed, a case like this, that went on appeal from a county quarter sessions with all the accompanying paper work, is one of the ways in which maddening gaps in the local records were produced, for there seems to be no way of telling what happened to the case once the papers were deposited in King's Bench filing system.

Charlotte Howe was brought to England in 1781 when very young, probably when she was about fifteen years old, by Captain and Mrs Howe, who settled in Thames Ditton.[41] She had been purchased in America as 'a negro slave', and continued in the couple's service until the death of Captain Howe in June 1783. His dying evidently brought about a change in the household's perception of its circumstances – as the death of a master often did – for Charlotte (or perhaps her mistress arranged it) got herself baptised in

December of that year, the churchwarden recording in the baptism register that she was 'Charlotte, an african servant to Mrs How'.[42] Some time in the new year, Mrs Howe moved to Chelsea, taking her black servant with her. In June, Charlotte walked out (we cannot tell whether this was done with encouragement or not) thus perhaps, making herself free, which Lorimer Douglas has suggested was a major route to the end of slavery in Britain, brought about by the actions of slave-servants themselves, rather than by the more conventionally evoked abolition brought about by legislation.[43]

This young woman may have freed herself (and certainly, no one went after her), but she was without means of subsistence, for in the late summer of 1784 she returned to Thames Ditton, and applied to the parish officials for poor relief (though she does not appear to have been examined by the magistrates as to the state of her settlement). In October, she was removed to St Luke's (this must have been on the order of a magistrate) and was placed in the parish workhouse. The Thames Ditton authorities paid St Luke's for three months keep of Charlotte Howe in January 1785, though the 1s. 5d. expended was vastly less than the monies that went to the local attorney, briefed to attend Surrey Quarter sessions where her case was disputed, and the immense sum that preparation for the appeal to King's Bench cost them.[44]

The Chelsea parish won its appeal against Surrey, and in January 1785, Charlotte Howe was carted back to Thames Ditton. At the end of the month, the vestrymen determined to take the opinion of King's Bench, a decision that was to cost them over £50, and brought no one much satisfaction, for the churchwarden and magistrates of Thames Ditton learned from Lord Mansfield and his fellow judges was that their attempts to deal with Charlotte Howe in terms of her settlement or lack of it had been completely erroneous. It had been argued most eloquently at Quarter Sessions and again at King's Bench that as she had 'lived as a servant from year to year, and therefore is to be considered a servant as far as the laws of England will permit', and that 'it would be hard if a person of this description should not be maintained and taken notice of by the law'.[45] She had acted as a servant, displaying a clear idea of the nature of her obligation, 'as she never thought of quitting the service of the family till her master's death: [and] that to deprive her of her settlement, the court must hold that she might have gone away at any time'.[46] But Mansfield cut briskly through the narration of her circumstances, with the observation that 'it cannot be contended that this was a voluntary hiring, and [is] therefore not a service'.[47] Whether she had been paid wages or not was irrelevant, for wages were not necessary to make a settlement, indeed, there was no entitlement to wages anyway, whether cash was handed over or no, 'because there never was a contract for wages'. All of this – with whom and how she had lived, the money she may have received – was irrelevant, and so were clever arguments by the lawyers from Chelsea and Surrey that the English legal system recognised the condition of slavery, or at least serfdom, and should thus recognise Charlotte Howe.[48] None of this would do, for indeed though the Poor Law was a 'subsisting positive law [statute law], enforced by statutes which began to be made about the time of Queen Elizabeth, when villeinage was not abolished, and villeins … [might] … in point of law … subsist to this day', nevertheless, 'the statutes do not relate to them, nor had they them in contemplation'. The point was rather that for Charlotte Howe to 'bring herself under a positive law, she must answer the description it requires'. Further, 'her colour or [her] being a slave, or [her] having become such will not affect the question'. Her case was indeed, 'very plain': 'the statute says there must be a hiring, and here there was no hiring at all. She does not come within the description'; or as another transcription has it, 'There is nothing in it.'[49] As the notes on the back of the King's Bench papers tersely summarise: 'Easter term 25th Geo: 3d a black who was purchased abroad and continues to live with Mar [Master] or his Exectr for years in England without any Hiring does not gain a *Settlement*.'[50] The case of Charlotte Howe thus became no case at all; neither Thames Ditton nor Chelsea was responsible for her, and (for the time being) she disappears from the records leaving behind fragments of a story made for her by the legal system.

There were literary forms, Grub-Street products, that exploited these everyday, enforced narratives of the self, most frequently told before a magistrate or a judge. There was the criminal tale, best known through *The Newgate Calendar*, but more widely distributed in chapbook form.[51] Mary Saxby's *Memoirs of a Female Vagrant, Written by Herself* (1806) is notable for two reasons. One is that in the massive microfilm publishing venture 'The People's History. Working Class Autobiographies, … 1729–1889' of 1986, a series of facsimiles of all such volumes deposited in the British Library, hers is the first woman's story reproduced. It is part of the on-going project, inaugurated in the twentieth century, to uncover and circulate the life-stories of the plebeian, the subaltern, the female. In this recovered working-class narrative, Saxby's pain at losing eight of her ten children, and the guilty anguish of coming slowly and creepingly to God, certainly structure a conventional Methodist conversion tale. But a surer and tighter structure for the narrative on the page is the writer's detailing of her contact with the law, and the central and local state. Her bids for settlement, appearances before the justices, encounters with the overseers of the poor (as well as with numerous philanthropic doctors and clergymen, likely to make a cash exchange for her story), dates and places of baptism and burial, births and deaths but on only one occasion, marriage (her cohabitations and fornications provide the book's insistent throb of shame) are listed and recorded, with a detail and precision of recall that the *genre* simply does not demand.[52] Mary Saxby's written autobiography was structured by all the other involuntary accounts she had delivered up, over the course of fifty years.

The narrative of a life, which when told, explains something of the person, here, now, telling a tale (much more rarely, writing it down) was articulated again and again, by men and women like these, from the seventeenth century onwards. The basic structures of the modern literary character were – perhaps – laid down in these numerous enforced autobiographies. This is a large claim; and as yet, we know very little about the way in which an understanding of what a character was (what an informal theory of 'character' looked like) moved into the emergent novel, and out again, into the wider society, to be taken and used in innumerable acts of self-fashioning and self-perception. There is suggestive work on stage melodrama of the nineteenth century, and the understanding it may have brought about, that a working-class character was a he or she buffeted by fortune and extraneous events: a someone to whom things *just happen.*[53] And in discussing fictional realism's fixation on 'character' Bruce Robbins has observed that as 'character was the mask that people were expected to don in the face of power', 'it seems more than a coincidence that from the time … when modern criticism took shape, a "character" was a statement in which one employer described to another … the habits and qualities of a servant'.[54]

The assumption of the modern 'autobiographical turn', that there exists and has existed an *urge* to tell the self, and that it comes from within, is of very little help in hearing these eighteenth-century cases of enforced narration. And for the moment, it is impossible to move beyond these a suggestions, that the modern literary articulation of selfhood and character had one of its origins among the poorer sort, when their verbal accounts of themselves, told before a magistrate, were recorded by others. What we can be clearer about is one of the sites of this storytelling, the Magistrate as the necessary and involuntary story-taker, and why it is the Archive contains what it does.

Sarah Maza has described stories something like these, shaped and articulated through legal process in pre-Revolutionary France, in *Private Lives and Public Affairs*.[55] The printed and published *mémoires* which made private cases into public reading matter and *causes célèbres*, emerged from a legal system that emphasised privacy, and in which plaintiff and defendant usually faced the Magistrate alone: here, witnesses did not confront each other, prosecuting council had no right to question a defendant and there was no cross-questioning. The *mémoires* were the major part of the paper work emerging from a procedurial system that was based on the written rather than the spoken (and haphazardly transcribed) word. They were originally handwritten and their technical function was in the courtroom, where they were read aloud to the Magistrate, or consulted by him, before he made his final judgement. They escaped the censorship laws and when published and circulated, translated the private court room into the public sphere, perhaps replacing the theatre as the stage on which monarchical government and absolutism and their effect on private persons and private lives were held up for scrutiny and questioned.[56] These stories (of love, sex and property, of obligation and *force majeure*) thus had a social role, and their articulation now contributes powerfully to the understanding provided by narratology: that narrative shapes 'our understanding of ourselves and of our world' and to the historian's understanding of their meanings, that held sway in one society, two and a half centuries ago.[57]

These differences, between two Magistrates and two legal systems, between spoken and written language, and between what was voluntary and what was not, force a greater specificity in the questioning of self, self-fashioning and narration. Charlotte Howe's story was made for her by legal process. Her being a slave makes her an extraordinary example of the ordinariness of these proceedings: having had the story taken, it was not returned to her, not even in the formulaic autobiography of the settlement certificate, but rather left behind, in the case books and the Archive.[58]

Notes

1 Benedict Anderson, *Imagined Communities. Reflections on the Origin and Spread of Nationalism* (London, Verso, [1983] 1991), p. 198.

2 Anderson's source for his formulation is Roland Barthes's *Michelet par lui-même* (Paris, Seuil, [1954] 1968), p. 92.

3 Jules Michelet, 'Jusqu'au 18 Brumaire' (1872–74), *Oeuvres Complètes*, XXI (Paris, Flammarion, 1982), p. 268.

4 Geoffrey Bennington and Jacques Derrida, *Jacques Derrida* (Paris, Seuil, 1991), pp. 299–302. Y.C. Aouate, 'Les mesures d'exclusion anti-juives dans l'enseignement public en Algerie, 1940–1943', *Pardès*, 8 (1988), 109–28. For the uses of history under Vichy see Robert O. Paxton, *Vichy France. Old Guard and New Order, 1940–1944* (New York, Knopf, 1972), pp. 150–68. Jean-Michel Barreau, 'Vichy, Ideologue de l'école', *Revue d'Histoire Moderne et Contemporaine*, 38 (1991), 590–616, and Jean-Michel Barreau, 'Abel Bonnard, Ministre de l'éducation nationale sous Vichy, ou l'éducation impossible', *Revue d'Histoire Moderne et Contemporaine*, 43:3 (1996), 464–78. See also Jean-Michel Guiraud, *La Vie intellectuelle et Artistique à Marseilles à l'époque de Vichy et sous l'occupation, 1940–1944* (Marseille, CRDP, 1987), pp. 144–55. See W.D. Hall, *The Youth of Vichy France* (Oxford, Clarendon Press, 1981), pp. 8, 19, 40, 216–19 for the uses of history in the inter-war years.

5 G. Bruno (Mme Alfred Fouillé), *Le Tour de la France par deux enfants. Devoir et Patries* (Saint-Cloud, Belin, 1922) – this was its *386th* edition – preserved the France that Michelet had helped to shape, though it nowhere mentions his name. See L.C. Syms, *Le tour de la France, par G. Bruno ed. for school use by L.C. Syms* (New York, American Book Company, 1902). Also Jacques and Mona Ozouf, 'Le Tour de la France par Deux Enfants. Le petit livre rouge de la République', in Pierre Nora, *Les Lieux de mémoire sous la direction de Pierre Nora. I. La*

République (Paris, Gallimard, 1984), pp. 292–321 for impossibilities of appropriating the republican Michelet to the Right.

6 See Nadia Margolis, 'The "Joan Phenomenon" and the French Right', in Bonnie Wheeler and Charles T. Wood (eds), *Fresh Verdicts on Joan of Arc* (New York, Garland, 1996), pp. 265–87, for Michelet's work on Joan of Arc. See also Robert Gildea, *The Past in French History* (New Haven and London, Yale University Press, 1994), pp. 154–65. The passage above concerning the Magistrate (from the unfinished *Histoire du XIXe Siècle* is quoted in full in Barthes's *Michelet par lui-même* under the title 'Magistrature de l'histoire'.

7 Victor Ehrenberg, *The Greek State* (London, Methuen, [1960] 1969), pp. 66–74, 77–80. Orlando Patterson, *Slavery and Social Death. A Comparative Study* (Cambridge MA, Harvard University Press, 1982), pp. 4–5, 29, 87.

8 William Doyle, *The Parlement of Bordeaux and the End of the Old Regime, 1771–1790* (London and Tonbridge, Ernest Benn, 1974), pp. 308–9. David A. Bell, *Lawyers and Citizens. The Making of a Political Elite in Old Regime France* (New York, Oxford University Press, 1994), pp. 22–4. Richard Mowery Andrews, *Law, Magistracy and Crime in Old Regime Paris, 1735–1789. Volume 1. The System of Criminal Justice* (Cambridge, Cambridge University Press, 1994), pp. 417–504.

9 Andrews, *Law, Magistracy*, pp. 417–94. See also Anthony Crubaugh, 'Local Justice and Rural Society in the French Revolution', *Journal of Social History*, 34:2 (2000), 327–50.

10 Andrews, *Law, Magistracy*, p. 494.

11 Sarah Maza, *Private Lives and Public Affairs. The Causes Celèbres of Prerevolutionary France* (Berkeley, Los Angeles and London, University of California Press, 1993), pp. 34–5.

12 Andrews, *Law, Magistracy*, p. 434.

13 Ibid., p. 502.

14 Bell, *Lawyers and Citizens*, p. 24; Steven Laurence Kaplan, *Provisioning Paris. Merchants and Millers in the Grain and Flour Trade during the Eighteenth Century* (Ithaca and London, Cornell University Press, 1984); *Bread, Politics and Political Economy in the Reign of Louis XV*, 2 vols (The Hague, Martinus Nijhoff, 1976).

15 Doyle, *The Parlement of Bordeaux*, pp. 308–9.

16 Eugéne Buret, *De la Misère des classes labourieuses en Angleterre et en France*, 2 vols (Paris, Paulin, 1840), 1, pp. 208–9. (In England, it is the government of the society itself, its legislation, that reveals the existence of poverty over the course of two centuries. Since the famous Act of 43 Elizabeth, there has not been a single year in which the law has not intervened to regulate the condition of the poor.)

17 Ibid., pp. 138–151, p. 209.

18 Sir William Blackstone, *Commentaries on the Laws of England. In Four Books* (Dublin, Company of Booksellers, [1765] 1775), 1, pp. 422–32. S.F.C. Milsom, 'The Nature of Blackstone's Achievement', *Oxford Journal of Legal Studies*, 1 (1981), 1–12. John W. Cairns, 'Blackstone, an English Institutionalist. Legal Literature and the Rise of the Nation State', *Oxford Journal of Legal Studies*, 4 (1984), 318–60. For the 'Roman' tendencies of the Lord Chief Justice, see James Oldham, *The Mansfield Manuscripts and the Growth of English Law in the Eighteenth Century*, 2 vols (Chapel Hill and London, University of North Carolina Press, 1992), 1, p. 204. For the Roman Law perspective on questions of English service and servitude, see John Taylor, *Elements of the Civil Law* (Cambridge, privately printed, 1767), pp. 247–63, 407–47.

19 Blackstone, *Commentaries*, 1, pp. 427–8. Justices of the peace were more likely to learn their law not even from one of the many editions of Richard Burn's *The Justice of the Peace and the Parish Office* published after 1756, but from volumes of tear-out blank warrants, and summonses, like Burn's own *Blank Precedents Relating to the Office of Justice of the Peace, Settled by Doctor Burn* (London, T. Cadell for the King's Law Printer, 1787). But in 1751, Ward probably referred to Michael Dalton, *The Country Justice. Containing the Practice, Duty and Power of the Justices of the Peace, as well as in as out of their sessions* (London, Henry Lintot, 1742), p. 139.

20 'An Act containing Divers Orders for Artificers, Labourers, Servants of Husbandry and Apprentices' (1562); 'An Act for the Better Adjusting and more easy Recovery of the Wages of certain Servants and for better Regulation of such Servants' (1747). A vast body of legislation governed the relationship between employers and servant. Elizabethan legislation was still found routinely useful in the second half of the eighteenth century, and many believed that these two acts of Parliament applied to all servants, not just the farm servants they

specified. It is clear that magistrates routinely ignored distinctions between types of servant and used these two acts as universal legislation for their regulation. Indeed, there were frequent calls for the provisions of 'that excellent statute [5 Eliz.c.4] and that of 20 Geo.III to our menial servants'. Anon., *Reflections on the Relative Situations of Master and Servant, Historically and Politically Considered; the Irregularities of Servants; the Employment of Foreigners; and the General Inconveniencies Resulting from the Want of Regulations* (London, W.Miller, 1800), p. 23. Richard Burn, *The Justice of the Peace and the Parish Officer*, 13th edn, 4 vols (London, A. Strahan and W. Woodfall, 1776), 1, pp. 151–8.

21 Lincoln's Inn Library, Misc. Manuscript 592, Manuscript Diary of Philip Ward of Stoke Doyle, Northamptonshire, 1748–1751.

22 Nottinghamshire County Record Office, M 8050, Notebook of Sir Gervase Clifton, JP, 1772–1812. Entry for 14 October 1785. PR 1093, Constable's Account Book, Staunton-on-the-Wold, 1748–1800. Again, for the vexed question of whether or not magistrates had rights of jurisdiction in the domestic service relationship as well as farm service (a point returned to again and again in eighteenth-century legal treatises), see n. 20 above; and James Barry Bird, *The Laws Respecting Masters and Servants, Articled Clerks, Apprentices, Manufacturers, Labourers, and Journeymen* (London, W. Clarke, 3rd edn, 1799), pp. 3, 139; and Thomas Waller Williams, *The Whole Law Relative to the Duty Office of a Justice of the Peace*, 4 vols (London, John Stockdale, 1812), 3, 887–93. Williams thought that in the previous century, magistrates simply assumed that all servants 'were servants in husbandry, and thus exercised jurisdiction' (p. 893).

23 Anon., *Reflections*, p. 23.

24 Thomas Gisborne, *An Inquiry into the Duties of Man in the Higher and Middle Classes of Society in Great Britain, Resulting from their respective Situations, Professions and Employments*, 2 vols (London, B. & J. White, 2nd edn, 1795), 1, p. 140.

25 J.M. Beattie, *Crime and the Courts in England, 1660–1800* (Oxford, Clarendon Press, 1986), pp. 5–6, 71.

26 Keith Snell, *Annals of the Labouring Poor. Social Change and Agrarian England, 1660–1900* (Cambridge: Cambridge University Press, 1985).

27 Warwickshire County Record Office, DR 223/327/33. Parish of Bed-
    worth, Settlement Examinations 1754–1779, Examination of Samuel
    Holyday, 14 June 1766.

28 Warwickshire Country Record Office, DR 19/433–493. Parish of
    Astley. Overseers of the Poor, Removal Orders and Settlement Exam-
    inations. DR 19/480, Mary Manton's Examination.

29 The Statute Fair: a hiring fair, at which servants in husbandry and, to
    a lesser extent, domestic servants, made verbal contracts with
    employers for a year's employment.

30 Nottinghamshire Record Office, M8051, Notebook of Sir Gervase
    Clifton, JP, 1805–1810, 37. Entry for 26 October 1809. For the law relat-
    ing to settlement, and a large number of cases which, unlike that of
    Elizabeth Wells, made case-law, see Francis Const, *Decisions of the Court
    of the King's Bench, Upon the Laws relating to the Poor, Originally pub-
    lished by Edmund Bott*, 2 vols (London, Whieldon & Butterworth,
    3rd edn, 1793), 1, pp. 315–515. See the case of Hannah Wright of
    Derbyshire, pregnant and out of place in 1778, in ibid., pp. 516–18, and
    in Thomas Caldecott, *Reports of Cases relative to the Duty and Office of
    a Justice of the Peace, from Michaelmas Term 1776, inclusive, to Trinity
    Term 1785, inclusive* (London, His Majesty's Law Printer's, 1785),
    pp. 11–14. Bastardy examinations are a major source for Mark Jackson's
    *New-born Child Murder. Women, Children and the Courts in Eighteenth-
    century England* (Manchester, Manchester University Press, 1996).

31 David Vincent, *Bread, Knowledge and Freedom. A Study of Nineteenth-
    century Working-class Autobiography* (London, Methuen, 1981). For
    Anthony Giddens it is irrelevant that these stories were not written
    down by their tellers. See his comments on the 'self … reflexively
    understood by the person in terms of his or her biography', and the
    claim that 'autobiography whether written down or not is actually the
    core of identity in modern life'. Anthony Giddens, *Modernity and Self-
    Identity. Self and Society in the Late Modern Age* (Cambridge, Polity,
    1991), pp. 52–4.

32 Anon., *A Proposal for the Amendment and Encouragement of Servants*
    (London, J. Shuckburgh, 1751), p. 10.

33 Cecil Fifoot, *Lord Mansfield* (Oxford, Clarendon Press, 1936), 206–7.
    Oldham, *The Mansfield Manuscripts*, 1, p. 108. John Impey, *The New
    Instructor Clericalis. Stating the Authority, Jurisdiction and Modern*

Practice of the Court of the King's Bench. With Directions for commencing and defending Actions, entering up Judgements, suing out Executors, and proceeding in Error (London, W. Strahan & W. Woodfall, 1782). 'Attorney', *An Attorney's Practice Epitomized; or, the Method, Times and Expenses of Proceeding in the Courts of King's Bench and Common Pleas* (London, Henry Lintot, 8th edn, 1757). For a clear account of procedures that followed on the King's Bench 'hearing an appellant, jurisdiction in consequence of its general superintendency over all inferior magistrates and courts', and the peculiar consequences of the 'judgement of justices of the peace in questions on the *poor laws* [being] not conclusive on the parties', see Williams Hands, *The Solicitor's Practice on the Crown Side of the Court of the King's Bench. with an Appendix Containing the Forms of the Proceeding* (London, J. Butterworth, 1803), pp. 27–31.

34 Buret, *De la Misère*, 1, p. 144. (A dispute between two parishes over one pauper has often cost more money than would have the entire support of the poor of both of them.)

35 Richard Burn, *The History of the Poor Laws: With Observations* (London, H. Woodfall & N. Strahan, 1764), pp. 211–12. *The Justice of the Peace and Parish Officer* (London, Henry Lintot for A. Millar, 1756) had gone through fifteen editions by 1785. See Richard Burn, *The Justice of the Peace and Parish Officer. Continued to the Present Time by John Burn Esq., his Son*, 4 vols (London, A. Strahan & N. Woodfall, 1793). See Sidney and Beatrice Webb, *English Local Government. Volume 1. The Parish and the County* (London, Cass, [1906] 1963), p. 406 for the popularity of Burn's manual. See also Snell, *Annals*, p. 115.

36 'It would be highly meritorious in the heads of parishes, to discourage all frivolous suits, those chiefly respecting *settlements*, which are often set on foot from interested motives, and prosecuted with a spirit of malevolence which ought everywhere to be repressed. The Earl of Mansfield hath reprobated contests of this kind, which have been brought before him, in the most pointed and indignant terms.' Henry Zouch, *Hints Respecting the Public Police, Published at the Request of the Court of Quarter Sessions held at Pontefract, April 24, 1786* (London, John Stockdale, 1786), p. 8.

37 Oldham, *Mansfield Manuscripts*, 1, pp. 164–8; and for unreported

cases (which Oldham calls a possible 'lively repository of social history' of little use to the legal historian) see pp. 183–5.

38 Joseph Burchall, *Arrangement and Digest of the Law in Cases Adjudged in the King's Bench and Common Pleas from the Year 1756 to 1794, inclusive* (London, J. Jones, 1796), pp. 232–40.

39 Francis Const, *Decisions of the Court of the King's Bench, Upon the Laws Relating to the Poor, Originally Published by Edmund Bott Esq. of the Inner Temple, Barrister at Law. Revised … by Francis Const Esq. of the Middle Temple*, 2 vols (London, Whieldon & Butterworth, 3rd edn, 1793), 2, pp. 315–515. The remark about legal activity in the second half of the eighteenth century is Joseph Burchell's. Burchell, *Arrangement and Digest*, Preface. On this point, see T.C. Hansard (ed.), *The Parliamentary History of England, from the Earliest Period to the Year 1803, Volume XIX, comprising the period from … January 1777 to … December 1778* (London, T.C. Hansard, 1814), Preface. See also Sir William Holdsworth, *A History of the English Law* (London, Methuen, 1938), 10, p. 100; and Oldham, *Mansfield Manuscripts*, 1, p. 163.

40 For settlement as possession, or a kind of property, see Edmund Bott, *Digest of the Laws Relating to the Poor, by Francis Const*, 3 vols (London, Strahan, 4th edn, 1800), 1, pp. 160–2, 164–6.

41 Sylvester Douglas, *Report of Cases Argued and Determined in the Court of the King's Bench, Volume 4 (1784–1785)* (London and Dublin, Sweet, Stevens & Millikins, 1831), pp. 301–2.

42 Surrey History Centre, Thames Ditton Parish Records. Baptisms, entry for 17 December 1783.

43 Lorimer Douglas, 'Black Slaves and English Liberty. A Re-examination of Racial Slavery in England', *Immigrants and Minorities* 3:2 (1984), pp. 121–50.

44 London Metropolitan Archives, St Luke's Chelsea, P74/LUK/111. Workhouse and Discharge Register, January 1782–December 1800. Entries for 25 October 1784, 20 January 1785. Surrey History Centre, Thames Ditton Parish Records, 2568/8/4. Overseers Accounts, 1773–1805. Entries for 10 December 1784, 2 April 1785 and undated entries 1786. 2568/7/4. Poor Rate Assessment and Vestry Minutes, 1778–1796. Entry for 31 January 1785. Surrey Quarter Sessions Order Books, QS2/6.

45 Douglas, *Report of Cases*, p. 301.

46 Thomas Caldecott, *Reports of Cases Relative to the Duty and Offices of a Justice of the Peace, from Michaelmas Term 1776, inclusive to Trinity Term, inclusive* (London, His Majesty's Law Printers for P. Uriel, 1785), pp. 516–20.

47 Douglas, *Report of Cases* (1831), p. 301.

48 Granville Sharp, *A Representation of the Injustice and Dangerous Tendency of Tolerating Slavery; or of Admitting the Least Claim of Private Property in the Persons of Men, in England. In four parts* (London, Benjamin White, 1769), pp. 108–11 rehearses these arguments which he suggests were widely known among lawyers.

49 Douglas, *Report of Cases*, p. 301. Caldecott, *Reports*, p. 520.

50 Lincoln's Inn Library, Dampier Manuscripts, B.P.B., 377. 'Surrey. The King agt the Inhabitants of Thames Ditton.'

51 J. L. Rayner, *The Complete Newgate Calendar*, 5 vols (London, privately printed, 1826); Victor E. Neuberg, *Chapbooks* (London, Woburn Press, 1976). One example plucked from the myriad is *An Account of the Execution of Mary of Shrewsbury for the Murder of Her Bastard Child* of 1775. The British Library's copy of *An Account of the Execution of Mary of Shrewsbury for the Murder of Her Bastard Child – God's Judgement Upon False Witnesses* (London, Alston, 1775), is bound with a series of chapbooks, among them *The Merry Life and Mad Exploits of Captain James Hind, the Great Robber of England*, *The Battledore, or, First Book for Children*, and *The High German Fortune Teller*. There is some discussion of the relationship of this kind of literature to the criminal biography in L.B. Faller, *Turned to Account. The Forms and Functions of Criminal Biography in Late Seventeenth and Early Eighteenth Century England* (Cambridge, Cambridge University Press, Cambridge, 1987). See also the discussion in V.A.C. Gattrell, *The Hanging Tree. Execution and the English People, 1770–1868* (Oxford, Oxford University Press, 1994). For the strange dislocations of chronology and voice in a form that allowed the condemned man or woman (like Mary of Shrewsbury) to be publicly hanged to the accompaniment of the ballad that recorded their last dying words (which they had not, and would not, utter), see Lennard Davis, *Factual Fictions. The Origins of the English Novel* (New York, Columbia University Press, 1986), pp. 42–84.

52 Mary Saxby, *Memoirs of a Female Vagrant, Written by Herself* (London, J. Burditt, 1806). People's History, 'The People's History. Working Class Autobiographies from the British Library, Part I: 1729–1889; Part II: 1890–1920' (Brighton, Harvester Press Microform Publications and the British Library, 1986).

53 Michael Booth, *English Melodrama* (London, Herbert Jenkins, 1965). Carol Mackay, 'Melodrama and the Working Class', in Carol Hanbery MacKay (ed.), *Dramatic Dickens* (London, Macmillan, 1989), pp. 96–109.

54 Bruce Robbins, *The Servant's Hand. English Fiction from Below*, (Durham and London, Duke University Press, [1986] 1993), p. 35.

55 Maza, *Private Lives*, pp. 34–5.

56 Ibid., pp. 116-17, 130–1.

57 Ibid., pp. 1–19.

58 For the taking of stories and their return to the dispossesed, see Carolyn Steedman, 'State Sponsored Autobiography', in Becky Conekin, Frank Mort and Chris Waters (eds), *Moments of Modernity. Reconstructing Britain 1945–1964* (London, Rivers Oram, 1999), pp. 41–54. See Adriana Caverero's comments on the he or she who takes the other's story, and fulfils the desire of the subject for 'a narratable self', in *Relating Narratives. Storytelling and Selfhood* (London, Routledge [1997] 2000), pp. 55–66, and passim.

4

The space of memory: in an archive

MNEMOSYNE WAS THE MOTHER of all the Muses including Clio, History's own, at least according to some authorities of the Ancient World. Modern historiographers have for the main part followed the ancient authorities, in giving their accounts of how History (a way of thinking; an academic discipline) came into the world, and what its relationship to Memory has been, over the last 300 years or so. Jacques Le Goff used the Mnemosyne myth in order to begin his account of how History usurped the functions of Memory; a long usurpation indeed, but accelerating in the nineteenth century, with the development of history as a subject of inquiry in the academy and, later, as information to be imparted to whole populations in European systems of mass education.[1] The account that Le Goff gives in *Memory and History* suggests – though he does not make this point explicitly – that History in its modern mode might be understood as just one more technology of memory, one of a set of techniques developed in order that societies might remember. In the 1960s Michel Foucault indicated the way in which History both shapes and occupies the function of Memory:

> History ... is certainly the most erudite, the most aware, the most conscious, and possibly the most cluttered area of our memory; but it is equally the depths from which all beings emerge into their precarious, glittering existence. Since it is the mode of being of all

that is given us in experience, History has become the unavoidable element in our thought.[2]

The charm and elegance – and possibly the perspicacity – of this observation lies in its partial reversal of the chronology we take for granted, in which modern historical understanding replaces older, informal ways of comprehending the past (in which History replaces Memory). Foucault suggests on the other hand, that History clutters up and occupies our memory.[3] At the same time, History (the formal written history, or history-writing) has provided a way of thinking about what is in a particular place – a place which for the moment shall simply be called Memory.

To interrogate that place, we have to be less concerned with History as *stuff* (we must put to one side the content of any particular piece of historical writing, and the historical information it imparts) than as *process*, as ideation, imagining and remembering. We need to accept the old stories about Clio's parentage (proceed on the assumption that the practices of Memory gave rise to History in its modern mode), but also, at the same time begin to disinter the ways in which, over the last 300 years or so, History has shaped Memory. This involves giving an account that is itself historical, of how this happened, and what is happening now to the History that people do these things with: think by, imagine by, remember with. A discussion of what has happened to time and to space in Clio's modern dominion returns us to the Archive, and to Derrida's Archive in particular.

That Archive – we have witnessed this – is associated with legal administration, with the beginning of things (government, police, magistracy), and with the rule system of the law.[4] But there is still room left for wonder at an etymology curiously dislocated from one of Derrida's purposes in 'Archive Fever', which is to provide some account of the structure of Freudian thought by analogy with the

Archive. It is a common desire – it has been so since at least the end of the nineteenth century – to use the Archive as metaphor or analogy, when memory is discussed. But the problem in using Derrida discussing Freud in order to discuss Archives, is that an Archive is not very much like human memory, and is not at all like the unconscious mind. An Archive may indeed take in stuff, heterogeneous, undifferentiated stuff … texts, documents, data … and order them by the principles of unification and classification. This stuff, reordered, remade, then emerges – some would say like a memory – when someone needs to find it, or just simply needs it, for new and current purposes.

But in actual Archives, though the bundles may be mountainous, there isn't in fact, very much there. The Archive is not potentially made up of *everything*, as is human memory; and it is not the fathomless and timeless place in which nothing goes away that is the unconscious. The Archive is made from selected and consciously chosen documentation from the past and also from the mad fragmentations that no one intended to preserve and that just ended up there. (The Warwickshire Quarter Sessions Rolls, 1842–1882; one torn testimonial for a serving maid pushed into the back of the gentry wife's Commonplace Book from 1822.) And *nothing happens to this stuff, in the Archive.* It is indexed, and catalogued, and some of it is not indexed and catalogued, and some of it is lost. But as stuff, it just sits there until it is read, and used, and narrativised. In the Archive, you cannot be shocked at its exclusions, its emptinesses, at what *is not* catalogued, at what was – so the returned call-slip tells you – 'destroyed by enemy action during the Second World War', nor that it tells of the gentry and not of the poor stockinger. Its condition of being deflects outrage: in its quiet folders and bundles is the neatest demonstration of how state power has operated, through ledgers and lists and indictments, and through what is missing from them.

A prosaic definition is useful; a definition that for the moment, is not about analogies and does not involve questions of meaning, that understands it simply as a name for the many places in which the past (which does not now exist, but which once did actually happen; which cannot be retrieved, but which may be represented) has deposited some traces and fragments, usually in written form. In these archives someone (usually from about 1870 onwards, across the Western world) has catalogued and indexed these traces.[5]

But the Archive is older than the English county record offices and the municipal and *départemental* archives of provincial France that are thus evoked. There is no need to return to the Greek city state, nor to the *archon* and his house cluttered up with municipal documents, in order to know that the modern European public archive came into being in order to solidify and memorialise first monarchical and then state power: the House of Savoy established an archive in Turin in the early eighteenth century; Peter the Great did the same at St Petersburg in 1720, Maria Theresa in Vienna in 1749. Princely and civic archives were instituted in Warsaw, Venice and Florence in the 1760s and 1770s. The National Archives were founded in France in 1790; the Public Record Office in 1838.[6] These are the origins of a prosaic place where the written and fragmentary traces of the past are put in boxes and folders, bound up, stored, catalogued …

And: the Archive is also a place of dreams.

In January 1824 Jules Michelet read the work of the eighteenth-century Neapolitan philosopher Giambattista Vico (1668–1744) and recorded in his diary that: 'I was seized with a frenzy caught from Vico, an incredible intoxication with his great historical principle.'[7] Later, at L'Ecole Normale, teaching his students made the principle clearer to him. It was, in his own summary of Vico, that

'Humanity is its own creation'.[8] He referred to the early and striking passages of the third edition of Vico's *The New Science* (1744), which assert that

> In the light of thick darkness enveloping the earliest antiquity, so remote from ourselves, there shines the eternal and never failing light of a truth beyond all question: that the world of civil society has certainly been made by men, and that its principles are therefore to be found within the modifications of our own human mind.[9]

Though Michelet's moment of understanding (the shocking, sudden *seeing* of something) can easily be made the symbolic birth of social history in its modern mode, the better contender for the title is the day the historian goes to the Archives, to the quietly folded and bundled documents of state and judicial administration, but where he believes the past lives: where he can make ink on parchment *speak* ... where he will rescue the unconsidered myriads of the past and write the People into being. Edmund Wilson described how Michelet 'went into the Records, with Vico and the echoes of July [the July Revolution of 1830] in his head, [and] a new past, for the first time, seemed to revive for the imagination'.[10] And in 1869 in a new *Préface* to his *L'Histoire de France* Michelet told of how, before the enlightenment that came through reading Vico, he had wandered in 'those solitary galleries' of the Archives 'in ... deep silence', until with Vico there had come to him 'the whispers of the souls who had suffered so long ago and who were smothered now in the past'.[11]

To enter that place where the past lives, where ink on parchment can be made to *speak*, still remains the social historian's dream, of bringing to life those who do not for the main part exist, not even between the lines of state papers and legal documents, who are not really present, not even in the records of Revolutionary bodies and fractions. But for Michelet, historical subjects like these signalled something beyond their mere absence. As the lost myriads of the past had never really lived, Michelet found himself able to give them actual life rather than mere resurrection. One of Michelet's more recent biographers is eloquent on this point, telling how in 1841, Michelet inscribed the Historian's dream by remembering another one, of the Ancient World:

> He recalled Caesar's dream of a weeping, beseeching army of the dead, and how, when waking [he] … wrote down the names of two lost cities, Corinth and Carthage, and rebuilt them. He … compared that rebuilding with that of the historian, who also resurrected the dead: 'men of a hundred years, nations of 2,000 years, infants who died when nursing, they all say that they hardly lived, that they barely began … They say that if they had the time to know themselves and prepare, they might have accepted their lot; they would have ceased to wander around us, they would have gently allowed their urns to be closed up, lulled by friendly hands, going back to sleep and rebinding their dreams'.

According to Mitzman, Michelet understood the Historian's task as pacifying the spirits of the dead, exorcising them 'by finding the meaning of their brief existences'.[12]

Michelet understood the dead as ghostly presences (shades of what might have been more than emblems of anything that might have happened); and what he could do for them was, as we have seen, what he most profoundly wished for himself:

> J'ai donné à beaucoup de morts trop oubliés l'assistance dont moi-même j'aurai besion. Je les ai exhumés pour une seconde vie … Ils vivent maintenant avec nous qui sentons leurs parents, leurs amis. Ainsi se fait une famille, une cité commune entre les vivants et les morts.[13] (I have given to many of the disregarded dead the assistance that I shall myself need. I have exhumed them for a second life … They live now among we who feel ourselves to be their parents, their friends. Thus is made a family, a city community of the living and the dead.)

It was in a very great solitude that Michelet dreamed his dream of those who could not themselves dream in peace. 'He worked at night', observed Edmund Wilson, 'and made the centuries of the dead keep him company and lend him their strength'.[14] He was the first to show us this capacity among historians to be alone, not only in the act of writing, but in the Archive itself. The Archive allowed the imagining of a particular and modern form of loneliness, which was perhaps analagous to the simultaneous conception of the Historian's relationship to the past 'as one of irretrievable dispossession'. Stephen Bann has described this sense of alienation, and disinheritance, and the way in which in the nineteenth century, it was 'widely and effectively diffused through the various media of representation'.[15]

But the Historian goes to the Archive to be at home as well as to be alone.

In August 1969 Douglas Johnson reviewed Richard Cobb's *A Second Identity* under the title 'The Historian as Frenchman'.[16] This brief notice still offers one of the best accounts of the Archival Romance, tells most clearly what it is historians (some historians) want from the Archive. Johnson noted Cobb's comparison between two investigative trades: 'the historian arriving in the small French provincial town, looking round the cafés before proceeding to the archives', was like 'Maigret putting his nose to the wind and getting the feel of the place'.[17] And then Johnson continues: 'It is deeply moving to find him [Cobb] quoting Georges Lefebvre's feeling that the supreme satisfaction was that of untying the string on the bundles of archives in the attic of a village *mairie*.'[18]

With this solitary undoing of the bundles Johnson lauded a most moving and odd and peculiar way of being in the world. Early on in *A Second Identity*, Cobb describes an extraordinary kind of aloneness emerging in the Archive, when the Historian ponders on the historical subject who is most interesting to him: 'the individual unrelated to any group, the man, the girl, or the old woman alone in the city, the person who eats alone, though in company, who lives in a furnished room, who receives no mail, who has no visible occupation, and who spends much time wandering the streets'.

Cobb made the act of identification waiting to be made, said that the Historian's main problem 'is that of loneliness, especially loneliness in the urban context'. He then went on to discuss in some detail his fondness for the *chronique judiciaire* of *Le Monde*, which provided him with modern examples of the desperation, madness and isolation that marked his favourite historical subjects and he, himself, the Historian:

> Madeleine, a Lyonnaise, in Paris only for the previous three months, has been shot dead, coming out of a Cours Pigier. Marcelle has been found stabbed to death, in the Bois de Boulogne; she was from la Ferté-Bernard. And so on … The parents, back home, are bewildered. Sooner or later, the *dossier* is closed. But not for the historian. What road, terminating in violence, has been followed by the daughter of a *cheminot* from Saint-Germain-des-Fossés? Into what fearful trap has the lonely provincial girl stumbled?[19]

When the Historian works in the national archives, you may note and record her passage from the entry hall at half past five; in her journey through the streets of the Metropolis to the modest hotel, she may be joined by another nineteenth-century figure of the twentieth-century critical imagination, the *flâneur* and also by the recently-invented *flâneuse*, whose historical impossibility may have been firmly stated, but who has nevertheless been forced into being.[20] But neither the *flâneur* nor the *flâneuse* can help us follow the Historian through the streets, not because the one who really walked was a man,[21] but because Richard Cobb wrote of the Historian's aloneness, not in a great metropolis, but in a provincial place, the county or *départemental* town, the ancient centres of local administration and jurisdiction. The town that holds the county record office can be mapped in an hour's walking though the dusk, and in the long stretches of time after the Archive shuts for the night, and before a decent time for dinner, the streets are the only place to be.

The next morning, when the doors are opened at precisely nine o'clock and the little waiting huddle is admitted, then the Historian can untie the bundles that have been waiting, through the long night and for a hundred years. To understand this moment – 'the supreme satisfaction' – we could start with other untyings and undoings. We can consider the opening of justices' notebooks, quarter sessions bundles, files of settlement examinations, private account books, *cahiers de doléances, dossiers, archives policières, registres des délibérations du conseil municipal*, newspaper files … in relation to reading practices associated with the epistolary, that is with, the social and cultural experience of letters and letter-writing.

Twenty years ago, Terry Eagleton drew on another long tradition, one of a critical practice stretching back to Classical Antiquity, in order to understand the opening and reading of letters.[22] (In Eagleton's argument these letters may be fictional or real.) 'Nothing could be at once more intimate and more alienable' says Eagleton of the letter. 'The letter is part of the body which is detachable: torn from the very depths of the subject, it can equally be torn from her physical possession.' In this way, in the realm of the epistolary novel *and* in the social worlds that produce such fictions, 'the letter comes to signify nothing quite so much as sexuality itself, that folded secret place which is always open to violent intrusion … There is always within the letter's decorously covered body that crevice or fissured place where the stirrings of desire can be felt.'[23] Writing letters, reading letters, and the erotic have occupied the same critical space since at least the seventeenth century.[24]

The eighteenth-century reader of epistolary fiction always read something in which *the story of the letters* themselves involved their being lost, pilfered or misappropriated in some way or other. The letters told the reader that what was being read, right now, was not addressed to him or her, and had been intended for other eyes.[25] In the long stretch of time in which the novel came into being and its narrative conventions were incorporated into other forms of prose narrative, this device of epistolarity disappeared, and readers of the nineteenth-century novel became the *intended* readers of the book in their hands, listening to a narrator who knew the story, all of it, from beginning to end, and who was now telling it to countless readers.[26] But the Historian who goes to the Archive must always be an unintended reader, will always read that which was never intended for his or her eyes. Like Michelet in the 1820s, the Historian always reads the fragmented written traces of *something else*, and in the long, whispering gallery must forever be a reader unimagined by the justices' clerk, the examining magistrate, the census enumerator or the guardian of the poor, who made those more-or-less legible registers, and lists and observations. The Historian always reads an unintended, purloined letter.

The two accounts above of the Archive (stories about what historians do in the Archive), one from the 1820s, the other from the 1960s, evoke recent discussions about modern uses of the past. To want to go to the Archive may be a specialist and minority desire (only a Historian's desire after all), but it is emblematic of a modern way of being in the world nevertheless, expressive of the more general fever to know and to have the past. Wanting the past can be attributed to certain turns of thought by which individual narratives of growth and development (particularly narratives of childhood) have become components of what we understand a modern self to be. 'History' is one of the great narrative modes that are our legacy from the nineteenth century, and as a way of plotting and telling a life (of giving shape and meaning to the inchoate items of existence) it is useful to compare it with the modern idea of childhood, and the way in which the remembered childhood – the narrative of the self – has become the dominant way of telling the story of how one got to be the way one is. In the practices of history and of modern autobiographical narration, there is the assumption that *nothing goes away*, that the past has deposited all of its traces, somewhere, somehow (though they may be, in particular cases, difficult to retrieve).[27]

This is the mode described by Stephen Bann in *The Clothing of Clio*, where he tells us about the move from eighteenth-century *vraisemblance* in historical representation, to nineteenth-century *vérité*. In the eighteenth-century understanding of historical representation (in the written history) there was a gap between things and their meaning; but in the nineteenth century we see all kinds of historian striving for a representation in which there was no gap between the thing and its image: in which the representation *was* the thing that 'actually happened'. Bann describes a desire for the lifelike in nineteenth-century historical representation: in the museum, the collection, the pageant, and in the formal written work of history, so that the representation might inscribe 'how things really were', and as 'they really happened'.[28] In the everyday world of the early twenty-first century, we operate within this mode by means of a politics of the imagination in which the past has become a place of succour and strength, a kind of home, for the ideas people possess of who they really want to be. In the 1980s and in a terminology that has now largely been lost, these new uses of the imagination came to be called 'identity politics'.

'Identity' as a term follows the same curious semantic path that Sigmund Freud traced in his essay on 'The Uncanny' where the word for the utterly strange, the *unheimlich* (translated as 'the uncanny') in fact 'leads back to what is known of old and long familiar', where the *unheimelich* 'finally coincides with its opposite', the *heimelich*, the most familiar and homely of things.[29] A modern 'identity', constructed through the process of identification, is at once a claim for absolute sameness, a coincidence and matching with the desired object, group, or person (perhaps a historical identity, located in the historical past) and at the same time, in the enclosed circuit of meaning, is a process of individuation, the modern making of an individuality and a unique personality.

In the project of finding an identity through the processes of historical identification, the past is searched for something (someone, some group, some series of events) that confirms the searcher in his or her sense of self, confirms them as they want to be, and feel in some measure that they already are. The search is for all the ideas, and times, and images that will give us, right now, solidity and meaning in time, and they are as various as: a great queen's passing, a story of gender relations in a household of the 1840s; or faces illuminated by the gas-flares at a union meeting, the travails of all the century before last's child labourers. It seems that we do this quite obdurately, in the face of the hard and clear advice from psycho-analysis, which tells us that the quest is impossible, that what we are searching for is for a lost object, which really cannot be found. The object (the event, the happening, the story from the past) has been altered by the very search for it, by its time and duration: what has actually been lost can never be found. This is not to say that *nothing* is found, but that thing is always something else, a creation of the search itself and the time the search took. These are Jean Laplanche's comments on the search for the lost object. The experience of psycho-analytic practice shows him the ways in which, through the processes of displacement and repression, the object sought is bound to be 'not the lost [one], but a substitute'.[30] The very search for what is lost and gone (in an individual past or a public historical past) alters it, as it goes along, so that every search becomes an impossible one.

Nevertheless, affective use of the historical past developed rapidly in the 1970s and 1980s in the UK.[31] In Raphael Samuel's account this was a time when the old historical epics, of 'classes fulfilling (or failing to fulfil) their appointed historical mission' became the mere echo of a story half-understood. The setting for this momentous abandonment was the changing cultural meaning of the past in post-war Britain, and developments in the means for visualising and imagining the stuff of the past that had been made available to populations in the post-war period.[32] In earlier accounts of this development, in 'On the Methods of History Workshop' (1980) and 'Reading the Signs' (1991) Samuel had started to reveal history become a well-spring of the modern self: history become pleasure.[33]

A new way of thinking and feeling had emerged, that Samuel charted by a kind of minute, slightly disaligned looking at material reworkings of the past in contemporary culture: something he glimpsed through a momentarily illuminated Spitalfields door, the texture of a brick, a devastating analysis of the absurdity of historical reconstruction in Christine Edzard's 1987 film of *Little Dorrit*. He charted the change by reading Dickens himself, and seeing that the heaped curiosities of the novelist's interiors, the great city of the world made magical by the act of walking it and scanning the ghostly faces encountered there, was the novelist's own reading of the signs: was the sign itself that the novelist had understood something about the meaning of the past and all the trifles it strewed in its wake for the *menu peuple* of the nineteenth century. The *things* in Dickens's writing described *their* understanding of the industrial capitalism that had brought them into being and the simultaneous means it had given them for knowing – through those heaped fragments of the past – what it was they were.

Theatres of Memory fulfilled its promise, to show what the modern British heritage industry reveals about 'the culture of the people', and about new makings of the past in the common imagination. But its intense observation of the *things* that make up this new past – the distressed bricks and Edwardian-lady tea-towels that riveted Samuel's gaze – were also the historian's acknowledgement that in late twentieth-century historical practice, time has been slowed down, compressed into the interior spaces of remembered things. It is for this reason that Samuel urged a 'molecular' vision on all historians, and the practice of 'micro-history'. The 'molecular' vision assumes that everything connects, that each entity and event contains the stuff that might illuminate another one. Time becomes solidified. Nothing goes away.[34]

In his much earlier note of 1980, on the social and historiographical effects of these new uses of the past, Samuel made the striking suggestion that a way out of the epistemological wasteland in which socialist historians found themselves, in the death throws of the Marxist epic, might be to remove historical explanation from the hypnotic fix of linear time. Historians, he suggested, could stop dealing with surface concordances, indeed, could rethink the notion of cause itself, which might also be 'more convincingly elaborated if it were removed from a temporal sequence'.[35] He lived – another sixteen years – to see this happen; but not perhaps to know how important a role he played in bringing a new history into being, in which time has been turned into something like the spaces and places of Gaston Bachelard's poetics.

In the practice of History (in academic history and in history as a component of everyday imaginings) something has happened to time: it has been slowed down, and compressed. When the work of Memory is done, it is with the *things* into which this time has been pressed. In *The Poetics of Space* (1958) Gaston Bachelard inaugurated what he called 'topoanalysis', an 'auxiliary of psychoanalysis', that is 'the systematic psychological study of the sites of our intimate lives':

In the theatre of the past that is constituted by memory … we think we know ourselves in time, when all we know is a sequence of fixations in the spaces of the being's stability – a being who does not want to melt away, and who, even in the past, wants time to 'suspend' its flight. In its countless alveoli space contains compressed time. That is what space is for.[36]

More than in any other place, Bachelard found compressed time in the house, which is the great resource for dreams, oneirically rich. The many rooms and levels of the house, its stairways and recesses, all allowed the topanalyst

to start to ask questions: Was the room a large one? Was the garret cluttered up? Was the nook warm? How was it lighted? How, too, in these fragments of space, did the human being achieve silence? How did he relish the very special silence of the various retreats of day-dreaming?[37]

The house was the focus of the poetics he inscribed; but he also paid attention to the nooks and crannies, cupboards, recesses and alcoves of the places in which we grow up and which provide the archive for our dreams and daydreams, during the rest of our life. He attributed particular resonance is to 'objects *that may be opened*. When a casket is closed, it is returned to the general community of objects; it takes its place in exterior space. But it opens! For this reason, a philosopher–mathematician would say that it is the first differential of discovery.'[38]

The Archive belongs to the kind of oneiric spaces that Bachelard described: alone in the Archive, in the counting house of dreams, the historian opens the bundles … . Bachelard told how

in … daydreams the past is very old indeed. For they reach into the great domain of the undated past. By allowing the imagination to wander through the crypts of memory, without realising it, we recapture the bemused life of the tiniest burrows in the house, in the almost animal shelter of dreams.[39]

The Archive is this kind of place, that is to do with longing and appropriation. It is to do with wanting things that are put together, collected, collated, named in lists and indices; a place where a whole world, a social order, may be imagined by the recurrence of a name in a register, through a scrap of paper, or some other little piece of flotsam.[40] Bachelard's description of these little things helps delineate the psychical phenomenology of the Archive, especially if one relies on the experience of historians like Michelet, who did actually breathe in the dust of old parchment, or Cobb, or someone like him, in an actual *archive municipale*, who is delayed a few minutes by the knot of faded pink tape that has not been undone since it was tied, a century and a half ago. Although few people visit archives, with professional historians a minority of those who do, and though the modern archive may be a sound or film library or a collection of post-cards, or a filing cabinet of oral history interviews, Bachelard's work can be instructive on the experience of working with materials like these, in the same way as it can enlighten on the pleasures of opening bundles in the county record office.

But it cannot help with what is not actually there, with the dead who are not really present in the whispering galleries, with the past that does not, in fact live in the record office, but is rather, *gone* (that is its point; that is what the past is for); it cannot help with parchment that does not in fact speak. It is a dream that the Historian makes in the Archive, and it is the dream to which we must return.

The Archive is a place in which people can be alone with the past and historians working there are taking part in an activity which has been scrutinised in its other guises. In his discussion of these matters, the psycho-analyst D.W. Winnicott operated within the long European tradition, of trying to understand those situations in which people are free, in a kind of suspension between the constraints of external and interior compulsions and dictates. Twentieth-century psychology located the genesis of this cultural form in childhood; but it was conceptualised as a way of being in the world long before Winnicott and other object-relations theorists did their work in the 1950s. Play has long been understood as a form of cultural experience that is above all, to do with the capacity to be alone. Paradoxically, this aloneness is dependent on the presence of someone else.[41] When Winnicott attempted a theoretical statement of his many discussions of this point, he made it in developmental terms, and wrote about the child reaching 'the stage of being alone in the presence of someone'. This someone is 'reliable', is 'available and continues to be available when remembered after being forgotten. This person is felt to reflect back what happens in playing'. Then a 'near-withdrawal state' can be achieved by children, 'akin to the *concentration* of adults'.[42] Winnicott further suggested that this activity takes place in a third dimension, not exactly inside the child who plays nor inside the adult who concentrates, nor in the external world, but somewhere else, in 'a third area of human living, one neither inside the individual nor outside in the world of shared reality. This intermediate living can be thought of as occupying a potential space, negating the idea of space and separation.'[43]

'The place where cultural experience is located', said Winnicott 'is in the *potential space* between the individual and the environment (originally the object).'[44] In his 'The Location of Cultural Experience' (1971), Winnicott expressed his anxieties about the term 'culture', noting that he had used it without being sure that he could define it, much beyond 'the inherited tradition ... something in the common pool of humanity, into which individuals and groups of people may contribute, and from which we may all draw if *we have somewhere to put what we find*'. In the Archive, in its deep silence, many historians have discovered that they do have *somewhere to put what they find*, which is the first thing and necessary thing to do with material derived from cultural activity.[45]

The place where what is found may be put, is History. It is in this way, and outside the walls of the Archive, that History has become the place where quite ordinarily and by remembering, we can find things where we have already put them. The processes that have been described here, and the traces of two historians working in archives, offer a striking reversal of the general impulse of modernity, to turn space into place, and to find a home in the world, by literary and other means.[46] The Archive then is something that, through the cultural activity of History, can become Memory's potential space, one of the few realms of the modern imagination where a hard-won and carefully constructed place, can return to boundless, limitless space, and we might be released from the house arrest that Derrida suggested was its condition.

Notes

1 Jacques Le Goff, *History and Memory* (New York, Columbia University Press, [1977] 1992), pp. 81–90; K. Pomian, 'Les archives', in Pierre Nora, *Les Lieux de mémoire, sous la direction de Pierre Nora*, III, *Les France. 3. De l'archive à l'emblème* (Paris, Gallimard, 1992), pp. 163–233; P.W. Musgrave, 'Curriculum History: Past, Present and Future', *History of Education Review*, 17 (1988), 1–14; Marc Ferro, *The Use and Abuse of History, or, How the Past Is Taught* (London, Routledge, 1981) pp. 94–113; V.E. Chancellor, *History for Their Masters. Opinion in the English History Textbook, 1800–1914* (London, Adams & Dart, 1970).

2 Michel Foucault, *The Order of Things. An Archeology of the Human Sciences* (Tavistock, London, [1966] 1970), p. 219.

3 Nora, *Les Lieux*, pp. 14–15; N. Watchel, 'Memory and History', *History and Anthropology*, 2 (1986), 207–24, pp. 217–18; C.S. Maier, 'Surfeit of Memory? Reflections on History, Memory and Denial', *History and Memory*, 5 (1993), 136–52.

4 Jacques Derrida, *Mal d'archive: une impression freudienne* (Paris, Editions Galilée, 1995), pp. 9–36.

5 H.E. Barnes, *A History of Historical Writing*, (New York, Dover, 1963), pp. 207–38; J.R. Hale, *The Evolution of British Historiography* (London, Macmillan, 1967), pp. 56–7; Philippa Levine, *The Amateur and the Professional. Antiquaries, Historians and Archeologists in Victorian Britain, 1838–1886*, (Cambridge, Cambridge University Press, 1986), 101–34; Christina Crosby, *The Ends of History. Victorians and 'The Woman Question'* (London and New York, Routledge, 1991), pp. 1–11.

6 Le Goff, *History and Memory*, pp. 87–9; Jules Michelet, 'Rapport au Ministre de l'Instruction Publique sur les Bibliothèques et Archives des Départements du Sud-Ouest de la France', in *Oeuvres Complètes, Tome IV* (Paris, Flammarion, [1835] 1971), pp. 536–63; Pomian, 'Les archives', pp. 163–233; Levine, *The Amateur*, pp. 100–19.

7 Edmund Wilson, *To the Finland Station. A Study in the Writing and Acting of History* (New York, Doubleday, [1940] 1953), pp. 1–2; Alfred Mitzman, *Michelet, Historian. Rebirth and Romanticism in Nineteenth-Century France* (New Haven and London, Yale University Press, 1990), pp. 24–5; Arthur McCalla, 'Romantic Vicos: Vico and Providence in Michelet and Ballanche', *Historical Reflections/Reflexions Historiques*, 19 (1993), 389–408.

8 McCalla, 'Romantic Vicos', pp. 41–2.

9 Giambattista Vico, *The New Science of Giambattista Vico*, trans. Thomas Goddard Bergin and Max Harold Fisch (New York, Doubleday, [1744] 1961), pp. 52–3; McCalla, 'Romantic Vicos', pp. 401–2; Wilson, *To the Finland Station*, p. 3.

10 Wilson, *To the Finland Station*, p. 7.

11 Michelet, 'Préface de l'Histoire de France' [1869], *Oeuvres Complètes, Tome IV* (Paris, Flammarion, 1974), pp. 11–127; Wilson, *The Finland Station*, p. 8.

12 Mitzman, *Michelet*, pp. 42–3; Michelet, 'Préface', 281.

13 Benedict Anderson, *Imagined Communities. Reflections on the Origin and Spread of Nationalism* (London, Verso, [1983] 1991), p. 198; Jules Michelet, 'Jusqu'au 18 Brumaire' (1872–74), *Oeuvres Complètes, Tome XXI* (Paris, Flammarion, 1982), p. 268.

14 Wilson, *To the Finland Station*, p. 26.

15 Stephen Bann, *The Clothing of Clio. A Study of the Representations of History in Nineteenth Century Britain and France* (Cambridge,

Cambridge University Press, 1984), pp. 15–16; *Romanticism and the Rise of History* (Boston, Twayne, 1995), p. 110.

16 Douglas Johnson, 'The Historian as Frenchman', *New Society* (7 August 1969), 223–4. Richard Cobb, *A Second Identity. Essays on French History* (Oxford, Oxford University Press, 1969).

17 Cobb, *A Second Identity*, p. 45.

18 Cobb, *A Second Identity*, p. 92; Georges Lefebvre, *Etudes sur la Révolution Française* (Paris, Presses Universitaires de France, 1963).

19 Cobb, *A Second Identity*, p. 17.

20 The nineteenth-century city was first figured, discussed, described and made a matter of investigation by the idea of a man walking it and gazing upon it, as Raymond Williams suggested long ago. Raymond Williams, *The Country and the City* (St Albans, Paladin, 1975), pp. 176–7, pp. 189–201. For the extensive modern literature on the *flâneur* (and the new *flâneuse*), see Deborah E. Nord, *Walking the Streets. Women, Representation and the City* (Ithaca and London, Cornell University Press) pp. 1–15; for the impossibility of the *flâneuse*'s existence, see Janet Wolff, 'The Invisible *Flâneuse*: Women and the Literature of Modernity', in Andrew Benjamin (ed.), *The Problems of Modernity. Adorno and Benjamin* (London, Routledge, 1991), pp. 141–56.

21 Recent complaints about the 'gender of history' (male) have had the unfortunate effect of actually preventing the imagining of female historians; and this is despite Bonnie Smith's brilliant resurrection of large numbers of Michelet's female contemporaries. 'Since I have invented this figure', says Katherine Kearns of her historian, 'he is male, and thus representative both statistically and attitidinally.' Indeed. Katherine Kearns, *Psychoanalysis, Historiography and Feminist Theory. The Search for Critical Method* (Cambridge, Cambridge University Press, 1997), p. 15.

22 Linda S. Kauffman, *Discourses of Desire. Gender, Genre and Epistolary Fiction* (Ithaca, Cornell University Press, 1986), pp. 30–61.

23 Terry Eagleton, *The Rape of Clarissa. Writing, Sexuality and Class Struggle in Samuel Richardson* (Oxford, Blackwell, 1982), pp. 54–5.

24 Peggy Kamuf, 'Writing Like a Woman', in S. McConnell-Ginet *et al.* (eds), *Women and Language in Literature and Society* (New York, Praeger, 1980), pp. 284–309; Nancy K. Miller, '"I"s in Drag. The Sex of

Recollection', *The Eighteenth Century. Theory and Interpretation*, 22 (1981), 47–57. For the entry of letter-writing practices and the reading of letters into political theory, see Nicola Watson, *Revolution and the Form of the British Novel, 1790–1825. Intercepted Letters, Interrupted Seductions* (Oxford, Clarendon Press, 1994); Deena Goodman, *The Republic of Letters. A Cultural History of the French Enlightenment* (Ithaca, Cornell University Press, 1994); Elisabeth Cook, *Epistolary Bodies. Gender and Genre in the Eighteenth Century Republic of Letters* (Stanford CA, Stanford University Press, 1996). Rebecca Earle, *Epistolary Selves. Letters and Letter Writers, 1600–1945* (Aldershot, Ashgate, 1999).

25 The epistolary novel contained two narratives: the story told by the letters that made it up; and the story of the letters themselves (their writing, sending, loss, going-astray, theft, concealment, destruction). The distinction between the 'in' and the 'of' of letters was originally Todorov's. Tsven Todorov, *Littérature et la signification* (Paris, Larousse, Paris), pp. 11–49.

26 For the peculiarities of epistolary narrative (for what Samuel Richardson called 'writing to the moment') and for some suggestions about the reading practices it engendered, see Ian Watt, *The Rise of the Novel* (London, Chatto & Windus, 1957); R.A. Day, *Told in Letters. Epistolary Fiction before Richardson* (Ann Arbor, MI, University of Michigan Press, 1966); Lennard Davis, *Factual Fictions. The Origins of the English Novel* (New York, Columbia University Press, 1983); Michael McKeon, *The Origin of the English Novel, 1600–1740* (Baltimore, Johns Hopkins University Press, 1987); Paul J. Hunter, *Before Novels. The Cultural Contexts of Eighteenth-century Fiction* (New York, Norton, 1990); Cook, *Epistolary Bodies*. See also J. Raven and Naomi Tadmor (eds), *The Practice and Representation of Reading in England* (Cambridge, Cambridge University Press, 1996).

27 Carolyn Steedman, *Strange Dislocations. Childhood and the Idea of Human Interiority, 1780–1930* (Cambridge, MA, Harvard University Press, 1995), pp. 9–15, 77–95; Mark Freeman, *Rewriting the Self. History, Memory, Narrative* (London, Routledge, 1993); Anthony Giddens, *Modernity and Self-Identity. Self and Society in the Late Modern Age* (Cambridge, Polity, 1991), pp. 53, 76; Charles Taylor, *Sources of the Self. The Making of the Modern Identity* (Cambridge, Cambridge

University Press, 1989), pp. 288–9; Franco Moretti, *The Way of the World. The Bildungsroman in European Culture* (London, Verso, 1987), pp. 6–7.

28 Bann, *The Clothing of Clio*, pp. 15–16.
29 Sigmund Freud, 'The Uncanny', *The Standard Edition of the Complete Psychological Works of Sigmund Freud*, 17 (London, Hogarth Press, [1919] 1955), pp. 217–56.
30 Jean Laplanche, *Life and Death in Psycho-analysis* (Baltimore, Johns Hopkins University Press, 1976), pp. 19–20.
31 Carolyn Steedman, 'Living Historically Now?', *Arena* (Australia), 97 (1991), 48–64.
32 Raphael Samuel, *Theatres of Memory. Volume 1: Past and Present in Contemporary Culture* (London, Verso, 1994), pp. 139–202.
33 Carolyn Steedman, 'Raphael Samuel, 1934–1996', *Radical Philosophy*, 82 (1997), 53–5.
34 Samuel, *Theatres*, pp. 413–25.
35 Raphael Samuel, 'On the Methods of History Workshop. A Reply', *History Workshop Journal*, 9 (1980), 162–76.
36 Gaston Bachelard, *The Poetics of Space* (Boston, Beacon, [1958] 1994), 8.
37 Ibid., p. 9.
38 Ibid., p. 85.
39 Ibid., p. 141.
40 For a poetics of littleness, see in addition to Bachelard's work, Frances Armstrong, 'Gender and Miniaturization: Games of Littleness in Nineteenth-Century Fiction', *English Studies in Canada*, 16 (1993), 403–16; E.Liebs, 'Between *Gulliver* and *Alice*: Some Remarks on the Dialectic of GREAT and SMALL in Literature', *Phaedrus*, 13 (1988), 56–60; S. Millhauser, 'The Fascination of the Miniature', *Grand Street*, 2 (1983), 128–35; Susan Stewart, *On Longing. Narratives of the Miniature, the Gigantic, the Souvenir, the Collection* (Durham NC, Duke University Press, 1993), pp. 37–69. For a brief account of social and psychological uses of littleness, see Carolyn Steedman, 'Inside, Outside, Other: Accounts of National Identity in the Nineteenth Century', *History of the Human Sciences*, 8 (1995), 59–76. For the way in which archives miniturise things ('l'objet historique') see Arlette Farge, *Le Goût de l'archive* (Paris, Editions du Seuil, 1989), p. 59, and passim.

41 D.W. Winnicott, 'The Capacity to Be Alone', in *The Maturational Process and the Facilitating Environment* (London, The Hogarth Press, [1958] 1965), pp. 29–36.

42 D.W. Winnicott, 'Playing: A Theoretical Statement', 'The Location of Cultural Experience' and 'The Place Where We Live', in *Playing and Reality* (Harmondsworth, Penguin, 1971), pp. 44–61, 112–21, 122–9, 129.

43 Winnicott, *Playing and Reality*, pp. 55, 60.

44 Ibid., p. 118.

45 Ibid., p. 116.

46 Moretti, *The Way of the World*, 19–24; K. Platt, 'Places of Experience and the Experience of Place', in L.S. Rouner (ed.), *The Longing for Home* (Notre Dame IN, University of Notre Dame Press, 1996), pp. 112–27.

~ 5

To Middlemarch: without benefit of archive

MARY ANN EVANS WAS BORN in 1819 in Arbury, Nuneaton – just north of the city of Coventry – where her father was land agent to the Newdigate family. 'Middlemarch' is Coventry, the fictionalised version of the place in which she grew up. Warwickshire, the county that Henry James called the 'the core and centre of the English world; midmost England, unmitigated England' is named 'North Loamshire' in the novel, and is the countryside surrounding the fictional parishes of Tipton and Lowick, the country houses, granges and rectories in which the plot of *Middlemarch* is played out.[1] The last time Marian Evans[2] visited Coventry – Middlemarch – was in 1853. After her family learned of her relationship with the physiologist and psychologist George Henry Lewes (who could not marry her, as the divorce law made it impossible for him to break with his wife), their profound disapproval prevented her ever going home again. She avoided the city during her last Midlands visit, in 1855.[3] *Middlemarch* was her seventh novel, one of the three she set in fictionalised versions of the time, place and politics of her own childhood (the others were *Mill on the Floss* (1860) and *Felix Holt* (1866)). It was the last of her Warwickshire novels, published in parts in 1871 and 1872.

'This', says one of Eliot's more recent biographers, 'is that very rare thing: a successful historical novel. In fact, it is so successful that we scarcely think of it in terms of that sub-genre of fiction.'[4] In

Eliot's novel, Middlemarch is a silk-ribbon manufacturing town, just as Coventry was in her lifetime. We know about the ribbon manufacture from the text, by the number of times we see the dyers' hands stained red in the Green Dragon Inn; by the narrator's comments on the trades that support Middlemarch's best families; and also by Rosamond Vincy's thoughts on the likes of young Plymdale, which tell us not only what kind of town but also what kind of cultural space we're in:

> [These] young [Middlemarch] men had not a notion of French, and could speak on no subject with striking knowledge, except perhaps the dyeing and carrying trades, which of course they were ashamed to mention; they were *Middlemarch gentry*, elated with their silver-headed whips and satin stocks, but embarrassed in their manners, and timidly jocose (emphasis mine) (300).[5]

They are supported in their imperfect acquisition of cultural capital by a system of rural outworking. The city's economic hinterland makes a brief eruption in the text, in Chapter 34, when Rosamond's father, Mr Vincy, is described as 'one of those who suck life out of the wretched handloom weavers in Tipton and Freshitt'. Eliot gave the book the subtitle *A Study of Provincial Life*. It is a historical study of Coventry and Warwickshire in the late 1820s and early 1830s, taking as its frame the period between September 1829 and May 1832.[6] The author wrote in the wake of the Second Reform Act of 1867, about the First Reform Act of 1832, setting her story in a period when she was herself eleven and twelve years old.

Twentieth-century commentators were not much interested in the novel's precise and peculiar temporal dissonance, though Walter Scott (who wrote many more historical novels than did George Eliot) explained its uses well enough in 1814, in his Introduction to *Waverley; or 'Tis Sixty Years Since*.[7] Too great a temporal distance would give his novel the stamp of the antique, the utterly remote; a modern setting would produce a mere novel of manners. Scott's chosen setting ('sixty years since', forty in George Eliot's case) was not very far removed from current experience, yet distant enough to arouse the reader's nostalgia. If you wrote at this remove, there would no exotic setting to distract the reader from the internal time of human passion. You could make the past live for the reader: your novel could then effect the integration of the external time of history with the beat of human interiority.

With Scott's exegesis in place, it is possible to see nineteenth-century historical novels – like *Middlemarch* – as part of a commodification of longing and nostalgia: a commodification of the bourgeois desire, newly emerged at the end of the eighteenth century and the beginning of the nineteenth, for many kinds of past. 'Bourgeois society tried to consume the past,' explains Donald Lowe in his *History of Bourgeois Perception*, 'in order to attenuate somewhat its estrangement in the mechanical, segmented present.'[8] Longing for the past was expressed in many ways in the first half of the nineteenth century: records and documents were preserved and catalogued; the Archive was born; museums, collections, historical pageants and antiquarian societies came into being; the disciplines of anthropology, archaeology, mythology and History itself, all developed as means of inquiry into the past. Nostalgia – longing temporalised in the desire for a *particular* past – was formalised, and the historical novel was part of the process.

In this historical novel, agitation for the Reform Bill and its turbulent progress through the Upper and Lower Houses of Parliament, provide the structure for George Eliot's story. The passage through Parliament of a party measure, carried by one section of the ruling elite (the Whigs) in opposition to the other (the Tories) against a background of great popular turmoil throughout the country and riots in many towns, punctuates and structures Eliot's text.

The narrator appears to be perfectly aware of the historiographical questions involved in writing a social and political history of provincial life. Indeed this narrator (who may not be – probably is not – George Eliot) makes very high claims for him or herself, comparing the novel to a work of Herodotus, the most famous historian of the ancient world. The narrative voice tells us that

> Old provincial society had its share of [a] subtle movement … its striking downfalls, its brilliant young professional dandies who ended living up an entry with a drab and six children … Some slipped a little downward, some got higher … Municipal town and rural parish gradually made fresh threads of connection – gradually, as the old stocking gave way to the savings-bank … while squires and baronets, and even lords who had once lived blamelessly apart afar from the civic mind, gathered the faultiness of closer acquaintance. Settlers too, came from distant counties … In fact, much the same sort of movement and mixture went on in old England as we find in … Herodotus, who also, in telling what had been, thought it well to take woman's lot for his starting point. (122)

Writing *Middlemarch* quite effaced another of Eliot's projects, a long biographical poem concerning Timoleon, the fourth-century BC liberator of Syracuse.[9] By the time she came to work on her novel of English provincial life, she had read very widely indeed in the historians of the ancient world, including Herodotus. It is possible then, that a 'woman's lot' is a classical reference, to Fortune, Fortuna, Destiny, Providence or – in the modern mode – to 'radical contingency', not to the common nineteenth-century meaning of 'woman's lot', as some kind of sad, familiar female story. All the central women characters in *Middlemarch* do quite nicely in the end, attaining reasonable incomes and some moderate degree of sexual satisfaction. Indeed, to support the view that it is something grander and more portentous that Eliot has in mind than the 'relative creature' of our modern historical imagination, we may note that just before the narrator evokes Herodotus's bustling Ancient Society, we are told to observe Destiny, standing by with 'our *dramatis personae* folded in her hand'.

Destiny may brood over the West Midlands, but something far less elevated opens Herodotus's work. Are we meant to know that a shopping expedition inaugurates his world history? In Argos, in the beginning – not of things, but of History – the Phoenician traders arrive, and display their wares on the seashore. After several days of brisk trading, when they are nearly sold out, a group of women from the royal household, including Io the King's daughter, come down to the beach. They are standing about, buying what takes their fancy, when the Phoenicians make a rush at them, and abduct Io and some of the others. There follows half a century of response, revenge, repercussions, to-and fro-ing and small wars, which involve much more famous abductions than that of Io. Herodotus tells us two things at this point, only the first of which has been consistently noted down the ages, as the principle and wisdom of the historian's enterprise: that this is the Persian account; there is at least one other version of these events, but Herodotus is quite clear that this is not the one he is recounting here. The second point is more interesting. Herodotus tells how the Phoenicians simply don't understand the political and military repercussions of that abduction from the shore, do not understand why the Greeks reacted the way they did. They know that abducting young women is not a legal act, but 'it is stupid after the event to make a fuss about avenging it. The only sensible thing to do is take no notice, for it is obvious that no young woman allows herself to be abducted if she does not wish to be.'[10] The History pauses, turns in upon itself, implodes, in this moment where it need not have happened the *way it did*.

According to Michael Mason, *Middlemarch* is an expression of Eliot's interest in the structure of time, in 'critical moments that determine future developments'.[11] But what did Eliot do with this proposition of Herodotus – with his potential negation of event, causation and the historical enterprise itself (which is to write narrative out of things that happen, relating the relationship between those happenings)? Not yet clear about the answer, we may look to the event that does in fact, start things, which is not an abduction, nor a war about the abduction, but is to do with women going shopping. After the traders arrive, this is the first happening that Herodotus relates. Carolyn Dewald has reckoned up the appearance of women in the *Histories* (there are 375 of them), and categorises Io and her women at the market on the shore under the heading of 'Passive Women' (128 of them), subjected to 'External aggression' (25 in number) … 'Abduction'.[12] New sociologies of shopping, and indeed, Eliot's use of this moment suggest, on the other hand, that shopping is an *activity* (perhaps the paradigmatic activity of capitalist modernity), of great social significance and affective importance. Tertius Lydgate will certainly end up recognising this, as he sits silently in his own disintegration amidst the stiff furnishings and fabrics that Rosamond has purchased on one of her trips to the Middlemarch emporia. In a novel that really might be about sex and shopping, we can note that Eliot's passages about Destiny and her evocation of Herodotus lie between Lydgate's contemplation first of Dorothea Brooke and then of Rosamond Vincy. If women are to be used in this novel to embody social process, we may also interpret 'lot' as 'portion': as capital (monetary capital and cultural capital); as a marriage portion; as what the girl's got (and what it is, in this particular case, that Lydgate so very badly wants).

'I shall send Part VII in a few days,' wrote the author to her publisher in August 1872: 'Since Mr Lewes tells me that the Spectator considers me the most melancholy of authors, it will perhaps be a welcome assurance to you that there is no unredeemed tragedy in the solution of the story.'[13] But its author was wrong; there is unredeemed tragedy in this book: the thought of the brilliant young doctor Lydgate becoming a fat-cat consultant to the gouty rich is insupportable. It is particularly unbearable because his decline is brought about by Rosamund (Eliot's publisher John Blackwood, called Rosamund a 'highly polished picture' of a 'heartless, obstinate devil, painted on the hardest possible piece of panel'[14]); but it comes about as well though a flaw of Lydgate, those 'spots of commonness' that the narrator's voice dwells on for such a very long time. (179) His commonness – his vulgarity – *is* to be deeply attracted to a daughter of a Middlemarch manufacturer. We watch her, as Lydgate watches her: that graceful, deadly turn of the neck. Towards the end we are told that he 'once called [Rosamund] his basil plant; and when she asked for an explanation, said that basil was a plant that flourished wonderfully on a murdered man's brains' (893).

The narrator continues to comment on the fate of men like Lydgate:

> In the multitude of middle-aged men who go about their vocations in a daily course determined for them in much the same way as the tie of their cravats, there is always a good number who once meant to shape their own deeds and alter the world a little … Nothing in the world more subtle than the process of their gradual change! In the beginning they inhaled it unknowingly; you or I may have sent some of our breath towards them infecting them, when we uttered our conforming falsities or drew our silly conclusions: or perhaps it came with the vibrations from a woman's glance.

It does indeed; Rosamund's glance ensnares Lydgate. But it is more than Rosamond the character that does this, for she embodies, or personifies, Middlemarch; as the town *belle*, she is its quintessence: she *is* its dreadful, self-regarding provincial vulgarity, despite thinking quite the opposite of herself, and having been a star pupil at Mrs Lemon's academy, just outside the county town of Warwick. (Here is the narrator's most cruel moment of condescension in a portrait of utter viciousness: if you are English, you *know* that Rosamond will pronounce it 'Le-Mon', in the faux genteel French manner, but that we the readers, must say 'lemon'.) (190) Through Rosamond, Middlemarch gets Lydgate. She shows that his grave error is to fail to take Middlemarch seriously. This brilliant young man who has studied in London, Edinburgh, Paris (he is the only true metropolitan in the book) cannot believe that this little town, peopled with mediocrities, can frustrate his plans … But it does: Middlemarch *gets* him, drags him down.

The action of this novel centres almost entirely on a few square miles of a Midlands county; what goes on in London and in the Houses of Parliament is introduced by the narrator to remind us that this story is set in a wider context; but like Dorothea's experience of Rome (another metropolis, of the ancient world) which is like that of a sleep-walker, this wider world is never realised in the text. The narrative voice makes it very clear indeed that what we are meant to do as readers is to connect the personal dramas going on at the Vincys', at Tipton, at Stone Court and at Lowick Manor, with political events taking place in the country as a whole. A typical and formulaic scene for the instruction of the reader: Rosamond is planning her wedding (curtains, sofas, carpets, silverware: she thinking about her Wedding List, about shopping indeed). Her father is a disappointment in this regard: '"I hope he knows I shan't give anything,"' he says, what with … '"Parliament going to be dissolved, and machine-breaking everywhere, and an election coming on."' Rosamond responds:

'Dear papa! What can that have to do with my marriage?'
'A pretty deal to do with it! We may be ruined for what I know – the country's in that state. Some say it's the end of the world, and be hanged if I don't think it looks like it.' (388)

Many proposals to reform the parliamentary system preceded the First Reform Bill; 'Old Corruption' had been under attack for at least half a century before 1832, during the long formation of a new class of society 'the industrial bourgeoisie', or, as we may have it for current purposes, 'Middlemarch Man', who is voteless under England's Ancien Régime. But many of the fictional Middlemarch men with whom we spend nearly a thousand pages *did* have a vote before 1832, because of Coventry's ancient system of 'Freedom by Servitude'. This manufacturing town returned two Members of Parliament in the 1820s. Freedom won by servitude brought with it the parliamentary franchise, earned by serving a registered apprenticeship to one trade for seven years. Any trade would do, though silk-ribbon weaving and watch-making predominated in the eighteenth century, when two acts of Parliament reiterated that Freemen were the only Coventry men permitted to exercise the franchise. As one historian of the city puts it, 'No matter how wealthy, no matter how respectable, no matter how influential you were, unless you had completed a seven years' apprenticeship to one trade you could not have the Parliamentary vote.'[15] Eliot is careful indeed to give us the life stories that allow us to know exactly who had the vote and who did not in Middlemarch. To add to all the items of his emasculation, Lydgate is rendered doubly voteless by settling in Middlemarch.

The Freeman's vote (which existed in other places besides Coventry) survived the final passage of the Bill through the House of Lords, and in the city (in Middlemarch) the Freemen and the new £10 householder voters took their place side by side on the electoral roll. On the new register of Coventry voters in 1833, there were nearly 3,000 Freemen and just 529 new £10 householders.[16] So Lydgate *will* gain a vote, but outside the time frame of the novel, which ends in early May 1832 in the 'dying gasp of ante-reform England'.[17] Within a few weeks, the Bill will pass, Dorothea will marry Ladislaw and Lydgate will get one of the 529 votes.

When the First Reform Bill reached the end of its turbulent progress in the early part of 1832 it achieved the political incorporation of the heads of middle-class households. The franchise was extended to some of the urban middle classes (those whose property was valued for rating purposes at £10 per annum). The number of potential voters was increased from about 500,000 across the country to something under a million. (Between 1832 and 1867, out of a male population of 6 million in England and Wales, about 900,000 men had a vote.)

Rosamund is indeed a starting point for a discussion of these questions; she (and all the women in the book) are foreshadowings of the larger exclusions and stratifications that shape British political life between 1832 and 1867, a period in which, despite the enfranchisement of the middle classes, a majority of the House of Commons would come from landed families until the very end of the century. Women had never voted in parliamentary elections, but the 1832 Act made the first explicit exclusion of them by its limit of the franchise to 'male persons', the first of many overt and legal exclusions that were made by Parliament between 1832 and 1867. A second effect of the Act of 1832, symbolic as much as political, was a profound alteration in perception and understanding of social structure in England. The Act implicitly defined all those who were not £10 householders as working class, and all those who were, as middle class. These terms efface enormous differences in wealth and status, but nevertheless, it was with the Act of 1832 that we enter the modern political world, the one we inhabit still. The English working class was certainly made in the years *before* 1832, in the *longue durée* of counter-Revolution, stretching from 1795, as Edward Thompson showed in *The Making of the English Working Class*; but it was made *after* 1832 as well, in the oppositions and exclusions set in place by the Reform Act.

Rosamund and her family represent an economic and social history, as well as the political and the cultural. They show how new forms of capital are introduced to the town; how money is accumulated and circulated in new ways (how mildly, how *domestically* is a relentless movement of money described, in the passage where the savings bank replaces the old sock under the mattress). Bulstrode's bank is built out of a history we now know well enough, though its specific texts were largely unwritten in 1870: a history of the relationship between capitalism, Protestantism and Judaism; out of fencing, shady dealing, semi-criminal activity, systems of debt and indebtedness stretching from a Midlands county right into central Europe.

In *Middlemarch* it is the clergyman Mr Farebrother who alerts us to the history of capitalism being written in its pages. In his hilarious piece 'Is Will Ladislaw legitimate?' John Sutherland shows how absolutely everybody in Middlemarch is related by sex and money to everybody else; except for Farebrother, who is given a voice (of 'uncharacteristic coarseness' notes Sutherland) to observe that 'our mercurial Ladislaw has a queer genealogy! A high-spirited young lady and a musical Polish patriot made a likely enough stock for him to spring from, but I should never have suspected a grafting of the Jew pawnbroker.' (He is being very coarse indeed.)[18]

George Eliot did all of this, wrote this history, without going to the Archive. It is believed that she did extensive research in the British Museum Reading Room, and in a wide range of secondary sources, but unable to go home, was prevented from using what local records were available in the late 1860s.[19] We may divide her research for the book into two forms of detailed empirical inquiry. She read very extensively indeed in the history of medicine and physiology, as it related to the training of a fictional young doctor in the 1820s.[20] It was extremely detailed and accurate research: *Middlemarch* explains better than any modern history of medicine

Bichat's tissue theory (for example) and why it held sway until cell theory was established in the 1840s. There is a very great deal *in* Lydgate as a character; he is an embodiment of the most perfectly understood theories and practices of medicine in the 1820s, in the way that other characters are not embodiments. The detailed history of medicine he represents is part of a tragedy: he falls hard, because of that detail.

For the political events that frame and shape the novel, Eliot's research was much more limited and superficial. She noted details of the passage of the Reform Bill and provincial reactions from the *Annual Register*, and perhaps used the backfiles of *The Times*, available in the British Museum Reading Room, though that reading, if it were undertaken, was a superficial one. In 1829, *The Times* reproduced many accounts from the *Coventry Herald and Observer*, describing the Riband Weavers' Dispute of that year – accounts of roads and bridges over the canal between Coventry and Nuneaton cut off, large-scale intimidation of the Nuneaton outworkers by the foreman of its main manufacturer, rough musicking, women smuggling ribbons in jars saying they were pickles for a friend, between Coventry, where the new engine looms were in operation, and Nuneaton and Bedworth, where ribbon was still produced on the single-hand loom.[21] Mary Ann Evans was at school in Nuneaton during these events, not yet at the Misses Franklins' in Coventry; but still, no one recalling this as a scene from her youth (or as related by the adults around her) could have translated these events into the mild-mannered election riot that features in the pages of *Middlemarch*).[22] Anyway, the train journey to Coventry could not be taken, and so unavailable to George Eliot were runs of the *Coventry Herald* for the late 1820s, and all the records of the unreformed Town Council: Coventry Council Minutes, the Town Clerk's correspondence, the Street Commissioners' records, and records of the system of policing operated by the aldermen and justices, in the years before the Municipal Corporations Act of 1835. Useless speculation really, but: had she used these records, *Middlemarch*'s extremely low-key election riot, the police methods used to control it and, indeed, the police force employed, might have been written differently.

There is a puzzle in the local history she *was* able to do. Pratt and Neufeldt, the editors of the Middlemarch *Notebooks* draw our attention to these entries:

> Brandreth a framework knitter so poor as to receive parish relief. The keen and constant sight and sense of suffering conspired with political enthusiasm & etc. (seduced into insurrection & hanged 1817)

and then

> Government spy; Oliver.[23]

Eliot's editors observe that she had been reading Carlyle on the French Revolution, and that she then 'turned closer to home even if only for a brief glimpse into British Reform agitation. These notes appear to be from a single unidentified source.' They go on to mention Archibald Prentice's *Historical Sketches and Personal Recollections of Manchester. Intended to Illustrate the Progress of Public Opinion from 1792 to 1832*, published in 1851; and then tell us regretfully that 'although most of the facts mentioned … are … in Prentice, the notes on this page do not come from this work. Indeed, there is no evidence that George Eliot ever read the book'.

We are forced to the conclusion that George Eliot's unknown source *had to be* Edward Thompson's *Making of the English Working Class*, even though it was not to be published for a century yet, for Thompson gives us a full account of the career of Jerry Brandreth, of the notorious spy Oliver and of the Pentridge Rising of June 1817.[24] Eliot's notes do indeed refer to the Rising, but do not name it. (In the space of the Timeless Universal Archive, Eliot – who read everything – probably did read Thompson: they are both probably reading each other, for their mutual edification; but in prosaic and material terms we had better settle for the speculation that the source for both of them was probably W.B. Gurney's *Trials of Jeremiah Brandreth* of 1817, which Thompson noted in 1963 as his authority on these events and which was received by the British Museum – the date stamp shows this – sometime before 1837.[25])

Middlemarch is made of fragments from an Unvisited Archive. The editors of the *Notebooks* suggest that it was Eliot's reading of Carlyle that deposits in *Middlemarch* the one trace of a history that Edward Thompson later chronicled, in that throwaway remark that 'Vincy is one of those who suck life out of the wretched handloom weavers in Tipton and Freshitt', and that 'that is how his family look so fair and sleek'.[26] It is the highly conservative, exorbitantly eccentric Mrs Cadwallader who makes this observation, no fictive weaver, no diseased dye-worker nor labourer (no Jeremiah Brandreth), as she employs the oldest narrative trick of the English bourgeoisie and evokes the sufferings of the poor in order in order to tell some other kind of tale, in this case to delineate the character and attributes of Middlemarch Man. So while it can be claimed that as a character Mrs Cadwallader represents the *form* of Thompson's later argument about the same historical developments, that is, of the new political understanding between middle and upper classes that emerged from the struggles of 1829–32, the *politics* out of which she was actually written prevents any realisation of the Tipton and Freshitt weavers; or at least prevents their being written in the way that Thompson wrote them ninety years later. *That* history, published in 1963, showed those spectral workers (and all the real ones too) agitating for what turned out to be middle-class reform out of their own hard-won consciousness of state, society, life and labour; out of the working-class consciousness that they made, between 1795 and 1832. With Eliot's own political analysis in place, her going to the Archive probably would not have changed anything at all.

Middlemarch is set in the period – the late 1820s – when the Archive and Social History came into the world, inseparable as developments, practices, ways of thinking and feeling. There are alternative ways of giving an account of European Social History and of the Archive, an account we need for a better understanding of what kind of thing *Middlemarch* is, and why, if you are English and living within the political and cultural structures laid down at the beginning of the nineteenth century, then wherever you are, you are always in Middlemarch as well. The story of European Social History could be told in several ways. Under other circumstances, a preferred route would be by way of the eighteenth-century 'philosophic historians' – James Millar and Adam Smith and Adam Ferguson are Scottish examples – who wrote about economic and social systems in their discussion of civil society and its origins. That is certainly a sexier origin than the one that is discussed here, and just possibly a truer one, too. But finding a beginning in the 1830s is to my purpose, for Mary Ann Evans and George Eliot knew Michelet's work. She reviewed Michelet's *Priests, Women and Families* for the *Coventry Herald* long before she left Coventry.[27]

Moreover, after a visit to Paris and conversations with Michelet in 1842, G.H. Lewes had reported on 'The State of Historical Science' in France.[28] He discussed Michelet's *Oeuvres Complètes* in comparison with the work of Thierry, Guizot, Hegel (and Michelet's translation of Vico's *Scienza Nuova* into French), reflecting on the charges brought against Michelet for want of gravity. Not hard, in this company, for Michelet to be called the most 'captivating' historian and writer; and Lewes's reading also allowed him to speculate on the sources for a history of everyday life, and the possibility of the historical vision that was later to inform *Middlemarch*.[29] 'History should be grave', conceded Lewes in 1844;

> but in a deeper sense than our 'classical historians' have understood … History must be grave, or it cannot be written; but this gravity does not *exclude* anything, which throws light upon the subject, whether a ballad, a legend, a custom, a silly fashion, or a secret anecdote; it holds nothing to be derogatory to its dignity, because it *includes* everything, as the greater does the lesser.[30]

Eliot probably undertook a sustained reading of the eighteenth-century historian whose work had so much influenced Michelet in the early 1860s, when she was working on *Romola*: 'Eliot and Lewes owned a number of Vico's works including his important *Principi di una Scienza Nuova* … in both Italian and in a French translation … which is heavily marked and annotated by both Eliot and Lewes.'[31] Indeed, the French translation they used was almost certainly Michelet's own. For many mid-Victorian readers like Eliot, Vico reinforced an understanding put in place by eighteenth-century philosophic and cultural history, that at any stage of human development, each aspect of culture – custom, law, government, morality, art, technology, religion, philosophy – takes a form that is different from the one that preceded it.[32] A reading of Vico might reinforce the notion that what had taken place in the past was a matter of human action and endeavour: was dependent on environment, and on what was available from the material world to do the work of living with.[33] This is an important conceptual framework for *Middlemarch*, as was Lewes's earlier perception of everything – habits, manners, customs, stray fragments of a culture, the clothes a woman wore – being grist to the historian's evidential mill.

But if Eliot used these perceptions to write a historical study of an only-half-invented provincial place, then the timing of understanding must also be taken into account. She wrote her novel (her history) in the wake of the Second Reform Act. In 1867 in the UK, the franchise was extended to borough householders with a one-year residential qualification, and to lodgers who paid an annual rent of £10 for at least a year: to – the iconic phrase of all the history books – 'the respectable working man'. In 1867, Eliot had not yet dreamed up her story (she would soon, some time in 1868); *Middlemarch* may be read as part of a common reaction to the Second Reform Act, that is, out of a re-imagining of class relations in Britain, though the lens of 'culture'. Matthew Arnold, poet and Inspector of Schools from 1852 to 1882, published *Culture and Anarchy* in 1869, as George Eliot was in the early stages of composition.[34] It set up the cultural terms for discussing a class society, terms which are still in use. Arnold's was the infamous division of English society into the Barbarians (the English aristocracy and landed gentry), the Philistines (the urban middle classes) and the Populace (the working-class).[35] It is his Philistine that has endured as an image, a figure made out of hundreds of train journeys to inspect schools in provincial places, thousands of cups of tea taken with the small-minded, uncultivated, mediocrities of Nonconformist and Evangelical manufacturers who managed those schools … in places like Coventry.[36] *Middlemarch* may be understood as a piece of writing that looks back to the past in the light of concerns of the late 1860s and 1870s; it is a portrait of Philistine Provincialism, defined in post-Second Reform Act terms.

Whilst *Middlemarch* is quite plainly a novel about political representation, in a much more interesting ways it embodies the extreme difficulties that the English have inherited from the moment of *Culture and Anarchy*, of directly representing the political, of writing about it in fictional terms, or dramatising it. There is George Eliot's difficulty in actually describing the move of Old Corruption into new corruption. She has nothing to say about it but in cultural terms; nothing to say about class formation but a note on the impoverished conversation of young Middlemarch man, his awkward manners, the folds of his cravat, the cut of his jib. Eliot reads class, class conflict, political struggle and questions of political agency through the filter of 'culture'. Francis Mulhern has noted the legacy of Matthew Arnold for the twentieth century, the development of a discourse 'whose foremost general cultural function is the repression of politics';[37] but *Middlemarch* shows how the moment was read backwards, from 1869 to the recent historical past, of 1832. It is a striking example of a difficulty experienced for over a century now, of actually talking and writing about the political without the occlusions of 'culture'. And then *Middlemarch* shows another extreme difficulty in writing about politics: the way in which everything has to be told in terms of something else, so that the awkward sons of the dyeing trade are called 'Middlemarch *gentry*' by Eliot, and English radicalism is figured by Will Ladislaw (instead of the impoverished hand-loom weavers who did actually make up the crowds agitating for reform in Coventry; Ladislaw, who does not even represent Polish political aspirations, but is really a way of saying something about Mr Causubon's want of German and his ignorance of new developments in European Higher Criticism).

E.P. Thompson tried this textual tactic in 1970, some seven years after *The Making of the English Working Class*, when he looked again at *Middlemarch* and at what the 'Middlemarch gentry' had become in the new mid-Atlantic world of the Midlands Motor and Aircraft Industry. He suggested that

> just as the great landed aristocracy of the eighteenth century exerted their power by manifold exercise of interest, influence … and purchase, so the new lords seem to infiltrate the command-posts of our society, including our educational institutions, not through any transparent democratic process, but quietly, in unnoticed ways. They

apparently share with their precursors the same assumptions that it is *their* world, to dispose of by ownership and by right of purchase.[38]

The legacy from this period is to make us see things in terms of something else; never as they actually are.

At the end of writing Part I, in July 1871, when Eliot still didn't know how the novel was going to work out, Eliot told her publisher that her 'design … [was] to show the gradual action of ordinary causes rather than exceptional';[39] and this may be what is claimed right at the end of the book, when the narrator tells us 'the growing good of the world is partly dependent on unhistoric acts'. (896) And yet: Eliot chose one of the most significant events of nineteenth-century British public and political history for her depiction of 'unhistoric acts'. Did she know about her own role of diminution and occlusion? – About a political story told in terms of something else?

At the beginning of the novel, the narrator makes his or her first leisurely survey of central Warwickshire and the story about to be told and speaks of Destiny: 'Destiny stands by sarcastic with our *dramatis personae* folded in her hand.' (122) Not ironically, we must note, but *sarcastically*. In Greek mythology Destiny – Moros – hovers above all the gods, above the Fates, far, far above the Muse of History, Clio, extending his invisible dominion over all. But Eliot makes Destiny a woman, with a sarcastic attitude. We anticipate Destiny using an elevated device like irony … but: *sarcasm*, that crude and blatant use of dispraise. There are two rather different things to say about this. First, Eliot's Destiny is much like Vico's Providence: something to assure the writer (though not, I think, us) that there is an order underlying the history of civil society.[40] And of course the other thing: that Middlemarch men and Middlemarch women are worth only sarcasm; if we are intended to learn nothing else by the end of the novel, it may well be this.

In the 'Finale', in a strange echo of the way in which Herodotus made the idea that History might *not be* flash briefly before the reader, the narrator seems to suggest that no one wrote this book nor told this story at all. Middlemarchers are convinced that Mary Garth (now Mary Vincy) couldn't possibly have written *Stories of Great Men, taken from Plutarch*, and that Fred must have done it; and that he just couldn't have produced *The Cultivation of Green Crops*, and it must have been written by his wife. 'In this way it was made clear … that there was no need to praise anybody for writing a book, since it was always done by somebody else.' Who wrote *Middlemarch*? – Who told this story? George Eliot? Mary Ann Evans? Destiny, in role as a girl with a sarcastic attitude? You can conclude perhaps, that *Middlemarch* denies itself in its very act of writing; see in that ending the same brief negation that is there to be found when Herodotus reports the Phoenician opinion on world events, and 'telling what had been' turns briefly, vertiginously, into something else, reminding us, as that earlier History did, that the writing and reading of it depends on the unsettling knowledge that nothing need have been said or written in the way it has been … nothing at all.

Notes

1 Henry James quoted in Valerie Dodd, *George Eliot. An Intellectual Life* (London, Macmillan, 1990), p. 69.
2 I follow the convention used by Rosemary Ashton in her biography of Eliot, of using the name she herself called herself, at different stages of her life. Rosemary Ashton, *George Eliot. A Life* (London, Hamish Hamilton, 1996), p. 9.
3 Ibid., p. 152.
4 Ibid., p. 139.
5 Page references in the text are to the 1965 Penguin edition of *Middlemarch*.

6 Jerome Beaty, 'History by Indirection: The Era of Reform in *Middlemarch*', *Victorian Studies*, 1 (1957), 173–9.

7 Sir Walter Scott, '*Waverley*: A Postscript Which Should Have Been a Preface', *The Prefaces to the Waverley Novels*, ed. Mark A. Weinstein (Lincoln and London, University of Nebraska Press, [1814] 1978), pp. 7–10.

8 Donald M. Lowe, *History of Bourgeois Perception* (Brighton, Harvester, 1982), pp. 40–1.

9 J.C. Pratt and V.A. Neufeldt (eds), *George Eliot's 'Middlemarch' Notebooks. A Transcription* (Berkeley, University of California Press, 1979), p. xxvii; Ashton, *George Eliot*, pp. 180–207.

10 Herodotus, *The Histories* (Harmondsworth, Penguin, 1954), pp. 3–4.

11 Michael Mason, '*Middlemarch* and History', *Nineteenth Century Fiction*, 25 (1970–71), 417–31.

12 Carolyn Dewald, 'Women and Culture in Herodotus' *Histories*', in Helene P. Foley (ed.), *Reflections of Women in Antiquity* (New York, London and Paris, Gordon & Breach, 1981), pp. 91–125; p. 120.

13 Gordon S. Haight (ed.), *The George Eliot Letters. Volume V, 1869–1873* (London, Oxford University Press; New Haven, Yale University Press, 1956), p. 296

14 Haight, *The George Eliot Letters*, 293.

15 J. Prest, *The Industrial Revolution in Coventry* (Oxford, Oxford University Press, 1960), pp. 26–31.

16 Ibid., p. 29.

17 Beaty, 'History', p. 179.

18 John Sutherland, 'Is Will Ladislaw Legitimate?', in *Is Heathcliff a Murderer? Puzzles in Nineteenth-Century Fiction* (Oxford, Oxford University Press, 1996), pp. 146–55; p. 148.

19 Mason, '*Middlemarch*', 417–31.

20 Anna Theresa Kitchel, *Quarry for 'Middlemarch'* (Berkeley, CA, University of California Press, 1950). See also Ashton, *George Eliot*, pp. 319–21.

21 'Riots at Nuneaton', *The Times*, 26 September 1829, p. 3; 'State of Spinning', *The Times*, 2 October 1829, p. 2; 'Riots at Nuneaton', *The Times*, 10 October 1829, p. 3. See also reports reprinted from the *Coventry Herald* in *The Times* for 18 and 19 September; 3, 17 and 31 October 1829; 1 March 1830; 9 and 10 November 1831; 26 November

and 12 December 1832. The first mention of the election in these reports of industrial disturbance was on 26 October 1829. See also 'Toryism Is Defeated Here', *The Times*, 12 December 1832, pp. 2–3.

22 According to Charles Bray, Mary Ann Evans's Coventry mentor and owner of the local newspaper, she met 'unemployed weavers' while at the Nuneaton school. Dodd, *George Eliot*, p. 73.

23 Pratt and Neufeldt, *George Eliot's 'Middlemarch' Notebooks*, pp. 46–7.

24 E.P. Thompson, *The Making of the English Working Class* (Harmondsworth, Penguin, [1963] 1991), pp. 686, 702–42.

25 W.B. Gurney, *The Trials of Jeremiah Brandreth* (London, Butterworth, 2 vols, 1817), 1, pp. 45, 109–12.

26 Pratt and Neufeldt, *George Eliot's 'Middlemarch' Notebooks*, pp. 46–7.

27 The review appeared in the 'Literary and Scientific Review of the Coventry Herald', *Coventry Herald and Observer*, 30 October, 1846, p. 2. See Kathleen McCormick, 'George Eliot's Earliest Prose: The Coventry *Herald* and the Coventry Fiction', *Victorian Periodicals Review*, 19:2 (1986), 57–62; see Ceri Crossley, 'Michelet and Quinet Reviewed by George Eliot', *French Studies Bulletin*, 8 (1983), 5–7; and Thomas Pinney (ed.), *Essays of George Eliot* (New York, Columbia University Press, 1963), p. 452.

28 Rosemary Ashton, *G.H. Lewes. A Life* (Oxford, Clarendon Press, Oxford, 1991), pp. 45–6. Edward K. Kaplan (ed.), *Mother Death. The Journal of Jules Michelet, 1815–1850* (Amherst, University of Massachusetts Press, 1984), pp. 135, 141, 144. Entries for 13, 22 and 26 May 1842.

29 (G.H. Lewes), 'The State of Historical Science in France', *British and Foreign Review; or, European Quarterly Journal*, 16 (1844), 72–118. Pratt and Neufeldt attribute George Eliot's social history to her reading of Alessandro Manzoni's *I Promessi Spozi*, in January 1867. Manzoni castigates historians who dealt only with 'the Enterprises of Princes and Potentates', rather than writing of 'Persons of low Condition and Ordinary Rank'. Pratt and Neufeldt, George Eliot's '*Middlemarch' Notebooks*, p. xxvii.

30 Lewes, 'The State of Historical Science', pp. 109–10.

31 Felicia Bonaparte, *The Triptych and the Cross: The Myth of George Eliot's Poetic Imagination* (Brighton, Harvester , 1979), p. 65.

32 Giambattista Vico, *The New Science of Giambattita Vico* (1744), trans. Thomas Goddard Bergin and Max Harold Fisch (New York, Doubleday,

[1744] 1961), pp. 52–3. Karl Marx's was the most famous use of this perception, in the much-quoted prolegomenon to 'The Eighteenth Brumaire of Louis Bonaparte', *Pelican Marx Library. Political Writings, Volume 2. Surveys from Exile* (Harmondsworth, Penguin, [1869] [1858] 1973), p. 146: 'Men make their own history, but not of their own free will; not under circumstances they themselves have chosen.'

33 Vico, *The New Science*, pp. 52–3; Arthur McCalla, 'Romantic Vicos: Vico and Providence in Michelet and Ballanche', *Historical Reflections/ Reflexions Historiques*, 19 (1993), 401–2; Edmund Wilson, *To the Finland Station. A Study in the Writing and Acting of History* (New York, Doubleday, [1940] 1953), p. 3.

34 Matthew Arnold, *Culture and Anarchy* (Cambridge, Cambridge University Press, [1869] 1954).

35 Patrick J. McCarthy, *Matthew Arnold and the Three Classes* (New York, Columbia University Press, 1964), pp. 106–38. Stefan Collin, *Matthew Arnold. A Critical Portrait* (Oxford, Oxford University Press, 1994), pp. 76–88, 110–19.

36 The Midland District was Arnold's first inspectorial district, in 1851–52. Cecil Y. Lang (ed.) *The Letters of Matthew Arnold*, 3 vols (Charlottesville VA, University Press of Virginia, 1996), 1, 227–81. Matthew Arnold, *Reports on Elementary Schools, 1851–1852* (London, HMSO, [1889]1908), pp. 1–17. Middlemarch could have prompted his notorious statement about 'the low degree of mental culture and intelligence' among pupil teachers, that 'number of young men, who at present, notwithstanding the vast amount of raw information which they have amassed are wholly uncultivated'. *Mathew Arnold*, 16–17. His thoughts run much like Rosamund's when she has Plymdale in prospect; however, he did not record any visit to Coventry in the letters he wrote from the field that year.

37 Francis Mulherne, *The Moment of 'Scrutiny'* (London, Verso, [1979] 1981), pp. 98–9.

38 E.P. Thompson, *Warwick University Ltd. Industry, Management and the Universities* (Harmondsworth, Penguin, 1970), p. 17.

39 Haught, *The George Eliot Letters*, V, p. 168.

40 Peter New, 'Chance, Providence and Destiny in George Eliot's Fiction', *Journal of the English Association*, 34:150 (1985), 191–208.

⌇ 6

What a rag rug means

Tearless, their surfaces appear as deep
As any longing we believe we had;
If shapes can so to their own edges keep,
No separation proves a being bad.
(W.H. Auden, 'Objects', 1966)

THIS STARTED OUT AS AN ERROR of transposition. However, the tense of the title – 'means' rather than 'meant' – was always correct. It is about what a rag rug means, rather than what a rag rug meant (though it is about that too); about the rag rug as an obscure object of desire, fashioned in some place between Memory and History, for all those who read the past, in their various ways, but particularly about historians as the readers in question.

The error of transposition is an introduction. I started thinking about the rag rug when I remembered the second chapter of Elizabeth Gaskell's *Mary Barton* (1848). As evening falls and the novel opens, two working-class families, the Bartons and the Wilsons, are returning from their May-time holiday walk in the countryside. Back in Manchester 'among the pent-up houses', the darkness seems to have come sooner than it would have in the fields they have just left. Mrs Barton takes the front-door key from her pocket and, 'on entering the house-place it seemed as if they were in total darkness, except [for] one bright spot … a red-hot fire, smouldering under a large piece of coal' (49).[1] Soon, the stirred fire illuminates the whole room, and with the addition of a candle we see its dimensions, its appurtenances, its furnishings, its decorations. It is an immensely detailed description of an interior space made up of: a window, a ledge, blue and white check curtains; geraniums on the sill; plates, dishes, cups, saucers, glassware; a japanned tea-tray, a crimson tea-caddy. This is a space crammed with furniture, though some of it is broken, and made only of deal in the first place. The fire-light provides depth, brightness and – the author seems to tell us as much – the intense interior glitter of the Victorian tale for children, when we first enter any old giant's castle, or this cottage in the woods, or that little house.

From this warm, richly coloured room, doors lead to a little back kitchen, where the functions assigned to the shelves evoke pantries and storerooms, sculleries and larders (though there is in fact, only the one little back kitchen). There is a staircase, so we know that we are in a house, and not a one-level dwelling: that we are not here in one of those places that in *The Poetics of Space*, Gaston Bachelard called oneirically incomplete, in which 'the different rooms that compose living quarters jammed into one floor all lack one of the fundamental principles for distinguishing and classifying the values of intimacy'.[2] We are emphatically *not* in a dwelling that, by this criterion, fails to provide the working material for dreams.

We shall return to Bachelard, to the poetics of space in general, and of this kind of space in particular. But the immediate concern has to be the fact that *there isn't a rag rug in the Barton parlour*. Rather, between the slanting cupboard under the stairs, which the Bartons use as a coal-hole, and the fireplace, there is 'a gay-coloured piece of oil-cloth laid'. No rag rug; and yet I *remember* a rag rug.

The process of my misrecollection is in fact, quite easy to reconstruct: I once wrote a paper in which I connected Elizabeth Gaskell's description of the Barton parlour – 'simple and heart-wrenching detail upon domestic detail called up to make us understand a simplicity and sadness in this form of life', I wrote in 1986 – with a passage from Richard Hoggart's *Uses of Literacy* (1958 [1957]), where – I suggested – 'a rag rug comes to symbolise a great and enduring simplicity of working-class life'.[3] I simply forgot the hundred and ten years between the two texts, and put the rag rug down on the Barton parlour floor.

The passage from Hoggart that I transposed belongs to a long section called 'There's No Place Like Home', which details in a manner strikingly similar to Gaskell's 'a good [working-class] living room'.[4] There *are* moments of historicisation and chronology in these pages of *The Uses of Literacy*, when for instance, Hoggart reminds the reader that what he writes is 'largely based on memories of twenty-years ago', that is of his own 1930s Hunslet childhood; but they are followed by immediate disavowal, in the typical statement that 'the basic pattern of working-class life remains as it has been for many years'. The rag rug (Hoggart calls it a clip rug) comes at the end of his depiction of the house as a cluttered and congested setting, 'a burrow deeply away from the outside world'.

Its sounds shape the inwardness and harmony of the house: the quiet noise of the wireless and the television, 'intermittent snatches of talk'; the thump of the iron on the table, the dog scratching itself; the rustle of a letter being read.[5] And then, Hoggart observes that

> in a few of the more careful homes this unity is still objectified in the making of a clip-rug by the hearth. Clippings of old clothes are prepared, sorted into rough colour groups and punched singly through a piece of harding [sacking]. Patterns are traditional and simple, usually a centre circle or diamond with the remainder an unrelieved navy blue ... or that greyish-blue which mixed shoddy usually produces ... The rug will replace at the fireplace one made a long time ago.[6]

The rag rug of *my* imagination lasted the ninety years between Manchester in the 1840s (the fictional time of *Mary Barton*) and the Leeds working-class community of the inter-war years that Hoggart recalled in the 1950s; and whilst the aetiology of my error would no doubt be fascinating (especially to myself), I think that in order to proceed it is best to see the transformed oilcloth on the Barton floor as *a likely rug*, and Hoggart's remembered rug as the personification of the way of living that he actually says it is: a feature of the poetics of a timeless and dehistoricised working-class life, available for use by British social historians and cultural critics of the twentieth century.

As a poetics, it was partly derived from works like *Mary Barton*, that is, from social observation translated into fictional realism (in the industrial novel), and from – we must strongly suspect – the gothic vision which informed the writing of so many of Dickens's Metropolitan interiors. However, though the restless bricolage of the fairy-tale does appear in his writing (one thinks in particular of the Boffins's kitchen in Chapter 5 of *Our Mutual Friend*) Dickens *doesn't really do it*. First of all, those interiors (Chapter 5 of *Barnaby Rudge*, Chapter 6 of *Dombey and Son*, Chapter 3 of *David Copperfield*) are not really working-class, and more significantly – a point to which I shall return – there is *usually somebody in them*. But for the visual depth that Dickens's writing seems to promise but not – in this instance – quite deliver, and for the delight provoked by seeing it *for the first time*, there is always Henry Mayhew's sudden, swift moment of aesthetic surprise at the harmony and comfort of a costermonger's dwelling, at an interior where the wall over the fireplace was entirely 'patched up to the ceiling with little square pictures of saints'. And then

> on the mantel-piece, between a row of bright tumblers and wine glasses filled with odds and ends, stood glazed crockeryware images … Against the walls, which were papered with 'hangings' of four different patterns and colours, were hung several warm shawls … A turn-up bedstead thrown back, and covered with a many-coloured

patch-work quilt, stood opposite to a long dresser with its mugs and cups dangling from the hooks, and the clean blue plates and dishes ranged in order at the back.[7]

There is no rest for the eye in these descriptions, however lovingly they are detailed. Hoggart emphasises the harmony of the 1930s terrace house by dwelling on the pattern of the rug, the 'centre circle or diamond with the remainder an unrelieved navy blue (except for the edging)'. But the rag rug is irreducibly a thing made from the torn scraps of other things, from rags, indeed. It returns us, no matter what coherence and peace Hoggart gives it in his mind's eye, to Mayhew's vision in *Life and Labour of the London Poor*, of a vast Metropolis, an entire way of life built upon the scavengings of the poor: bones retrieved for boiling down, dog shit collected from the street, mud dredged for tiny fragments of metal, rag yards heaped with old clothing on its way to becoming some other kind of object, some other sort of thing.[8] When this is done knowingly, when the story-teller, or potter, or weaver, or other kind of craftsman brings together the shards and fragments of the world in order to remake it, then he may be praised for taking part in 'montage praxis, using debris and rubbish, ... broken pots and torn scraps'.[9] But what went into the rag that makes the rag rug, its own history of production, ownership and consumption, of wearing and tearing, deflects the use of this aesthetic, as we shall see.

Hoggart's rug was the product of longing. It was made partly out of nostalgia for his own past, from the oneiric richness of his own childhood space. With this perspective it is useful to counterpoise Hoggart's dream of the rag rug with another extremely rare first-hand account of living in a working-class interior, that is, with Leonora Eyles's *The Woman in the Little House* (1922), in which she records that for five years of my life I was never alone for a single instant; in bed, in the kitchen, shopping, gardening, always someone very near to me, touching me most of the time. I felt sometimes as though I could come to hate the crowding people who were really so dear to me. Is it in one of these momentary spasms of impatient desire to get alone for a few minutes that murders are sometimes done?[10]

We shall reluctantly leave that alternative story, in which blood soaks the rag rug, taking from this conjunction of Hoggart with Eyles two points: that there is bound to be a distinction between the sexes in relation to the little house, and all that is symbolised by the rag rug before the hearth; but that we are never likely to find out very much about that difference because voices *from* the working-class interior are an extraordinary rarity. All the descriptions we have are from observers, from those who penetrated the maze of greasy streets and stepped through the door of another kind of space. It is to observation of those spaces and places of the nineteenth-century imagination that our attention must now turn.

Historians have provided us with a poetics of this kind of encounter, observation and imagining (unwittingly, we must suppose: historians do not in the normal course of events do that sort of thing). Alain Corbin's work directly addresses *the ways of seeing* the homes of the poor that were evolved by the middle classes. In *The Foul and the Fragrant* he reports that 'the flood of discourse on the habitat of the masses' reached new dimensions after the 1832 cholera morbus epidemic.'[11] Using French (and particularly Parisian) evidence he traces in some detail the ways in which the sanitary reformer's denunciations of the odour and excrement of the quarters of the poor were used by popular novelists to write a new form of shock, that made its effect on the sensory borderline between smell and vision. 'The odour of stagnant urine, congealed in the gutter, dried on the paving, encrusted on the wall, assailed the visitor who had to enter the wretched premises of the poor.'

Corbin then goes on to provide an epitome of the journey to the lair, a journey that can be read (for Britain as well as France) in countless government reports, reports of charity organisations and by investigative journalism, from the 1830s onwards. It is the mode in which modern historians of working-class life write – *of course* – because they have learned their rhetoric from the nineteenth-century sources themselves. (David Rubinstein's book *Victorian Homes* (1974) is still the most useful compilation of such contemporary observations.) There is Corbin's epitome:

> The only means of entry was through low, narrow, dark alleys ... Gaining access to the poor man's stinking dwelling almost amounted to an underground expedition ... The narrowness, darkness and humidity of the small inner courtyard into which the alley opened made it look like a well, the ground carpeted with refuse. Inside the dwelling, congestion, a jumble of tools, dirty linen and crockery, prevailed ... In particular, writings focused on the aspect of narrowness. The crampedness of the sleeping area, the depth of the yard, and the length of the alley created in the mind of the bourgeois ... the impression of suffocation.[12]

Corbin also tells us that in all this complex of writing 'the cage rather than the den was the dominant image'. However, these powerful pages of his book suggest the imprisonment of the dungeon, not the animal cage, for Corbin evokes cage as prison; as underground prison, without air.[13]

Margaret McMillan can be found using this poetics of the working-class lair for overtly political purposes, as late as 1919. Her writing demonstrates a striking formality of vision, a vision made formulaic through the processes of official and fictional writing, from the mid-nineteenth century onwards. McMillan was making her usual plea to the Labour Party and its sympathisers, to rescue the child of the slum by placing him in a garden, specifically in the garden of her open-air nursery school in Deptford, South East

London. She usually did this, as in the passage below, by actually insisting on the child's enduring contact with the dark place that spawned him:

Dennis lives in a … street [that] is a huddle of houses with dark, greasy lobbies and hideous black stairs leading down into cellars. It is so dark that when one goes down one sees nothing for a few moments. Then a broken wall, and a few sticks of furniture appear, and a dark young woman with glittering eyes looks down [sic] at us. Dennis is a great pet in the Nursery. On his firm little feet he runs all round the big shelter and garden … he breaks into a kind of singing on bright June mornings … his eyes alight with joy. In the evening his older sister comes, and carries him back to the cellar.[14]

It is the cellar, the greasy walls, the stained and broken ceiling, that endure in the imagination. These are the spaces poeticised and used for rhetorical purposes, despite the wealth of alternative description from the nineteenth century available to historians. In fact, many a social investigator climbed a broken and stinking stair to find a small whitewashed room of endearing neatness, very close to the stars; or followed a child, fictional or real, into the fetid courts and alleys that generated it – to find, not malodorous horror, but a floor scrubbed 'three or four times a week' by Mayhew's Little Watercress Girl, or a 'poor upper room' – Nelly's lodging in Mrs Sewell's ballad of 1861, *Our Father's Care* – where 'A small fire is burning, the water is hot,/The tea is put into the little teapot,/ And all things are carefully set in their place.'[15]

Nevertheless, it is the lair we must consider, the small enclosed space between, and beneath, and at the end of something else: enclosed. Mayhew reported on the poetic dichotomies of this space quite as much as he did on an actual costermonger's dwelling in the first volume of *Life and Labour of the London Poor* (1851). 'Although these people were living, so to speak, in a cellar' he reported still every endeavour had been made to give the home a look of comfort. The window, with its paper-patched panes, had a clean calico blind. The side-table was dressed up with yellow jugs and cups and saucers, and the band-boxes had been stowed away on the flat top of the bedstead. All the chairs, which were old fashioned mahogany ones, had sound backs and bottoms.[16]

It lacks only the rag rug.

What kind of space is this?

Gaston Bachelard described 'the poetic depth of the space of the house'. He wrote about the house as 'one of the greatest powers of integration for the thoughts, memories and dreams of mankind'.[17] Its many rooms and levels, its stairways and recesses allow Bachelard's topanalyst 'to start to ask questions: Was the room a large one? Was the garret cluttered up? Was the nook warm? How was it lighted?'. We may ask these questions too, although it is not houses that we have been considering but *rooms* in houses – neglected, dirty houses – rooms in cellars, or rooms at the far reaches of a broken stair. Bachelard continued his questions about these spaces within houses, asking 'How, too, in these fragments of space, did the human being achieve silence? How did he relish the very special silence of the various retreats of day-dreaming?' We know the answer to that one, even though, lacking evidence from those who lived in narrow cluttered rooms we have to wait until the twentieth century for a voice to tell us about the lack of aloneness of the little house.

We have already seen that Bachelard considered some dwellings to be oneirically incomplete, incapable of providing material for the dream-work or even for daydreaming: 'the different rooms that compose living quarters jammed into one floor all lack one of the fundamental principles for distinguishing and classifying the values of intimacy'.[18] Here he found the Parisian apartment wanting; but we must suppose that the large numbers of Victorian poor who lived with their family and others in one room dwellings were also deprived of the 'fundamental principles for distinguishing … intimacy'.

'Overcrowding' was not officially defined in the UK until 1891, as a room containing more than two adults. Children under ten counted as half by this measure, and babies not at all. According to John Burnett in *A Social History of Housing*, 11.2 per cent of the population of England and Wales – about 3½ million people – was 'overcrowded' in 1891.[19] There are no reliable statistics on house building for the first half of the nineteenth century, and as Enid Gauldie suggests in *Cruel Habitations*, we have to steer a course between the statistical suppositions that Census figures allow, suggesting that building kept pace with the increased demand for housing (the Census shows that the average number of person per inhabited house held steady between 1801 and 1831, and actually dropped very slightly in 1841) and the overwhelming evidence deposited by the slum visitor, that working-class districts were becoming more overcrowded.[20] We must assume that throughout the middle years of the nineteenth century many more than 11.2 per cent of the population experienced oneiric deprivation.[21]

And yet … the Barton parlour *is* the stuff of dreams, its furnishings those of the imagination … *someone's* imagination, though whose is not yet quite clear. If, accompanied by *The Poetics of Space*, we turn into the alley, cross the stinking court and enter one of these many single-room dwellings (or even allow that pleasant walk home the Bartons take, on the level, in the clear light of day, along a street of houses so new that some of them are still half-finished, and have a working-class woman put the key in the lock and open the door) – if we do that with Bachelard's poetics of space in mind, then the objects we find in these numerous rooms present us with yet another puzzle.

Always, we see the objects in these working-class interiors as if for *the first time*. For Bachelard, the way in which quite ordinary objects are marked 'with the sign of "the first time"' by the writer is the highest form of poetic expression.[22] He suggests that when objects are lit in this way *as the first time*, they transmit a light to their surroundings, just as in this case, their evanescence fills the Barton parlour with radiance, once the glowing eye of the fire is made to blaze, and cast its illumination over the multitude of objects in the room. According to Bachelard, this intimate light is particularly manifest in things 'that are cherished', and he suggests that polishing, the giving of a bright appearance to things, is the best mark of cherishing:

> Objects that are cherished in this way really are born of an intimate light, and they attain to a higher degree of reality than indifferent objects, or those that are defined by geometric reality. For they produce a new reality of being, and take their place not only in an order but in a community of order.[23]

When the working-class interior is the object of the writer's desire, its multifarious bric-à-brac gleams and glitters in this way. The objects in the Barton parlour, ranged on the mantlepiece and towering up in the shelves of the open cupboard, while not possessing the oneiric depth of those 'objects *that may be opened*' like the caskets and boxes to which Bachelard draws our attention, are nevertheless, objects that curve themselves outwards (or inwards), that present their interior as well as their exterior to the world: cups, glasses, dishes. The phenomenology of earthenware, glassware and china does indeed allow the most interesting elaboration of Bachelard's thesis, for these everyday objects present inside and outside together, as on a continuum created by the uses to which they are put; they contain and emanate the has-been-opened. It is worth noting as well, that Gaskell has John Barton remember and grieve for his dear, dead wife in relation to these household objects. He remembers loving her, in her use of them. (57)

The question remains: whose dream-work is this? And there is still for the moment, the provisional answer to that question: that wherever we may come to locate the dream, we can be certain that it is *not* in the mind or heart of the fictional or real inhabitants of the rooms we are considering.

The overwhelming impression of the reader is that in these clean and itemised interiors, one has entered a fairy-tale. But it is not just the warmth, the fire filling the cluttered space with heat and light, each flame reflected back by the myriad surfaces, that we should note. It is the *smallness* of this house, this narrow room, the littleness of the objects depicted, that should give us pause. Bachelard mentions the fairy-tale as the beginning of his chapter on 'The Miniature', and starts by discussing those objects that are 'so easily made smaller through literary means'. He understands the role of the reader and of course, above all, of the writer in this process, perhaps even signalling that it is writing itself that has a major part to play in miniaturising the world. 'Is it possible' he asks 'for the conscious[24] of both writer and reader – to play a sincere role in the very origin of images of this kind?' – for it is indeed the case that everything is made smaller in imagination, in the mind's eye.[25]

The attraction of the miniature object, the deep pleasures of littleness, have been noted by literary scholars attempting to create a poetics of relative size and smallness. Claude Lévi-Strauss considered that miniaturisation was the very foundation of the aesthetic.[26] But perhaps Susan Stewart's work is the most useful here, not only because the title of her book *On Longing* inscribes so clearly the desire involved in making small the world, but also because she understands the relationship of pleasure in the miniature to childhood and history. She writes that 'the miniature, linked to nostalgic versions of childhood and history, presents a diminutive, and thereby manipulatable, version of experience, a version which is domesticated and protected from contamination'.[27] These are extraordinary insights and an understanding of littleness that is historically located; a reading that forces us to think of the ways in which the pleasures of interiority and smallness inscribed in Elizabeth Gaskell's (and Henry Mayhew's and many, many others') description of the neat fairy-tale parlour, emerged in a particular historical period and for – this point will be returned to – particular historical purposes.

But none of these theorists of littleness do what Bachelard did so eloquently, in 1962. His overall turn of thought, announced in the introduction to *The Poetics of Space*, was to delineate the house by the structure of individual memory, and a return in imagination to the security of childhood. Much of the exegesis that follows in *The Poetics of Space* is to do with the way in which 'childhood remains alive and poetically useful within us'. And yet when Bachelard comes to concentrate on the miniature in Chapter 7 of his book, he puts to one side the proposition that 'the tiny things we imagine simply take us back to childhood, to familiarity with toys and *the reality of toys*'.[28] He dismisses this idea by telling us that 'the imagination deserves better than this'. (He means: the imagination deserves a better kind of explanation than this.) 'In point of fact,' he claims, 'imagination in miniature is natural imagination which appears at all ages in the daydreams of born dreamers.'

The question now forces itself: why does Elizabeth Gaskell poeticise the Barton interior in this particular way – and why – by means of metonymy – does she do what she does to the people who enter the house-place just before us, who step over the threshold after Mrs Barton's turn of the key, but who then strangely, disappear, so that what we are left to contemplate is the stillness and unpeopled nature of the fairy-tale house? (The one belonging to the Three Bears that Goldilocks enters is the most obvious example to hand.) However, Bachelard disapproved of metaphor so much that he surely would disapprove of any recourse to metonymy as a device explanatory of the dream process.

Why? Why desire for this parlour, these things, this life, in a room emptied of people, though usually (in the time of social reality) full of them? The silence is held within the cups, glasses, teapots, boxes, tables, trays, tea-caddies, and polished chairs, that send forth their light into the room. Why desire then, for a life that is actually emptied out of the picture we are presented with, as the ghosts of Gaskell's imagination fall silent on the threshold, and we step into the little room?

We must pursue childhood a little further. Childhood – this has been established elsewhere – was brought into being in Western culture, as ideation, as an idea, as memory, as image, at the same time as history was brought into being; and the poetic depth of childhood has been attested to by many literary scholars.[29] But the adult desire for the working-class interior needs further elaboration, by considering a remembered child's use of the poetic space of the working-class interior.

It is Manchester, in the late 1850s. The remembered child – it is Frances Hodgson Burnett writing her nauseatingly entitled *The One I Knew Best of All* (1893) – lives in the Square (the chapter referred to is entitled 'Islington Square', a 'a sort of oasis in the midst of small thoroughfares and back streets, where factory operatives lived').[30] The Square is cut off from these surroundings by iron gates, but the child Hodgson Burnett remembers (who is even more nauseatingly referred to as The Small Person) finds infinite delight in getting out, straying into a forbidden back street and luring 'a dirty little factory child into conversation'. Even *in* the Square the surrounding streets provided entertainment:

'A row in Islington Court!' or, 'A row in Back Sydney Street. Man beating his wife with a shovel!' was a cry which thrilled the bolder juvenile spirits of the Square with awesome delight. There were even fair little persons who hovered shudderingly about the big gates, or even passed them, in the shocked hope of seeing a policeman march by with somebody in custody. (69)

But none of this provides the dream-work. Something else does. In a quite extraordinary scene, the child brings the desired working-class interior into her own house, as shadow play: as dream. Burnett describes the Nursery floor, and in particular, one room of it at the rear, which 'looked down upon the back of the row of cottages in which operatives lived. When one glanced downwards it was easy to see into their tiny kitchens and watch them prepare their breakfasts, and eat them too.' The narrative voice continues:

> Imagine then, the interest of waking very early one dark morning and seeing a light reflected on the ceiling of the Nursery bedroom from somewhere far below.
> The Small Person did this once, and after watching a little, discovered that not only the light and the window itself were reflected, but two figures which seemed to pass before it or stand near it. (76–7)

The child wakes her sister: 'It's a man and a woman ... Back Street people in their kitchen. You can see them on our ceiling. *This* ceiling; just look.'

The children whisper about what they see on the screen above them: the loaf in the woman's hand, the man washing his face at the dresser. They know that 'they're factory people, and the man's wife must be getting his breakfast before he goes to work. I wonder what poor people have for breakfast.' 'Ah the charm of it!', continues Burnett.

> The sense of mystery and unusualness ... How could one go to sleep ... when the Back Street woman was awake and getting her husband's breakfast? One's own ceiling reflected it and seemed to

include one in the family circle ... What each figure was really doing when it was near enough to the window to be reflected, what it did when it moved away out of the range of reflection, and what it was possible they said to each other, were all things to be excitedly guessed at. (78)

The chapter closes with Burnett recalling that

it became a habit to waken at that delightful and uncanny hour, just for the pleasure of lying awake and watching the Woman and the Man. That was what they called them. They never knew what their names were, or anything about them ... but the Small Person was privately attached to them, and continually tried to imagine what they said. She had a fancy that they were a decent couple, who were rather fond of each other, and it was a great comfort to her that they never had a fight. (79)

It was all a very great comfort to those social investigators and novelists who wrote the working-class interior in the way I have described. The child's particular achievement in this case was to people the strange, magical interior of her reverie, have the Man and the Woman move across the screen, preparing food, eating it, washing in a bowl placed on the dresser (though they do not – cannot – speak and their conversation is only to be guessed at).

There is probably not much more to say about these matters at this juncture. Except for one thing, which is to do with the ways in which, with the development of a modern class society, working-class people, their image, their appurtenances, were used to tell other people's stories: to tell some kind of story of the bourgeois self. Following the trajectory of this tradition, of representation and use of the working-class story, all that can be suggested for the moment, is that perhaps the working-class domestic is read and written out of the same obscure desire: that desire means you understand – and write – the self through others, who are not like you. You want to enter that little space, as Elizabeth Gaskell did, with all its miniature bricolage, and in doing so, you will take something away, though what that thing might be is as yet uncertain. What we can be certain of, is that these modes of desire and representation have no necessary connection at all with the people who actually, in time and social circumstance, occupied the cruel habitations. Which is why I like the rag rug, and my mistake about it, for the rag rug is made from the torn fragments of other things, debris and leavings, the broken and torn things of industrial civilisation. The rag rug carries with it the irreducible traces of an actual history, and that history *cannot be made to go away*, but ways of writing it and wanting it (and what it represents) are actually somebody else's story.

∽

And there is a coda, for this cannot be left alone. *Why* isn't there a rag rug in the Barton parlour? There *ought to be one*, laid before the fire. Clip-, peg-, or rag-rug-making is an old domestic craft. Hooked or progged rugs (a progger is the implement – in appearance rather like a fat little awl – used for pulling the piece of rag through the hessian backing) were simple copies of expensive looped and cut-pile carpeting. The flexibility and give of the rag rug was in any case a good choice for covering the uneven brick and stone floors of working-class interiors, better than carpeting would have been, could it ever possibly have been afforded.[31]

The history of domestic production in nineteenth-century Britain is uncertain, and we know very little about the regional development of rag-rug-making, though existing accounts suggest that developments in textile production and in the ready-to-wear clothing market gave great impetus to the practice. Cotton had been commonly worn in Britain in the seventeenth century,[32] and jute-hessian sacks were easily available in the 1830s. Mainly produced in Scotland, they were distributed across the UK as containers for loose foodstuffs, and could probably be obtained from any grocer's shop, anywhere, in the 1840s. In any case, the Lancashire sacking trade had developed in the mid-eighteenth century. In his tour of the county in 1771, Arthur Young noted the vitality of the Warrington sailcloth and sacking manufacture, and also that it was largely the province of women and girls.[33]

And surely, in Manchester, in the 1840s, there *should be* such a rug on the Barton's house-place floor? The production of woven cotton cloth, in this great centre of cotton production, rose expeditiously in the 1840s. Total UK exports of cotton piece goods doubled between the late 1830s and 1850.[34] The earlier century witnessed a growing localisation of the cotton industry in Lancashire.[35] By the 1840s, some 70 per cent of those employed nationally in the production of cotton lived in Lancashire. Counting the ten major Lancashire concentrations of cotton manufactures, Manchester was superseded only by Oldham in the number of its factories in the 1830s and 1840s.[36]

However, it appears that the bags of loom ends and ready-cut spoiled cloth that by the 1890s could be purchased from the mills were not available fifty years before. (By the early 1900s, according to some authorities, ready-stamped hessian could also be purchased by the yard, along with commercially produced hooks and proggers.) A *length* of cheap – because flawed – cloth is not what you want for making a rag rug. You want bits and pieces, a variety of colours and textures, otherwise there would be just that unrelieved, solid colour of the border of Richard Hoggart's rug. The tailor and the dressmaker were probably a source for bits and pieces long before the side-door of the mill. (And yet: Mary Barton is *apprenticed* to a dressmaker. *Why* doesn't she bring home bundles of off-cuts, bits of selvage, the awkward little pieces that remain, however economically you place the pattern?)

Or perhaps, by looking to Lancashire, we are looking in the

wrong place for the development of the rag rug. Over the Pennines, or in the woollen districts up round Rochdale, the woollen textile industry was older, looms were not always the latest in modern technology that Lancashire aspired to, there was a much bigger variation in size of unit of production, a wider variety of size of loom (for broadcloth, and narrow cloth), and theft was 'accepted as an integral part of outwork systems by merchant manufacturers'.[37] In short, where wool was woven, there were perhaps many more opportunities for spoilage and wastage, and the sale and purchase of remnants and off-cuts.

But the truth of the matter (and of the rag rug's absence from the Barton parlour floor) probably lies in the history of an industry other than textiles, that is, in the history of paper production and in the voracious demand of the paper manufacturers for linen and cotton rags. After 1860 usable and commercially viable substitutes *were* found for cotton rags in paper making, but the large-scale, bulk import of wood pulp was a development of the much later century.[38] What is more, in the very early 1860s, the first machinery designed to render old cotton fit for spinning came into production, so the consequent diminution in demand for cotton rags by the paper trade came in tandem with a new demand for them from the cotton industry. (The technology had been available for woollen cloth rendering since 1813, but it was cotton that was needed prior to 1865, for the making of paper.)[39]

From the middle of the eighteenth century, cotton rags had been at a premium, and UK paper manufacturers imported vast quantities from abroad to feed the insatiable appetite for their products. Prices rose to a peak in the early 1850s, and a report to the Board of Trade in 1854 noted 'the great and increasing scarcity of the raw material used in paper making'. The government official from the Department of Art and Science compiling the Report went on to observe that the cause of the scarcity was not just the 'growing thirst for literature', but also a raw material that was 'the product of wear and tear of a substance of very advanced manufacture', that is, cotton cloth, and the rags that were its eventual detritus. Even a partial stoppage in the cotton or linen trades (he mentioned recent lock-outs in Wigan and Preston) could account for scarcity and a rise in prices of rags, and of paper.[40]

All those involved in any form of tailoring or dressmaking had been exhorted, for at least the previous half century, to save every scrap of cotton and linen cloth they could. In 1799 *The Times* 'particularly recommended to Ladies and every person employed in Needlework, not to burn even the smallest pieces which they may cut', for

> the Rags annually collected in this kingdom amount in weight to several tons. Doubtless a much greater quantity might be preserved by the care of individuals. – The paper Manufacturers would not then depend on the uncertain importation from foreign countries for an article which could be easily produced in our own.[41]

There's romance in the rag of course, as Mrs Paull acknowledged in the title to her temperance tract of 1876, *The Romance of a Rag*, but even at this late date, when rags were no longer at the premium of unique source, the rag that tells the tale of a working-class family and a hand-me-down dress ruined by a drunken father (the handful of rags that remain of the dress is subjected to a process of severe purification and turns into a temperance pledge card!) becomes paper, not reconstituted thread for cotton spinning.[42]

Nearly all our knowledge of the rag rug comes framed by a romance. Romance frames knowledge about the period that oral, labour and social history of the 1960s and 1970s located as the origin of the 'traditional working class', that is, the end of the nineteenth century.[43] In this terrain of the historical imagination, the rug is connected with flat-caps, pigeon-fancying, fish and chips, the kind of domestic interior that Hoggart described in *The Uses of Literacy*, and the great monolithic industries (coal, steel, textiles) that gave birth to such a culture. But even Elizabeth Roberts's informants, speaking from the heartland of industrial Lancashire, and remembering the period 1890–1940, never recall purchasing ready-cuts for the peg rugs they made. Rather, they remember cutting up 'old coats, they were kept specially.'[44]

We should return to the economy that Mayhew described, built on the scavenging, exchange and trading of tiny things. The rag rug has to do, more than anything else perhaps, with the second-hand clothing market, that half-hidden motor of an industrial economy that Beverly Lemire has described as a 'well-established, organized system of redistribution, founded on the demand of those in more straitened circumstances'. She goes on to remark that 'identification of the characteristics of this second tier of demand are crucial for an understanding of the British home market in the eighteenth century'.[45] In the eighteenth century the second-hand market in clothes was 'a key intermediate trade', for those in 'straitened circumstances' and for anyone who wanted to raise a bit of ready money. By the nineteenth century and the period of *Mary Barton*, it was a consumer economy of the poor and very poor who – perhaps – found a domestic use for the final tatters of the seventh-hand shirts and shifts in which they clothed themselves, though it does seem that up until the 1870s even a small quantity of rags was worth more on the open market to the vendor than the value of a painstakingly-made floor covering could possibly have been. You needed a lot of rags to make a rug. Offering advice to the USA on the making of hooked rugs as part of a programme of national regeneration, the American Ivan Crowell suggested that 'roughly a square yard of worn clothing will make a square foot of hooked rug'.[46] The value of even a tiny quantity of rags was one of the messages of Mrs Paull's *The Romance of a Rag*.[47]

We could suggest, then, that the rag rug has its origins in the Metropolis, or more widely, in centres of commerce, trade and distribution older than Manchester, where the trade in second-hand clothing first established itself: South, not North. And maybe we shouldn't be looking at the (absent) rag rug *at all*, but rather at what is actually *there*, in the parlour of Elizabeth Gaskell's dream, which is that 'gay-coloured piece of oil-cloth'. This is the badge of the Barton's modernity; it symbolises the fact that they are doing quite nicely, and suggests that their neat house-place does not have a broken, uneven, cracked brick floor, that would need the soft contours of the rug but, rather, that it is well made-up, even and smooth, able to take the relative stiffness of canvas coated with oil-based paint.[48] Nor was oil-cloth particularly cheap, and its maintenance demanded a well-ordered – and comfortably financed – domesticity.[49]

And beyond all of this – the absent rag rug, the present oil-cloth – is the question of whether this is the thing to start – or end – with, at all. This room, this space is Elizabeth Gaskell's dream after all: her fiction. We should note the particularities of her interior, the glowing enchantment of its surfaces, textures and details, and then pay attention to what she said of its origins, and of the novel as a whole.

Gaskell was one of the first voluntary district Visitors of the Manchester and Salford District Provident Society,[50] and after the publication of her novel, she told a fellow worker that

> the one strong impulse to write 'Mary Barton' came to her one evening in a labourer's cottage. She was trying hard to speak comfort, and to allay those bitter feelings against the rich that were so common with the poor, when the head of the family took hold of her arm and grasping it tightly said, with tears in his eyes: 'Ay, ma'am, but have ye ever seen a child clemmed to death?'[51]

She probably started to write her novel in the last months of 1845 at the suggestion of her husband, 'to divert her mind from the morbid thoughts which [then] assailed her', for she had lost her little boy Willie, just ten months old, in August that year.[52] She always asserted that it was John Barton's tragedy rather than the love-interest and melodrama provided by his daughter's tale that should be read as the centre of the novel.[53] Barton's story inscribes a tragedy; and he is one of the few working-class tragic heroes in English literature, because he is Elizabeth Gaskell's story, her dream and her compensation. What she took away from the labourer's cottage in which she tried to speak comfort was herself, and a new way of understanding her own story, of parenthood, love and loss.[54]

What had she just said to the man who responded (in the moment when the story was born) '"Ay, ma'am, but have ye ever seen a child clemmed to death?"' Surely not that she had recently lost a child? The etiquette of talking to the poor – the nice reticence learned by the philanthropic bourgeoisie, about one's own, always more comfortable sorrows – was surely exercised here. There is certainly nothing in Gaskell's correspondence or other personal writing to suggest that she ever – could ever have – behaved in such a boorish and thoughtless way. More likely she had said something general, as she would in *Mary Barton*, about the trials of the well-to-do being as great as those of the poor, as Mr Carson has it rather more specifically right at the end of the novel, when he exclaims '"How in the world can we help it? We cannot regulate the demand for labour. No man or set of men can do it. It depends on events which God alone can control. When there is no market for our goods, we suffer just as you can do."' (456) But the separation between Gaskell and her interlocutor, and between her and her invention John Barton proved (to use W.H. Auden's formulation) 'a being bad'. The hand pressed on another in sympathy, eyes and hearts meeting across the wastes of class relations, are acknowledgement of that separation.

The things in the little room of Gaskell's imagination have surface and depth only out of her longing. But they keep their shape, which is the shape of *what they are*, no matter who imagines them, because they are things, with histories of their making, purchase, consumption (and, in the Barton case, as tragedy tightens its grip and the household goods are sold, one by one, their dispersal). And all the systems of Cottonopolis – economic and social – stretching far beyond its boundaries, into the great world of trade and commerce, colonialism and slavery, and all the human relationships made and sustained out of those systems, are what make the separation that the novelist strives to dissolve but that remains in place, between Gaskell and her dream, between Gaskell and the labourer who gripped her arm, between John Barton and the Manchester masters who are to blame for it all.

In the verse used as epigraph to this chapter, Auden's deliberate phonemic ambiguity will tell us as much. Are the objects of his poem things that shed no tears, or things untorn? In the case of this particular object, there is no doubt, for what makes up the rag-rug that isn't there is – rags. The pieces of cloth are torn, and they make up the rug that cannot to its own edges keep: it intrudes in the dream of the novelist, the dream of the historian: the dreams of all the sympathetic visitors to those heart-wrenching rooms on the other side of the borderline. It is the object that mediates, and that promises the capacity to see what is oneself, and what is not oneself, but that, unlike the 'blankets, rags, and other soft objects' of the object relations theory poeticised by Auden, cannot allow a final disengagement from itself.[55]

Using Walter Benjamin's work, Esther Leslie has persuaded us to add stories (and perhaps rag rugs) to the more conventional list of crafted objects (pots and carvings and products of the loom) so that we might pay attention to the experiences people have with these objects, and the memories that they contain.[56] But when the novel that is crafted is taken and remade out of *other people's* stories, and when the rag rug is itself a re-making by twentieth-century historians, of a working-class experience that probably never happened – what then? We may say two things: that the *absent* rag rug is the truth of Gaskell's novel, is the history it cannot escape, and its tragedy; and that as a crafted object (like the gleaming and glittering cups and dishes that *are* actually present), and in its own absence, it shapes the rhythms and structures of the tale.[57] Reading the nineteenth-century domestic space, the historian has made the mistake of carpeting it with a rug that, in fact, could not be made in an economy in which such a tiny number of things circulated again and again, among so many people; where scarcity and technological underdevelopment created a shortage, not of the poor, but of the traditional symbols of the poor, their rags; and where even a handful of tattered clothing was worth a trip to the rag merchant, reckoned as it was until the late nineteenth century, as half a loaf of bread.

Notes

1 References in the text are to the 1970 Penguin edn of *Mary Barton*.

2 Gaston Bachelard, *The Poetics of Space* (Boston, Beacon, [1958] 1994), p. 27.

3 Carolyn Steedman, *Past Tenses. Esays on Writing, Autobiography and History* (London, Rivers Oram, 1992), p. 197.

4 Richard Hoggart, *The Uses of Literacy* (Harmondsworth, Penguin [1957] 1958), pp. 20–6.

5 In the Barton parlour, Elizabeth Gaskell has Alice Wilson note the same 'comfortable sounds of a boiling kettle, and the hissing, fizzling ham'. (53)

6 Hoggart, *The Uses of Literacy*, p. 23.

7 Henry Mayhew, *Life and Labour of the London Poor*, 1 and parts of 2–3 (London, George Woodfall, 1851), pp. 47–8, quoted in David Rubinstein, *Victorian Homes* (Newton Abbott, David & Charles,

1974), pp. 115–21. Mayhew was drawn by the same smells and sounds of quiet domestic comfort as Gaskell and Hoggart, noting the 'savoury smell of stew' as he mounted the stairs, and the rattling lid of the tin saucepan, placed on the bright coke fire. See above p. 14, and n. 5.

8 For the strange dislocations of perspective that come from Mayhew's classificatory and statistical obsessions, see Gertrude Himmelfarb, *The Idea of Poverty. England in the Early Industrial Age* (London, Faber, 1984), pp. 312–54.

9 Esther Leslie, 'Dreams, Toys and Tales (a paper on Walter Benjamin first given at the conference Obscure Objects of Desire, UEA, 1997', *Crafts*, 146 (1997), 26–31.

10 Leonora Eyles, *The Woman in the Little House* (London, Grant Richards, 1922), p. 54.

11 Alain Corbin, *The Foul and the Fragrant* (Leamington Spa, Berg, 1986), pp. 151–2.

12 Ibid., pp. 152–3.

13 Ibid., pp. 151–7.

14 Margaret McMillan, *The Nursery School* (London, Dent, 1919), p. 182.

15 Mayhew, *Life and Labour*, pp. 151–2; Mrs Sewell, *Our Father's Care. A Ballad* (London, Jarrold, 1861), p. 14.

16 Mayhew, *Life and Labour*, 48.

17 Bachelard, *The Poetics of Space*, pp. 8–9.

18 Ibid., p. 27.

19 John Burnett, *A Social History of Housing, 1815–1970* (London, Methuen, 1978), pp. 142–3.

20 Enid Gauldie, *Cruel Habitations. A History of Working Class Housing 1780–1918* (London, Allen & Unwin, 1974), pp. 82–92.

21 It would be more elegant not to have an end-note explaining that the writer does *know* that there were far worse deprivations suffered by the Victorian poor than the oneiric – deprivations of food, warmth, adequate clothing, clean water, to name only the most pressing. But I cannot make the words work with the irony that speech allowed, when this argument was first delivered.

22 Bachelard, *The Poetics of Space*, p. 27.

23 Ibid., p. 68.

24 'La conscience – celle de l'écrivain, celle du lecteur – peut-elle sincère-
ment être en acte a l'origine même de telles images?' (140). This
should surely be translated as 'consciousness'.

25 Bachelard, *The Poetics of Space*, p. 148.

26 See above, p. 87, n. 40. Claude Lévi-Strauss, *The Savage Mind* (London, Weidenfeld & Nicholson, 1966), pp. 22–5.

27 Susan Stewart, *On Longing. Narratives of the Miniature, the Gigantic,
the Souvenir, the Collection* (Durham, NC, Duke University Press,
1993), p. 69.

28 Bachelard, *The Poetics of Space*, p. 149.

29 Carolyn Steedman, 'Inside, Outside, Other: Accounts of National
Identity in the Nineteenth Century', *History of the Human Sciences*, 8
(1995), 59–76, for a summary of this literature

30 Frances Hodgson Burnett, *The One I Knew Best of All* (London, Frederick Warne, 1893), pp. 62–79. Page references in the text are to this
edition of 1893.

31 There is a brief pre-history of the modern tufted carpet to be found in
Judy Attfield, 'The Tufted Carpet in Britain: Its Rise from the Bottom
of the Pile', *Journal of Design History*, 7 (1994), 205–16. See also Shipley Art Gallery, *Ragtime. Rugs and Wallhangings* (Shipley, Tyne and
Wear Museums Service, 1988), p. 8.

32 'By the late seventeenth century, cotton was commonly found in the
humblest pedlars' packs, and its place as a cheap alternative to linen
was firmly established.' Sarah Levitt, 'Clothing', in B. Rose (ed.), *The
Lancashire Cotton Industry. A History Since 1700* (Preston, Lancashire
County Books, 1996), p. 155. She cites Margaret Spufford, *The
Great Reclothing of Rural England. Petty Chapmen and their Wares in
Seventeenth-century England* (London, Hambledon, 1984), p. 92.

33 Rose, *The Lancashire Cotton Industry*, pp. 5–6, quoting Arthur Young,
A Six Months Tour Through the North of England, 4 vols (London, W.
Strahan, [1770] 1771), 1, pp. 211–12.

34 B.R. Mitchell and P. Deane, *Abstract of British Historical Statistics*
(Cambridge, Cambridge University Press, 1962), p. 182.

35 D.A. Farnie, *The English Cotton Industry and the World Market*
(Oxford, Clarendon Press, 1979), pp. 45–77; Rose, *The Lancashire
Cotton Industry*, pp. 13–26.

36 Rose, *The Lancashire Cotton Industry*, pp. 13, 17; Edward Baines,

History of the Cotton Manufacture in Great Britain (London, Cass, [1835] 1966), p. 386.

37 Rose, *The Lancashire Cotton Industry*, p. 11.

38 D.C. Coleman, *The British Paper Industry 1495–1860. A Study in Industrial Growth*, Oxford, Clarendon Press, 1958), pp. 337–44; 'M. Canrinade's Substitute for Rags in Making Paper', *The Times* (10 October 1865), 10.

39 'Machine to Render Old Cotton Rags Fit for Spinning', *The Times* (27 April 1863), p. 10; R. Thornton and Sons (Dewsbury) Ltd, *A Story of Woollen Rag Sales, 1860–1960* (London, Harley, 1960), p. 7.

40 Coleman, *The British Paper Industry*, p. 338; British Parliamentary Papers (1854), 'Copy of the Correspondence between the Departments of the Treasury and Board of Trade, in regard to the Scarcity of Materials in the Fabrication of Paper'; and 'An Account of the Total Quantity of Rags Imported into the United Kingdom and the Total Quantity Exported from the United Kingdom, in each Year, from 1801–1853, inclusive', 1854, lxv, 491–5, 505. 'The Budget and Free Trade in Rags', *The Times* (20 February 1860), 7; 'Meeting of Paper Manufacturers to Consider Export Duties on Foreign Rags', *The Times* (22 March 1860), 12; 'Rags from India' and 'Importation of Foreign Rags', *The Times* (26 March 1860), 6. Rag Tax, *The Rag Tax. The Paper Makers' Grievance and How to Redress It, for Private Circulation* (London, privately printed, 1863), p. 5; British Parliamentary Papers, 1854, lxv, 494–5.

41 'High Price of Paper, On Account of the Scarcity of Rags', *The Times* (17 December 1799), 4.

42 Mrs Paull, *The Romance of a Rag and Other Tales* (London, Kempster, 1876), pp. 53–82, 72.

43 Eric Hobsbawm, *Worlds of Labour. Further Studies in the History of Labour* (London, Weidenfeld & Nicolson, 1984), pp. 176–93, 194–213; Elizabeth Roberts, *A Woman's Place. An Oral History of Working-class Women 1890–1940* (Oxford, Blackwell, 1984), pp. 128, 131, 151; K. Walker, 'Starting With Rag Rugs. The Aesthetics of Survival', in G. Elinor *et al.*, *Women and Craft* (London, Virago, 1987), 27–30; Shipley Art Gallery, *Ragtime*, pp. 10–12. The wartime injunction to Make Do and Mend gave some impetus to a history of the rag rug, but its most thorough treatment was in the American folklore

movement of the early twentieth century. Here the rag rug was given the most diverse and spectacular of world histories (attributed to Vikings, belonging 'absolutely to America, none ever having been found in the Old World', 'wrapped in a veil of mystery) and – in one account – with the power to dispel 'Chaos' and bring about its 'antonym, order, Heaven's primary law'. I. Crowell, *Design and Hook Your Own Rugs* (New York, Macmillan, 1945), p. 1; E. Foley and E. Waugh, *Collecting Hooked Rugs* (New York, Century, 1927), p. 4; M.L. Phillips, *Hooked Rugs and How to Make Them* (New York, Macmillan, 1925), 9. See also E.S. Bowles, *Handmade Rugs* (Boston, Little Brown, 1927), A. Miall, *Make Your Own Rugs*, (New York, Woman's Magazine Handbooks, 4, 1938), and B. Hawker-Smith, *Thrifty Rug Making. Including Surrey Stitch Rugs. With a Foreword by Lady Dowson* (Pitman, London, 1940).

44 Roberts, *A Woman's Place*, p. 128.
45 Beverley Lemire, *Fashion's Favourite: The Cotton Trade and the Consumer in Britain, 1660–1800* (Oxford, Oxford University Press, 1991), p. 62.
46 Crowell, *Design*, p. 7.
47 Paull, *The Romance of a Rag*, p. 67.
48 Temple Newsam House, *Country House Floors* (Leeds, Leeds City Art Galleries, 1987), pp. 101–11.
49 Jenny Calder, *The Victorian Home* (London, Batsford, 1977), pp. 88–9; Temple Newsam House, *Country House Floors*, pp. 110–11.
50 M.C. Frykstedt, 'Mary Barton and the Reports of the Ministry to the Poor: A New Source', *Studia Neophilologica*, 52 (1980), 333–6.
51 J.G. Sharps, *Mrs Gaskell's Observation and Invention. A Study of Her Non-Biographic Works* (Fontwell, Linden, 1970), p. 56.
52 Sharps, *Mrs Gaskell's Observation*, 52; Jenny Uglow, *Elizabeth Gaskell. A Habit of Stories* (London, Faber and Faber, 1993), pp. 15–155.
53 Sharps, *Mrs Gaskell's Observation*, pp. 57–9.
54 John Hawley points out that on questions of political economy, class consciousness and working-class political activism '*Mary Barton* may well have been written to console, not the workers, but the middle classes from which Gaskell came'. J.C. Hawley, '*Mary Barton*: The View from Without', *Nineteenth Century Studies*, 3 (1989), 23–30, p. 28.

55 M. Davis and D. Wallbridge, *Boundary and Space. An Introduction to the Work of D.W. Winnicott* (Harmondsworth, Penguin, 1981), pp. 69–72; D.W. Winnicott, 'Transitional Objects and Transitional Phenomena', in *Playing and Reality* (Harmondsworth, Penguin, 1974), pp. 1–30.

56 Leslie, 'Dreams', pp. 26–31.

57 For a resonant reading of the economy, circulation, and meaning of things in a very different kind of narrative, see S. Crehan, '*The Rape of the Lock* and the Economy of "Trivial Things"', *Eighteenth-Century Studies*, 31 (1997), 45–68.

7

About ends: on how the end is different from an ending

> … but we, at haphazard
> And unseasonably, are brought face to face
> By ones, Clio, with your silence. After that
> Nothing is easy.
> (W.H. Auden, 'Homage to Clio', 1948–57)

YOU CAN NEVER BE QUITE SURE whether Auden has seen
something of very profound importance, or whether what you
have before you is simply an extraordinarily moving string of
phonemes; but perhaps it doesn't really matter which, as we are
given his Clio anyway, figured as the most mysterious of the Muses
(though mysterious, as it turns out in the end, only because she has
absolutely nothing to say). Indeed the poet wrote to a friend telling
her that in his view, his Clio was actually the Virgin Mary.[1]

'What icon/Have the arts for you?' the poet asks, 'Who look like
any/Girl one has not noticed and show no special/Affinity with a
beast?'

He continues:

> … I have seen
> Your photo, I think, in the papers, nursing
> A baby or mourning a corpse; each time
> You had nothing to say and did not, one could see,
> Observe where you were, Muse of the unique
> Historical fact, defending with silence
> Some world of your beholding.

It must be Clio's silence that is her most important attribute here, for the poem deals with reversals, with a disturbance of the taken-for-granted view of history as a *telling* of the past. Then a moment later, there is the grander and more striking reversal of the ordinary relationship between Memory and History (which we have already noted being observed by other commentators) when the poet entreats the Muse to 'teach us our recollections'.

But the silence is the more provoking, for what is left to us if Clio does not speak, if history is not to be something that is told about what has happened, – if really, Clio has nothing to say?

> … but we, at haphazard
> And unseasonably, are brought face to face
> By ones, Clio, with your silence. After that
> Nothing is easy.

The recent linguistic turn in historical studies came – as most of Clio's turns do – from outside the field, as the echo of an attention paid to history as a form of language by philosophers, literary theorists and cultural critics.[2] However, over the thirty years the turn took, while the question of telling – of narrative – was endlessly discussed, the dizzying proposal of Clio's silence seems never to have been contemplated. Slow turn, endless discussion … In 1986, for example, David Carr was concerned to answer the charge of narratologists and philosophers, that in the historical enterprise, narrative is no more than a kind of 'window dressing or packaging, something incidental to our knowledge of the past'.[3] He referred in particular to the work of Louis Mink, and Mink's judgement that stories are not things that are lived, so much as told; that what comes to be told about the past is not *part of* the events that are narrated: that telling is always something different from *what happened* (whatever that was).[4] Indeed, in this period of discussion, Hayden White thought that anyone who believed that 'sequences of real events possess the formal attributes of the stories we tell about imaginary events', was living in a fantasy, or daydreaming.[5] Paul Ricoeur had long paid attention to narrative as a kind of semantic innovation; to the way in which something new is brought into the world by language – the words that tell; to the ways in which narrative does not so much describe the world as redescribe – or re-make – it. In the accounts of the 1970s that Carr attempted to displace, the function of narrative was seen to be the way it attaches to the real world a shape and form that it does not intrinsically possess.

In *Time, Narrative and History*, Carr brought his understanding of an *event* to bear on the early orthodoxies. In his account, events are something so wrapped up in and with time that it cannot be denied. Time-consciousness pervades our very existence; narrative is thus not a clothing for something else but, rather, is the very structure of human existence and action.[6] Time-consciousness is rooted in the apprehension of now, of each and every moment of being; time is a structure that inheres in the very phenomena being narrated.[7] Indeed, to 'exist humanly' is not just to be *in* time, but rather is to 'encompass it or "take it in" as our gaze takes in our surroundings'. For Carr, all narratives – historical narratives and all sorts of narrative – are made out of this experience of time. Counter arguments (like those of Ricoeur and Mink) were probably less to do with the phenomenology of time, and more to do with the ways in which historical narratives have borrowed from other forms of mimesis and representation. Ricoeur believed this experience of temporality to be 'mute', for poetry and plot had the power to reconfigure confused and inchoate experience, but plot and poetry were the creative work of historians and other narrators, never actually *there* in the first place.[8]

In these opposing accounts, then, Clio had a very great deal to *say*, though most commentators had very severe doubts about her capacity to explain what it was she told. Ricoeur in particular emphasised the borrowed plots she used, pointing to the way in which historical narratives easily incorporated generalities, or theoretical and causal explanations that came from outside: 'every historical explanation is looking for an explanation to incorporate into itself because it has failed to explain itself'.[9]

Yet Clio *writes*. Auden pays attention to her silence, and the discussants of the linguistic turn endlessly debated her deficiencies as a narrator, because they forgot her typical stance, pen in hand, foot on the ground, glancing up from the page, momentarily *looking at you* – as she writes.[10] (Or maybe – we must just briefly consider this – the silence Auden hears comes from her not being Clio at all; it is possible that she really is – as he believed – the Virgin Mary.) But in the *Homage to Clio* collection, Auden encounters her again, in 'Makers of History' where he is utterly clear that she is the historian – the historian of the *miserabilis personae* – who cannot care for 'Greatness', the Kings, Senators and Generals who are the Names of History; rather:

> Clio loves those who bred them better horses,
> Found answers to their questions, made their things[11]

Clio may have nothing to say, but she has everything to write. The historian's massive authority as a writer derives from two factors: the ways archives *are*, and the conventional rhetoric of history-writing, which always asserts (though the footnotes, through the casual reference to PT S2/1/1 ...) that you *know* because you have been there. There is story put about that the authority comes from the documents themselves, and the historian's obeisance to the limits they impose on any account that employs them. But really, it comes from *having been there* (the train to the distant city, the call number, the bundle opened, the dust ...) so that then, and only then, can you present yourself as moved and dictated to by those sources, telling a story the way it has to be told. Thus the authority

of the historian's seemingly-modest 'No; it wasn't quite like that …
'

History (the work of historians; history-writing) could not (cannot) operate differently. There is everything, or Everything, the great undifferentiated past, all of it, which is not history, but just stuff.[12] The smallest fragment of its representation (nearly always in some kind of written language) ends up in various kinds of archive and record office (and also in the vastly expanded data banks that Derrida refers to in 'Archive Fever').[13] From that, you make history, which is never what *was* there, once upon a time. (There was only stuff, Everything, dust …) 'There is history,' says Jacques Rancière, after his long contemplation of Michelet,

> because there is the past and a specific passion for the past. And there is history because there is an absence … The status of history depends on the treatment of this twofold absence of the 'thing itself' that is *no longer there* – that is in the past; and that never was – because it never was *such as it was told.*[14]

It seems probable that history cannot work as either cognition or narrative without the assumption on the part of the writer and the reader of it that there is somewhere the great story, that contains everything there is and ever has been – 'visits home, heartbeats, a first kiss, the jump of an electron from one orbital position to another', as well as the desolate battlefield, the ruined village – from which the smaller story, the one before your eyes now, has simply been extracted.[15] This form of thinking and imagining – the way history is – was formalised by Robert F. Berkhofer as 'The Great Story'. He remarks that 'Although historians may be wary of Great Stories … it seems they cannot do without them. Their histories need the larger and largest contexts that Great Stories provide, especially if the Great Past is conceived of as the Great(est) Context of all stories, small and Great.'[16]

However, as Louis Mink told us in 1981, stories are only truly narrativised when they take on the same meaning for the listener as the teller; and they come to an end when there is no more to be said, when teller and audience both understand that the point that has been reached, this end-place, this conclusion, was implicit in the beginning: was there all along.[17] Considered in this light, all stories, no matter what their content, take part in the art of fiction. At the end of the novel, no matter how arbitrary and strange that ending might be, you know that there has been someone there all along, who knew the story, all of it, from beginning to end, and was able to bring you to this place, this ending, now. *This* extraordinary turn of thought and temporality which is not much more than 300 years old, and conventionally hidden by the labels 'the development of print culture', 'the rise of the novel' has been explored, notably by Benedict Anderson and Franco Moretti.[18] In the spoken or written life-story there is in operation a simple variant of this narrative rule. The man or woman, standing up against the bar (in a public house, or a court of law), is the embodiment of something completed. That end, the finished place, is the human being, a body in time and space, telling a story, a story that brings the listener or the reader to the here and now, or to this rounded and finished character in the pages of the book. Written autobiography ends in the figure of the writer, and the narrative closure of biography is the figure that has been created through the pages of the book.

In narrative terms like this, these forms of writing – biography and autobiography – must always remain in conflict with the writing of history, which does indeed come to conclusions and reach ends, but which actually moves forward through the implicit understanding that *things are not over*, that the story isn't finished, can't ever be completed, for some new item of information may alter the account as it has been given. (And also because – the most obvious of points – we have not yet come to the end of it: the Great

Story, Everything …) At the centre of the written history lies this recognition of temporariness and impermanence. And all historians, even the most purblind empiricists, recognise this in their acts of writing: they are *telling the only story that has no end.* Indeed, this was quite conventionally recognised when the modern profession established itself on a positivistic high in the middle years of the nineteenth century. It was understood for example, that history would never be able to furnish its own inductive laws, for to be sound, 'an induction must take in, actually or virtually, all the facts. But history is unlike all other studies, in this, that she can never have actually or virtually all the factors in front of her. What is past, she knows in part.'[19]

The apostles of 'scientific' history, Claude Langlois and Charles Seignobos, looked back to the 1850s from the 1890s to reflect on how every modern work of history needed to be 'continually recast, revised, brought up to date', for each one of them had superseded earlier works and would be 'sooner or later, superseded in their turn'.[20] Closures have to be made, in order to finish arguments and get manuscripts to publishers; but the story can't be finished because historians have as their stated objective exhaustiveness (finding out again and again, more and more about some thing, event or person), and they proceed upon the path of refutation by pointing to exceptions and to the possibility of exception. The practice of historical inquiry and historical writing acknowledges its own contingency (it will not last), and in this way is a quite different literary form from that of the life-story in both its modes – the fictional and the biographical – which presents momentarily a completeness, a completeness which lies in the figure of the writer or the teller, in the here and now, saying: that's how it was; or, that's how I believe it to have been. At the centre of the written history, on the other hand, lies a recognition of temporariness and impermanence.

History is not about ends. We have seen David Carr counter Ricoeur and Mink and Hayden White and their claims about stories being told things rather than lived things, about the power of narrative to attach to the real world an order and form it does not intrinsically possess. We could abandon this discussion about whether or not narrativity exists in the real world with the observation that Carr may be right, and Ricoeur (for example) may be wrong, but they all fail to take enough account of writing, and the extraordinary specificity of history as a written form. Whether it is life itself that has narrativeness embedded in it, or not – whether action, life and history have narrative form because they acquire it in some way by borrowing from other cultural artifacts, particularly literary ones (the novel again), or not – history does something most peculiar (as writing) and unique (as cognition): it turns what possesses narrative coherence into something without an end, possessing only an ending.

The question of biography complicates the question even more. At the end of a 300-year process of ideation it is difficult indeed to think outside the biographical mode, the telling of all stories *as if they were a life.* The figure of *personification* may offer more than a description of the way in which human shape has been given to abstract ideas and notions; it can point to the way in which new information about human bodies, their workings, their finitude, came to function as the representation of all events, happenings and plots, observed throughout the whole of the natural world.[21] Biography gives a name and a face to the subject that is its reference; history gives a habitation and a name to all the fragments, traces – all the inchoate stuff – that has ended up in the archive. History and biography came into being together as modes of perception and ways of thinking; the life is the analogy of history, for historians want ends, quite as much as anybody else. They, though, are the only narrators who cannot have what they want. And here is a problem: history and biography came into being together, make constant reference to each other, make us see the one in the other, make us think in the same way; but one is about the end, and the other can only ever be about endings.

If endings are what History deals in, then its mode of beginning always suggests a wayward arbitrariness: 'once upon a time' is the rhetorical mode: the unspoken starting point of the written history. The grammatical tense of the archive is not then, the future perfect, not the conventional past historic of English-speaking historians, nor even the *présent historique* of the French, but the syntax of the fairy-tale … 'once, there was', 'in April 1751' … 'once *upon* a time … in the summer of 1995'. And then there is the content of these tales: the release of muffled and occluded voices, 'the whispers of the souls who had suffered so long ago and who were smothered now in the past' – the voice of the People – has been the injunction laid on social historians for nearly two centuries now. This is what we do, or what we believe we do: we make the dead speak, we rescue the handloom-weavers of Tipton and Freshitt from the enormous indifference of the present. We have always, then, written in the mode of magical realism. In strictly formal and stylistic terms, a text of social history is very closely connected to those novels in which a girl flies, a mountain moves, the clocks run backwards, and where (this is our particular contribution) the dead walk among the living. If the Archive is a place of dreams, it permits this one, above all others, the one that Michelet dreamed first, of making the dead walk and talk.

The archive gives rise to particular practices of reading. If you are a historian, you nearly always read something that was not intended for your eyes: you are the reader impossible-to-be-imagined by Philip Ward keeping his justice's notebook as aide memoire (quite different from the way that Henry Fielding, who had a good deal of horrifying fun with what went on in the justice room, *did* imagine you, a reader, with *Joseph Andrews* in your hands, reading the novel he wanted someone to read). The vestryman recording an allowance of 6d. a week in bread to a poor woman, the merchant manufacturer's wife listing the payments-in-kind to her serving maid (silk ribbons, a pair of stays, a hat-box!) in Howarth 1794, had nothing like you in mind at all.[22] Productive and extraordinary as is Derrida's concept of the *carte-postale* (the idea of the relationship between language and truth that 'La Carte postale' explores), of messages gone astray, messages not sent in the first place, or unread because you can't see them for looking at them, as in Poe's 'Purloined Letter', none of it gives insight (indeed, it was not meant to) into the message that was never a message to start with, never sent, and never sent to the historian: was just an entry in a ledger, a name on a list.[23] Moreover, historians read for what is *not there*: the silences and the absences of the documents always speak to us. They spoke of course, to Jules Michelet (he was actually after the silence, the whisper, the unrecorded dead: what wasn't there at all, in the Archives Nationales); and they spoke to post-Second World War social and labour historians whose particular task it was to rescue and retrieve the life and experience of working-class people from the official documents that occlude them. An absence speaks; the nameless watchmaker's apprentice is important *because* he is nameless: we give his namelessness meaning, make it matter. Indeed, Rancière claims that it was Michelet who first formulated the proper subject of history: all the numberless unnoticed *miserabiles personae*, who had lived and died, as mute in the grave as they had been in life. According to Rancière, Michelet's modern reputation, as mere Romantic – indeed, sentimental – rescuer of 'the People', serves to repress both his startling originality as a historian, and History's proper topic.[24] Of course, Michelet was wrong, about the Dust, and about the life he believed he gave back to the People, by breathing it in. His dead were not there; or, not the dead he wanted, for they really had never really existed. He inhaled the dust of the animals and plants that provided material for the documents he untied and read; the dust of all the workers whose trials and tribulations in labour formed their paper and parchment. He did indeed, breathe in the People, giving them life by the processes of incorporation that resulted in his terrible headaches, his Archive Fever, but they were not the People he named in his histories.

On several occasions during the 1980s, it was very sensibly suggested by Christopher Norris that it was best for historians to have nothing to do with the manner of reading texts most closely connected with Derrida's name, best for them not to mess with deconstruction because, as a method devised for the interrogation of philosophical texts, its power lies solely in that particular terrain (and that of literature). Norris made this point for political purposes, when an extreme relativism wedded to a form of deconstruction allowed some historians (and others, using works of history as their evidence) to deny that certain past events had actually taken place.[25] They are presumably the historians Derrida had in mind when he raised questions about 'débats autour de tous les "révisionisms" … [les] séismes de l'historiographie' (debates about all the 'revisionisms' … seismic shifts in historiography) (and which questions force one to ask whether it is not historians and the history they write that he has in his sights, rather than the archives that he names as the trouble in *Mal d'archive*).[26]

What is clearer seven years on is that it was not historians who needed warning off by Norris, but rather a number of cultural critics and theorists who wanted to address the question of history, or historicity, or merely have something to say about its relationship to deconstructive practice. It was the question, or problem of diachronicity (in the realm of synchronic analysis and thinking) that was being raised. Or the problem of pastness, *tout court*.[27] It was the urgency with which Norris needed to make his strictures against revisionist historians that perhaps prevented him from looking at what happens when the traffic goes the other way, and deconstruction considers historians and the history they write. It has long been noted that when literary theorists alert historians to the fact that they write in the tragic mode, or as ironists; tell them that they emplot their stories in particular ways, and thus that they may produce meanings that work against overt and stated arguments – that all of this makes absolutely no difference at all to your dogged and daily performance of positivism. The text that is usually taken to stand in for the whole deconstructive endeavour (as far as historians are concerned) when observations like these are made, is Hayden White's *Metahistory*, a work now almost thirty years old. With Hayden White's work in view, it has been suggested that one of the reasons for the absence of meaning that deconstruction has for history, for the way in which deconstructive readings slither around the written history (or more plainly: do not touch it; cannot affect it) is that their analyses do not have reference in mind. History-writing, says Maurice Mandelbaum, does not refer to the Archive (nor to archives), nor to the documents they contain. Neither is the point of reference any existing account of those documents in already-existing works of history. Rather, says Mandelbaum, what is referred to are anterior entities: past structures, processes and happenings. The writings of historians 'refer to past occurrences whose existence is only known through inferences drawn from surviving documents; but it is not to those documents themselves, but to what they indicate concerning the past, that the historian's statements actually refer'.

Mandelbaum seems to suggest that the historian's statements are not inventive, nor creative, but rather that the history they write makes reference to History – to something that has a prior, pre-textual existence.[28] We should probably go beyond this, by allowing that it is, in fact, the historian who makes the stuff of the past (Everything) into a structure or event, a happening or a thing, through the activities of thought and writing: that they were never actually *there*, once, in the first place; or at least, not in the same way that a nutmeg grater actually once was, and certainly not as the many ways in which they 'have been told'. So there is a double nothingness in the writing of history and in the analysis of it: it is about something that never did happen in the way it comes to be represented (the happening exists in the telling or the text); and it is made out of materials that aren't there, in an archive or anywhere else. We should be entirely unsurprised that deconstruction made no difference to this kind of writing. The search for the historian's nostalgia for origins and original referents cannot be performed, because there is actually *nothing there*: she is not looking for anything: only silence, the space shaped by what once was; and now is no more.

Notes

1 John Fuller, *W.H. Auden. A Commentary* (London, Faber & Faber, 1998), pp. 464–5. For the Ischian poems, written between 1948 and 1957, see Edward Callen, *Auden: A Carnival of Intellect* (Oxford, Oxford University Press, 1983), pp. 218–37. 'Homage to Clio' was first published in *Encounter*, November 1955, and gave the title to the eponymous collection of 1960. Fuller, *W.H. Auden*, p. 463.

2 Robert H. Canary and Henry Kosiki (eds), *The Writing of History. Literary Form and Historical Understanding* (Madison and London, University of Wisconsin Press, 1978); 'Editorial. Language and History', *History Workshop Journal*, 10:2 (1980); Paul Ricoeur, 'The Narrative Function', in John Thompson (ed.), *Hermeneutics and the Human Sciences* (Cambridge, Cambridge University Press, 1981), pp. 274–96; Lewis O. Mink, 'Everyman His or Her Annalist', *Critical Inquiry*, 7:4 (1981), 777–83; Hayden White, 'The Question of Narrative in Contemporary Historical Theory', *History and Theory*, 23

(1984), 1–33; '"Figuring the Nature of the Times Deceased"', in *The Content of the Form. Narrative Discourse and Historical Representation* (Baltimore, Johns Hopkins University Press, 1987), pp. 1–25; 'Special Feature: Language and History', *History Workshop Journal*, 27:1 (1989); Bryan D. Palmer, *Descent into Discourse. The Reification of Language and the Writing of Social History* (Philadelphia, Temple University Press, 1990); Geoff Eley, 'Is All the World a Text?', in Terrence J. McDonald (ed.), *The Historical Turn in the Human Sciences* (Ann Arbor, University of Michigan Press, 1996), pp. 193–243.

3 David Carr, *Time, Narrative and History* (Bloomington IN, Indiana University Press, 1986), p. 9.

4 Mink, 'Everyman'.

5 Carr, *Time, Narrative*, p. 12.

6 Ibid. pp. 64–5, p. 25.

7 Ibid., p. 49.

8 Paul Ricoeur, *Time and Narrative* (Chicago, University of Chicago Press, 1983), p. xi.

9 Ibid., pp. 154–5.

10 Cesare Ripa, *Baroque and Rococo Pictorial Imagery* (New York, Dover [1758–60] 1971), 'Historia', Icon 22.

11 W.H. Auden, 'Makers of History', in *Homage to Clio* (London, Faber & Faber, 1960), pp. 30–1.

12 See P.A. Roth, 'Narrative Explanation: The Case of History', *History and Theory*, 27 (1988), 1–13.

13 But Arlette Farge found *things* as well as writing. See Arlette Farge, *Le Goût de l'archive* (Paris, Editions du Seuil, 1989), p. 49, and passim.

14 Jacques Rancière, *The Names of History. On the Poetics of Knowledge* (Minneapolis, University of Minnesota Press, [1992] 1994), p. 63.

15 Roth, 'Narrative Explanation', pp. 1–13 .

16 Robert Berkhofer, *Beyond the Great Story. History as Text and Discourse* (Cambridge, MA, Harvard University Press, 1995), p. 44.

17 Mink, 'Everyman', pp. 777–83.

18 Benedict Anderson, *Imagined Communities. Reflections on the Origin and Spread of Nationalism* (London, Verso, [1983] 1991), pp. 37–46; Franco Moretti, *The Way of the World. The Bildingroman in European Culture* (London, Verso, 1987), pp. 3–73.

19 J.B. Hale, *The Evolution of British Historiography: From Bacon to*

Namier (London, Macmillan, 1967), p. 51, citing Goldwin Smith, *The Study of History. A Lecture* (Oxford, privately printed, 1859), p. 29. For the positivistic high, see Bonnie Smith, *The Gender of History. Men, Women and Historical Practice* (Cambridge, MA, Harvard University Press, 1998), pp. 103–29.

20 Claude Langlois and Charles Seignobos, *Introduction to the Study of History* (London, Duckworth, 1898), pp. 302–3.

21 Carolyn Steedman, *Strange Dislocations. Childhood and the Idea of Human Interiority, 1780–1930* (Cambridge, MA, Harvard University Press, 1995), pp. 118–19.

22 For the historian as a reader – always this kind of reader – of the unintended, purloined letter, see Carolyn Steedman, 'A Woman Writing a Letter', in Rebecca Earle (ed.), *Epistolary Selves. Letters and Letter Writers, 1600–1945* (Aldershot, Ashgate, 1999), pp. 111–33.

23 Jacques Derrida, *The Post Card: From Socrates to Freud and Beyond*, trans. Alan Bass (Chicago, University of Chicago Press, [1980] 1987). The exception to the rule of the unintended letter, is of course, Hester Thrale, who quite clearly intended me to laugh at my own pretensions to Archive Fever, just as she laughed at Fanny Burney's to another kind. For the stays and the hatbox, see John Styles 'Involuntary Consumers? The Eighteenth Century Servant and her Clothes', *Textile History*, forthcoming, 2002.

24 Rancière, *The Names*, pp. 42–75. And see Hayden White's comments on these points, his Introduction to this work, pp. xiv–xviii.

25 Christopher Norris, *Uncritical Theory. Postmodernism, Intellectuals and the Gulf War* (London, Lawrence & Wishart, 1992); and *Deconstruction and the Interests of Theory* (London, Pinter, 1988), pp. 16–17.

26 Derrida, *Mal d'archive*, 'Prière d'insérer'.

27 See for example, Derek Attridge, Geoff Bennington and Robert Young (eds), *Post-structuralism and the Question of History* (Cambridge, Cambridge University Press, 1987).

28 Maurice Mandelbaum, 'The Presuppositions of Hayden White's *Metahistory*', *History and Theory*, 19 (1980), 39–54.

8

The story of the dust

'My dear Mr Boffin, everything wears to rags,' said Mortimer, with
a light laugh.

'I won't go so far as to say everything,' returned Mr Boffin, on whom
his manner seemed to grate, 'because there's some things that I
never found among the dust.'

(Charles Dickens, *Our Mutual Friend*, Chapter 34)

THERE ARE MANY DUSTS. Indeed, there emerges something
that may be called Dust Studies. There is the dust Karl Marx noted
as the most noxious and damaging of all the consequences of
industrialisation, that rose in great clouds as the rag-pickers
worked in the first stages of paper-making;[1] there is the malignant,
eternal dust of the Archive. And there is the novel that seems to be
most concerned with Dust, Charles Dickens's *Our Mutual Friend*.[2]
We are moderns – or something like that – inheritors of biological
accounts of the composition of things from the early twentieth
century; and so we are bound to think that the text of the novel
can't be – is bound not to be – quite candid about what's in the
Dustheap. We think there must be something really nasty – something excremental – in the Heaps, somewhere. As Stephen Gill
points out in his 1971 edition of the novel, there have been persistent attempts to find shit of some sort in the Harmon dustyard, that
lies between Kings Cross and the Holloway Road.[3] But Dickens's
sociology of dust was even more extensive and accurate than the

one Gill points to in that Penguin edition, and all the Dustheaps in *Our Mutual Friend* are contained within the parameters of Henry Mayhew's account of 1851 (reissued in the four-volume edition of *London Labour and the London Poor* of 1861–62).[4] In both editions, Mayhew is very clear that 'dust and rubbish accumulate in houses from a variety of causes, but principally from the residuum of fires, the white ashes and cinders, or small fragments of unconsumed coke, giving rise to by far the greater quantity'.[5]

He was clear as well, about the value of the product, before and after sifting; about methods of collection, storage and processing; about the labour process of the dustyards and the sub-contracting and putting-out by which it was organised, and about the family economy that the process maintained among many workers. He philogised the peculiar language of the dust trade (reading these passages from Mayhew is like being present at the birth of speech, as if in a kind of space in which gesture creates language, some Rousseau-esque realm of immediacy and plenitude, where if a woman sifts, she is a 'sifter' and if a man shovels the dust to fill her sieve, he is a 'filler-in').[6] And at the end of it all, he concluded briskly that 'A dust heap, therefore may be briefly said to be composed of the following things', and he went on to itemise brieze or cinders, sold to brickmakers; rags, bones and old metal, sold to marine store dealers; old tin kettles and the like, sold for japan-work (the corners of trunks, for example); old bricks and oyster shells sold to builders for sinking foundations and forming roads; old shoes, used as the in-filling between sole and insole in new ones; money and jewellery, 'kept, or sold to Jews' – and the item 'soil', which is what has probably given rise to some of the excremental confusion.

'Soil' – Mayhew is insistent on this point – is nothing to do with night soil, but is rather the name for the fine dust sold to farmers as 'manure of land of a particular quality'. This fine dust could be used to break up marshy or heathy land, and was in demand in the

1840s among agriculturalists no longer reclaiming land for crops, but turning what they already possessed into pasturage. It is not excremental nor decaying vegetable matter, but rather, a very fine powdered cinder.[7] The siting of dung-hills in the same yards as dust-heaps, which was common in the early century, *may* have continued after 1848 and the Nuisances Removal and Disease Prevention Act of that year (11 & 12 Vict. c.123), but not for long, and Mayhew did not find them contiguous in summer of 1850. He told his readers that dustmen may also happen to be night soil collectors; their master may also have contracted with a parish for the cleaning of cesspits, and with individuals for household collection; but that was work done under a different contract, at a different time, and was part of a quite separate economy. Dustmen, scavengers, nightsoil men and sweeps, all belong to distinct systems, and separate economies. No shit.

Of course, the pigs rooting in the North London yards that Mayhew visited in the summer of 1850 suggest that the divisions of rubbish were not as strict as the ones he laid down, though the point he was probably making through them was that a dustyard bore strict comparison with a farmyard, where a nice fat household pig could be kept going for free on what fell out in the normal way of business. There is the Golden Dustman's – Mr Boffin's – fragment of a memory, of Old John Harmon bringing many 'a bone and feather and whatnot' to Mr Venus, that also serve to blur the strict categorisation Dickens was working with.

And then there's the Inner Temple; and there 'Mr Boffin in Consultation', for he has 'frequently heard tell of the Temple as a spot where lawyer's dust is contracted for' (136). In the course of the meeting, he describes how feelings for poor Little John Harmon, last seen by him and Mrs Boffin when the child was but seven years old, have faded over the years. The young solicitor responds ('with a light laugh', the narrative voice notes):

'My dear Mr Boffin, everything wears to rags,' ...

'I won't go so far as to say everything,' returned Mr Boffin, on whom his manner seemed to grate, 'because there's some things I never found among the dust.'

'Dust' is one of those curious words that in its verb form, bifurcates in meaning, performs an action of perfect circularity, and arrives to denote its very opposite. If you 'dust', you can remove something, or you can put something there. Viz.: you cleanse a place – usually a room in a house – *of* dust, in a meaning that seems to have been established at the same time as that of its opposite action, which is to sprinkle something with a small portion of powdery matter, as in 'to make dusty' (1530), or later, 'to strew as dust' (1790). 'Dust' is established as a culinary term by the 1780s (to dust toast, or the surface of a pie, with nutmeg, or cinnamon, or sugar). The earlier, opposite, verb of removal – as in dusting a room – is established at the end of the sixteenth century, at the same time as the noun consolidates its meaning as 'a minute particle of dry matter'. The 'dry' is important, for the late sixteenth century inherited the meaning of dust as that which is first solid matter, but comes to be so pulverised or comminuted as to make it able to rise in a cloud.

What is there to say about strange semantic circularities like these? – except perhaps, that they were most strikingly discussed by Sigmund Freud in his essay on 'The Uncanny' (1919), in a kind of psycho-philology already noted, in which the word for the utterly strange 'leads back to what is known of old and long familiar', where the *unheimlich* finally coincides with its opposite, the *heimlich*, the most familiar of things: a woman's body ... 'the place where each one of us lived once upon a time and in the beginning'.[8] (All of this *must* be about narrative, and here with Freud – in the translation of Freud – the distinct possibility of a fairy-tale.) Yes, to be sure: the *heimlich* and the *unheimlich* do coincide; but not without a little labour on the part of the philologist-cum-psychoanalyst. Whilst 'dust' on the other hand, *verb transitive*, just does it for you, all at once: to remove dust; to sprinkle with dust.

In writing up his forays into the dust yards of North London, Henry Mayhew was dismissive of the new 'zymotic theorists' who saw danger lurking in the Heaps, and in the clouds that rose from them as they were worked. Indeed, he noted the healthy, rubicund appearance of the hill-men and hill-women, the fillers-in, the sifters, the carriers-off, and all the children 'helping' among the heaps.[9] Such insouciance about dust could not have lasted much beyond the beyond the 1860s, and Dickens's repetition of it. The suspicion of dust, that Kate Flint explores in her recent "'The Mote Within the Eyes'" is most intense in the 1880s and 1890s, but originates twenty years earlier, and for good reason, as we have seen.[10]

We have thus already explored one category of Dust, which knows no end, and which cannot be dispersed, as harbourer of the anthrax infection (which also knows no end, and cannot be dispersed). We have seen Jules Michelet breath in this Dust to find himself able to speak on behalf of the dead, and to interpret the words and the acts they themselves had not understood. Dust allowed him a perception of time as a kind of seamless duration in which past and future could not be sundered. In his journal, Michelet recorded amazement at perpetuity itself, at the marvellous continuity of things that brought him the gift of experiencing history.[11] Turning this sense perception to deliberate narrative purpose, he wrote to give the People shape and form (historical existence; a new life) through depiction of their revolutionary struggles. The narrative of Dust – the dust he inhaled in order to perform this task – was intimately tied to the French Revolution and its nineteenth-century reverberations. We may see Michelet as an extraordinarily vocal narrator of Dust, but not the only one. The seventh verse of the *Marseillaise* describes how:

Nous entrerons dans la carrière
Quand nos aînés ne seront plus
Nous y trouverons leur poussière
Et la trace de leurs vertus[12]
(We will enter on our career [the career of the citizen and the revo-
lutionary]/When our elders are no more/We will find there their
dust – *leur poussière* – /And the trace of their virtues)

There is a pun on *carrière*, which is both 'career' and 'quarry'. In
the Revolutionary period, the Paris quarries were filled in with the
bones of the dead to form the Catacombs. All the nineteenth-
century revolutions which followed on from 1789 added their
shrines to this underground realm of dust, which indeed the Catacombs may be called, for it is more common in French literary
language to use *poussière* for the remains of dead bodies, rather
than *os* (bones).

Michelet's breathing in of the dust of the dead thus has a double
meaning, or rather, a literalness, that does not pertain in English.
And the Catacombs were often visited as a tourist attraction (as
were the Morgue and the sewers). In nineteenth-century Paris,
then, we could say that the spectacle of dust thus existed, created by
the Revolution (which also created the national archives and the
duty of the state to provide them for the public).[13]

Michelet thus enacted some of the more material dimensions
of the Revolutionary order, at the same time as dust actually began
to be flushed out of the street by the new, Haussemannian sewer
system.[14] Dickens remarks on this newer, cleaner Paris, where
'nothing is wasted' in Chapter 12 of *Our Mutual Friend*, by way of
contrast with London, and London's 'mysterious paper currency
which circulates … when the wind blows'. But he attributes the
cleanliness of the Parisian streets to 'human ants [who] creep out
of holes and pick up every scrap', to leave – 'nothing but dust',
rather than to the regularly placed spigots that pushed Seine water

through the streets. Dickens's ants, by the way, pick up every scrap, and leave – dust. Dust, you see, will always do this: be both there and not there; what is left and what is gone.

Michelet was unaware of the precise components of his Dust, and yet he breathed it in, restored the dead to the light of day, and gave them justice by bringing them before the tribunal of History. This History was what Michelet himself wrote, out of the notes and the handfuls of dust he carried away from the Archive. This writing was also an idea, of the total justice of a narrative that incorporated the past and the 'when it shall have been', that is, when the dead have spoken and (Michelet's central interest as a historian) France has been made. Yet it is not his history of the French nation for which Michelet is now remembered. What promotes the bright, interested question 'Was he *mad*?' when you tell people that you are reading him, are all the volumes that do not seem to be works of history, to the modern, professional, historical eye: work on the sea, on birds, on women and witches, on mountains, insects, love …[15] These were the texts, an admixture of physiology and lyricism, that entertained Roland Barthes in the early 1950s. They will probably continue to be marked as odd, though in the nineteenth-century development of the modern practice of history, they were not so *very* strange.

As History, as a form of narrative and as a modern academic discipline, came to be formulated, it bore much resemblance to the life-sciences, where the task was also to think about the past – think pastness – about the imperishability of matter, through all the stages of growth and decay, to think these matters through to the point of recognition that 'within the system of nature existing as it is, we cannot admit that an atom of any kind can ever be destroyed'.[16] *Nothing goes away*. Physiology, in serious and popular ways, was conceived as a form of history, a connection exemplified by the American chemist and physiologist George William Draper, who followed his *Human Physiology* of 1856, with a *History of the Intellectual Development of Europe* in 1863. Here he sought to provide evidence for a concluding remark from his earlier work, that 'the history of men and of nations is only a chapter of physiology'.[17] Draper's panegyrics to the ever-moving, ever-changing sea and sky in this second work, his descriptions of the constant yielding of mountains to frost and rain, the passing of all things from form to form, suggest that Michelet's volumes on similar topics should not be read solely under the interpretive banner of Romantic lyricism, but as a form of history. They also make it very plain how Michelet *knew* that the unconsidered dead were to be found in the Archives Nationales; how he *knew* that the material presence of their dust, the atomistic remains of the toils and tribulations, the growth and decay of the animal body, was literally what might carry them, through his inhalation and his writing of History, into a new life. He knew that they were 'not capable of loss of existence'.[18]

This is what Dust is about; this is what Dust *is*: what it means and what it is. It is not about rubbish, nor about the discarded; it is not about a surplus, left over from something else: *it is not about Waste*. Indeed, Dust is the opposite thing to Waste, or at least, the opposite principle to Waste. It is about circularity, the impossibility of things disappearing, or going away, or being gone. Nothing *can be* destroyed. The fundamental lessons of physiology, of cell-theory, and of neurology were to do with this ceaseless making and unmaking, the movement and transmutation of one thing into another. Nothing goes away. Indeed, the death of the material body was but 'a final restoration of the compounds of the Human Organism to the Inorganic Universe', and the beginning of a new 'Life of the Soul'. 'If there is a point in natural philosophy which may be regarded as finally settled', wrote Draper, 'it is the imperishability of the chemical elements and the everlasting duration of force … we cannot admit that an atom of any kind can ever be destroyed'.[19]

Involvement in the everyday Dusty Trades, far away from the physiologist's laboratory, allowed access to this philosophy of indestructibility – what we may come to recognise as the Philosophy of Dust. In 1863 the trade association of master paper-makers mounted a campaign against the taxes on imported rags. One of their campaigning pamphlets, *The Rag Tax. The Paper Makers' Grievance and How to Redress It, for Private Circulation* (1863) outlined a grand system of the world, in which the waste of an industrial civilisation was caught in the same great cycle as was cultural production:

> Civilisation invents various and abundant clothing – the wear of clothing terminates in the production of rags – Rags are transmuted into Paper – Paper supplies the incessant Press, and the various activities of the Press sustain and extend Civilisation.[20]

This was a self-congratulatory description, for the Paper Makers went on to assert that where 'society is most civilised there will be most Rags for the Paper Maker, and most demand for his Paper … the Continent makes more Rags than it makes Paper … England makes proportionately much more Paper than the Continent, and [yet] does not get enough of its own Rags.'

These are nineteenth-century conclusions, about the imperishability of matter and the import of physiology for all sorts of imaginings, both philosophical and every-day. In *Strange Dislocations*, I was particularly interested in the complex history – of thought, of common imaginings – that led Sigmund Freud to muse (again, in 'The Uncanny') on the way in which 'biology [had] not yet been able to decide whether death is the inevitable fate of every human being, or whether it is only a regular but perhaps unavoidable event in life'.[21] Now, having breathed in the Dust, *knowing about it*, in a way that was not really possible in a period of attention to its opposite, Waste, the implications of this imperishability – this *not-going-away-ness* – of Dust for narrative, force themselves forward.

Cultural historians and commentators have been convinced by the idea of Waste. How could we not all be so convinced, when we pay attention to the nineteenth century, and its multifarious discourse on loss, mishap, mislaying, squandering, spending, ridding and surplus (perhaps above all, surplus, and its enthralling metonym, 'excess')? It is difficult to avoid the net of the Victorian imagination in this regard, with its multifarious discourse on what gets left over; outside, outwith the system (whatever that system might happen to be). And we are certainly under the net here with Henry Mayhew. After the *Morning Chronicle* survey was over he began his next publishing venture, the original *London Labour and the London Poor*, the one published in weekly parts between August 1851 and February 1852.[22] His readers were presented in alternate weeks with a sociology and history of prostitution and an account of the London sewer system. These analogies and connections are our taken-for-granted of mid-nineteenth social perception: that there were things and people done away with: put away, or put outside. Our understanding of all sorts of plot – fictional plots and social plots – our understanding of *how things happened* indeed, is bound up with this understanding: that there is sequence, event, movement; things fall away, are abandoned, get lost. Something emerges, which is a story. You can take this story from sewage systems, and systems of prostitution, and plans for the social incorporation or dispersal of surplus women and destitute children; but you can't take it from Dust. Dust – the Philosophy of Dust – speaks of the opposite of waste and dispersal; of a grand circularity, of nothing ever, ever going away. There were complex, articulate and well-understood languages developed to express this knowledge, a few of which I have mentioned. And I suggest that Dust is another way of seeing what Franco Moretti described as the nineteenth-century solution to the violent ruptures of the late eighteenth century, a solution found in narrative. He points to 'the centrality of *history* in nineteenth-century culture and … science as well; and … the centrality of *narrative* within the domain of literature'. He thinks that the reason for this is that narrative and history 'do not retreat before the onslaught of events, but demonstrate the possibility of giving them order and meaning'. The *Bildungsroman*, the novel of development, was in his view, the particular response to such an onslaught, with its extraordinary attempt to make time, sequence and linearality into a circle; to create harmony out of discordant, non-sequential, meaningless events.[23] To recognise and deal with the understanding that nothing goes away: to deal with Dust. And we have already noted History's solution, which is a more extraordinary one than achieved in the nineteenth-century novel. Historians, writing the narrative that has no end, certainly make endings, but as we are still in it, the great, slow moving Everything, in which nothing has gone away and never shall, you can produce only an Ending, which is a different thing indeed, from an End.[24] Michelet's solution to the constraints placed on him by History's narrative was to write in the future perfect, from the perspective of the 'when it shall have been'. This was an attempt to appropriate the perspective allowed to the novelist, to be the story-teller who has it all, the whole story, *there* and palpable, time ready to be made a circle, delivered up in parts to the reader, who doesn't know it yet.

Now we should look out these occasions when Dust is dealt with as an opposite principle, or philosophy, to Waste. Historians will be most interested in people *knowing* about these things, being conscious of the opposing principles of Waste and Dust and the spaces in between. So we will ponder overt statements about the plot of *Our Mutual Friend*, and the difference between them and the way the story actually works. The Mounds are probably meant to make the story. Dickens certainly tidies up and concludes his narrative as the final remnants of the Heaps are carted away from the yard. But it is the river that does it: the great open sewer of the

Thames is what makes everything happen, moves the plot towards its conclusion, and makes the story.

∾

It is impossible to discover when Mayhew went to visit the North London Dustheaps. Certainly not for the *Morning Chronicle* survey, and they are not mentioned in the weekly parts issue of *London Labour* of 1851–52, when the topics are sewage waste and prostitution. But there are internal references in the 1862 edition that show it to be written in 1850 – probably high summer, as the pigs appear full grown and rooting nicely, unaware of their autumn fate. It happened, there are traces of the visit. So though there were things that Mr Boffin 'never found among the dust', that doesn't mean they weren't – aren't – there to be found. Boffin was wrong on this score; but then, isn't Boffin's being wrong part of the story?

Notes

1 Karl Marx, *Capital. Volume 1* (Harmondsworth, Penguin, [1867] 1976), pp. 592–3.

2 References in the text are to the 1971 Penguin edition of *Our Mutual Friend*.

3 The most contemplative attempt is still Harvey Peter Sucksmith's, in 'The Dust-Heaps in *Our Mutual Friend*', *Essays in Criticism*, 23 (1973), 206–12. But see also John Sutherland, 'What Is Jo Sweeping?', in *Is Heathcliff a Murderer? Puzzles in Nineteenth-Century Fiction* (Oxford, Oxford University Press, 1996), pp. 90–8.

4 Henry Mayhew, *London Labour and the London Poor*, 4 vols (New York, Dover Publications, [1861–62] 1968), 2, pp. 166–79.

5 Ibid., p. 171.

6 Bertrand Taithe, *The Essential Mayhew. Representing and Communicating the Poor* (London, Rivers Oram, 1996), pp. 45–59. When Mayhew expressed a desire to write a history of the people 'in their own words' he was not behaving as an oral historian *avant la lettre*; rather, the

People's words embodied their history; words were the material traces of an actual history. For Rousseau's fantasy of the origins of language, see Jean-Jacques Rousseau, *Discourse on the Origin of Inequality* (Indianapolis, Hacket, [1755] 1992), and *Two Essays on the Origin of Language. Jean-Jacques Rousseau and Johann Gottfried Herder* (Chicago, University of Chicago Press, [1781] 1966), pp. 1–74.

7 Mayhew, *London Labour*, 2, p. 170.

8 Sigmund Freud, 'The Uncanny', *Standard Edition of the Complete Psychological Works of Sigmund Freud*, 17 (London, Hogarth Press, [1919] 1955), pp. 217–56.

9 Mayhew, *London Labour*, 2, p. 175.

10 Kate Flint, '"The Mote Within the Eyes": Dust and Victorian Vision', in Juliet John and Alice Jenkins (eds), *Rethinking Victorian Culture* (London, Macmillan, 2000), pp. 46–62.

11 Paul Viallaneix, 'Michelet: Le Magistère de l'Historien', *L'histoire au XIXe siècle. Cahiers de l'Association internationale des études françaises*, 47 (1995), 247–64.

12 'La Marseillaise', <http://www.premier-ministre.gouv.fr/HIST/MARSEIL.HTM>. See Laura Mason, *Singing the French Revolution. Popular Culture and Politics, 1787–1799* (Ithaca and London, Cornell Uniersity Press, 1996), pp. 93–103. Michel Vovell, 'La Marseillaise. La guerre ou la paix', in Pierre Nora, *Les Lieux de Mémoire sous la direction de Pierre Nora. I. La République* (Paris, Gallimard, 1984), pp. 85–136.

13 Lara Moore, 'Putting French History in Order. Archivists and Archival Classification in the 1840s', unpublished paper, 'Archives and Social Memory' Seminar, Institute of Advanced Studies, University of Michigan, September 2000.

14 David P. Jordan, *Transforming Paris. The Life and Labors of Baron Haussmann* (New York, Free Press, 1995), pp. 267–96.

15 There is a list of these more outré histories in Roland Barthes, *Michelet par lui-même* (Paris, Seuil, [1954] 1968), 13. George Eliot reviewed the less odd, in his book on women and priests. See p. 169, and Note.

16 John William Draper, *Human Physiology, Statistical and Dynamical; or, the Conditions and the Course of the Life of Man* (New York, Harper, [1856] 1868), p. 548.

17 Ibid., p. 604. John William Draper, *History of the Intellectual Development of Europe*, 2 vols (London, Bell Daldy, 1864). On the relationship of history to physiology, see Carolyn Steedman, *Strange Dislocations: Childhood and the Idea of Human Interiority, 1780–1930* (Cambridge, MA, Harvard University Press, 1995), pp. 43–95.

18 Draper, *Human Physiology*, p. 549.

19 Ibid., p. 548. See also George Henry Lewes, *Sea-side Studies at Illfracombe, Tenby, the Scilly Isles and Jersey* (Edinburgh, Blackwood, 1858), pp. 218, 322.

20 Rag Tax, *The Rag Tax. The Paper Makers' Grievance and How to Redress It, for Private Circulation* (London, privately printed, 1863), p. 5.

21 Freud, 'The Uncanny', p. 242.

22 Henry Mayhew, *The 'Morning Chronicle' Survey of Labour and the Poor*, 6 vols (Firle, Caliban, 1980–82). Taithe, *The Essential Mayhew*, 17–19.

23 Franco Moretti, *The Way of the World. The Bildungroman in European Culture* (London, Verso, 1987), pp. 6–7, 19, 63.

24 Carolyn Steedman, 'About Ends. On How the End is Different from an Ending', *History of the Human Sciences*, 9:4 (1996) 99–114.

Bibliography

Adcock, K. J., *Leather. From the Raw Material to the Finished Product* (London, Pitman, nd [1924]).

Aguiah, A., 'Meningitis caused by Anthrax in Boy of 11', *Bulletin de la Société de pédiatrie de Paris*, 26 (May 1928).

Anderson, Benedict, *Imagined Communities. Reflections on the Origin and Spread of Nationalism* (London, Verso, [1983] 1991).

Andrews, Richard Mowery, *Law, Magistracy and Crime in Old Regime Paris, 1735–1789. Volume 1. The System of Criminal Justice* (Cambridge, Cambridge University Press, 1994).

Anon., *A Proposal for the Amendment and Encouragement of Servants* (London, J. Shuckburgh, 1751).

Anon., *Reflections on the Relative Situations of Master and Servant, Historically and Politically Considered; the Irregularities of Servants; the Employment of Foreigners; and the General Inconveniencies Resulting from the Want of Regulations* (London, W. Miller, 1800).

Aouate, Y.C., 'Les mesures d'exclusion antijuives dans l'enseignement public en Algerie, 1940–1943', *Pardès*, 8 (1988).

Armstrong, Frances, 'Gender and Miniaturization: Games of Littleness in Nineteenth-Century Fiction', *English Studies in Canada*, 16 (1993).

Arnold, Matthew, *Culture and Anarchy* (Cambridge, Cambridge University Press [1869], 1954).

Arnold, Matthew, *Reports on Elementary Schools, 1851–1852* (London, HMSO, [1889]1908).

Ashton, Rosemary, *G.H. Lewes. A Life* (Oxford, Clarendon Press, 1991).

Ashton, Rosemary, *George Eliot. A Life* (London, Hamish Hamilton, 1996).

Attfield, Judy, 'The Tufted Carpet in Britain: Its Rise from the Bottom of the Pile', *Journal of Design History*, 7 (1994).

'Attorney', *An Attorney's Practice Epitomized; or, the Method, Times and Expenses of Proceeding in the Courts of King's Bench and Common Pleas* (London, Henry Lintot, 8th edn, 1757).

Attridge, Derek, Geoff Bennington and Robert Young (eds), *Post-structuralism and the Question of History* (Cambridge, Cambridge University Press, 1987).

Auden, W.H., 'Makers of History', in *Homage to Clio* (London, Faber & Faber, 1960).

Auden, W.H., *Homage to Clio* (London, Faber, 1960).

Bachelard, Gaston, *The Poetics of Space* (Boston, Beacon, [1958] 1994).

Baines, Edward, *History of the Cotton Manufacture in Great Britain* (London, Cass, [1835] 1966).

Balderston, Katharine C. (ed.), *Thraliana. The Diary of Mrs Hester Lynch Thrale (Later Mrs Piozzi) 1776–1809*, 2 vols (Oxford, Clarendon Press, 1951).

Bann, Stephen, *The Clothing of Clio. A Study of the Representations of History in Nineteenth Century Britain and France* (Cambridge, Cambridge University Press, 1984).

Bann, Stephen, *Romanticism and the Rise of History* (Boston, Twayne, 1995).

Barante, Le Baron de, *Etudes Historiques et Biographiques* (Paris, Didier, 4 vols, 1857).

Barnes, H.E., *A History of Historical Writing* (New York, Dover, 1963).

Barreau, Jean-Michel, 'Vichy, Idéologue de l'école', *Revue d'Histoire Moderne et Contemporaine*, 38:3 (1991).

Barreau, Jean-Michel, 'Abel Bonnard, Ministre de l'éducation nationale sous Vichy, ou l'éducation impossible', *Revue d'Histoire Moderne et Contemporaine*, 43:3 (1996).

Barthes, Roland, *Michelet par lui-même* (Paris, Seuil, [1954] 1968).

Bayley, Christopher, *Empire and Information: Intelligence Gathering and Social Communication in India, 1780–1870* (Cambridge, Cambridge University Press, 1996).

Beattie, J.M., *Crime and the Courts in England, 1660–1800* (Oxford, Clarendon Press, 1986).

Beaty, Jerome, 'History by Indirection: The Era of Reform in *Middlemarch*', *Victorian Studies*, 1 (1957).

Bell, David A., *Lawyers and Citizens. The Making of a Political Elite in Old*

Regime France (New York, Oxford University Press, 1994).

Bennington Geoffrey, and Jacques Derrida, *Jacques Derrida* (Paris, Seuil, 1991).

Berg, Maxine, *The Age of Manufactures, 1700–1820* (London, Fontana, 1985).

Berkhofer, Robert, *Beyond the Great Story. History as Text and Discourse* (Cambridge, MA, Harvard University Press, 1995).

Bird, James Barry, *The Laws Respecting Masters and Servants, Articled Clerks, Apprentices, Manufacturers, Labourers, and Journeymen* (London, W. Clarke, 3rd edn, 1799).

Blackstone, Sir William, *Commentaries on the Laws of England. In Four Books* (Dublin, Company of Booksellers, [1765] 1775).

Bonaparte, Felicia, *The Triptych and The Cross: The Myth of George Eliot's Poetic Imagination* (Brighton, Harvester, 1979).

Booth, Michael, *English Melodrama* (London, Herbert Jenkins, 1965).

Bott, Edmund, *Digest of the Laws Relating to the Poor, by Francis Const*, 3 vols (London, Strahan, 1800).

Bowles, E.S., *Handmade Rugs* (Boston, Little Brown, 1927).

Brachman, Philip, 'Inhalation Anthrax', *Annals of the New York Academy of Science*, 353 (1980).

Bruno, G., (Mme Alfred Fouillé), *Le Tour de la France par deux enfants. Devoir et Patries* (Saint-Cloud, Belin, 1922).

Bruynoghe R., and M. Ronse, 'Une Infection méningée par un bacille Anthracoide' ('Meninginal Infection due to Anthracoid Bacillus'), *Comptes rendus des séances de la Sociétée de biologie*, 125 (1937).

Burchall, Joseph, *Arrangement and Digest of the Law in Cases Adjudged in the King's Bench and Common Pleas from the Year 1756 to 1794, inclusive* (London, J. Jones, 1796).

Buret, Eugène, *De la Misère des classes labourieuses en Angleterre et en France*, 2 vols (Paris, Paulin, 1840).

Burn, Richard, *The History of the Poor Laws: With Observations* (London, H. Woodfall & N. Strahan, 1764).

Burn, Richard, *The Justice of the Peace and the Parish Officer*, 13th edn, 4 vols (London, A. Strahan & W. Woodfall, 1776).

Burn, Richard, *Blank Precedents Relating to the Office of Justice of the Peace, Settled by Doctor Burn* (London, T. Cadell for the King's Law Printer, 1787).

Burn, Richard, *The Justice of the Peace and Parish Officer. Continued to the Present Time by John Burn Esq., his Son*, 4 vols (London, A. Strahan & N. Woodfall, 1793).

Burnett, Frances Hodgson, *The One I Knew Best of All* (London, Frederick Warne, 1893).

Burnett, John, *A Social History of Housing, 1815–1970* (London, Methuen, 1978).

Burton, Antoinette, 'Thinking Beyond the Boundaries: Empire, Feminism and the Domains of History', *Social History*, 26:1 (2001).

Bynum, W.F. and Roy Porter, *Companion Encyclopaedia of the History of Medicine*, 2 vols (London, Routledge, 1993).

Cairns, John W., 'Blackstone, an English Institutionalist. Legal Literature and the Rise of the Nation State', *Oxford Journal of Legal Studies*, 4 (1984).

Caldecott, Thomas, *Reports of Cases relative to the Duty and Offices of a Justice of the Peace, from Michaelmas Term 1776, inclusive, to Trinity Term 1785, inclusive* (London, His Majesty's Law Print, for P. Uriel, 1785).

Calder, Jenny, *The Victorian Home* (London, Batsford, 1977).

Callen, Edward, *Auden: A Carnival of Intellect* (Oxford, Oxford University Press, 1983).

Canary, Robert H. and Henry Kosiki (eds), *The Writing of History. Literary Form and Historical Understanding* (Madison and London, University of Wisconsin Press, 1978).

Carr, David, *Time, Narrative and History* (Bloomington IN, Indiana University Press, 1986).

Casey, Catherine, *Work, Self and Society. After Industrialism* (London and New York, Routledge, 1995).

Caverero, Adriana, *Relating Narratives. Storytelling and Selfhood* (London, Routledge [1997] 2000).

Chancellor, V.E., *History for their Masters. Opinion in the English History Textbook, 1800–1914* (London, Adams & Dart, 1970).

Chatterjee, Indrani, 'Testing the Local Against the Colonial Archive', *History Workshop*, 44 (1997).

Cobb, Richard, *A Second Identity. Essays on French History* (Oxford, Oxford University Press, 1969).

Coleman, D.C., *The British Paper Industry 1495–1860. A Study in Industrial Growth* (Oxford, Clarendon Press, 1958).

Collini, Stefan, *Matthew Arnold. A Critical Portrait* (Oxford, Oxford University Press, 1994).

Combe, Sonia, *Archives Interdites. Les Peurs françaises face à l'histoire contemporaine* (Paris, Albin Michel, 1994).

Const, Francis, *Decisions of the Court of the King's Bench, Upon the Laws relating to the Poor, Originally published by Edmund Bott Esq. of the Inner Temple, Barister at Law. Revised ... by Francis Const Esq. of the Middle Temple*, 2 vols, (London, Whieldon & Butterworth, 3rd edn, 1793).

Cook, Elisabeth, *Epistolary Bodies. Gender and Genre in the Eighteenth Century Republic of Letters* (Stanford CA, Stanford University Press, 1996).

Cook, Terry, 'Electronic Records, Paper Minds: The Revolution in Information Management and Archives in the Post-custodial and Postmodernist Era', *Archives and Manuscripts*, 22:2 (1994).

Corbin, Alain, *The Foul and the Fragrant* (Leamington Spa, Berg, 1986).

Corn, Jacqueline Karnell, *Response to Occupational Health Hazards. A Historical Perspective* (New York, Van Nostrand Reinhold, 1992).

Crehan, S., '*The Rape of the Lock* and the Economy of "Trivial Things"', *Eighteenth-Century Studies*, 31 (1997), 45–68.

Crosby, Christina, *The Ends of History. Victorians and 'The Woman Question'* (London and New York, Routledge, 1991).

Crossley, Ceri, 'Michelet and Quinet Reviewed by George Eliot', *French Studies Bulletin*, 8 (1983).

Crossley, Ceri, *French Historians and Romanticism. Thierry, Guizot, the Saint-Simonians, Quinet, Michelet* (London, Routledge, 1993).

Crowell, I., *Design and Hook Your Own Rugs* (New York, Macmillan, 1945).

Crubaugh, Anthony, 'Local Justice and Rural Society in the French Revolution', *Journal of Social History*, 34:2 (2000).

Dalton, Michael, *The Country Justice. Containing the Practice, Duty and Power of the Justices of the Peace, as well as in as out of their sessions* (London, Henry Lintot, 1742).

Davis, Lennard, *Factual Fictions. The Origins of the English Novel* (New York, Columbia University Press, 1986).

Davis, M. and D. Wallbridge, *Boundary and Space. An Introduction to the Work of D.W. Winnicott* (Harmondsworth, Penguin, 1981).

Davis, Natalie, *Fiction in the Archives. Pardon Tales and their Tellers in Sixteenth-century France* (Oxford, Polity, 1987).

Day, R.A., *Told in Letters. Epistolary Fiction before Richardson* (Ann Arbor, MI, University of Michigan Press, 1966).

Deniker, Michel, Jean Patel and Bernard Jamain, 'Meningite au Cours du Charbon' ('Meningitis as a Complication of Anthrax'), *La Presse médicale*, 46 (13 April 1938).

Derrida, Jacques, *Grammatology*, trans. Gayatri Chakravorty Spivak (Baltimore and London, Johns Hopkins University Press, [1967] 1976).

Derrida, Jacques, 'Freud and the Scene of Writing', in *Writing and Difference*, trans. Alan Bass (London, Routledge & Kegan Paul, [1967] 1978).

Derrida, Jacques, *The Post Card: From Socrates to Freud and Beyond*, trans. Alan Bass (Chicago, University of Chicago Press, [1980] 1987).

Derrida, Jacques, 'Archive Fever. A Freudian Impression', *Diacritics*, 25:2 (1995).

Derrida, Jacques, *Mal d'archive: Une impression freudienne* (Paris, Editions Galilée, 1995).

Derrida, Jacques, *Archive Fever. A Freudian Impression* (Chicago, University of Chicago Press, 1996).

Derrida, Jacques, '"To Do Justice to Freud": The History of Madness in the Age of Psychoanalysis', in Arnold I. Davidson (ed.), *Foucault and His Interlocutors* (Chicago, University of Chicago Press, 1997).

Dewald, Carolyn, 'Women and Culture in Herodotus' *Histories*', in Helene P. Foley (ed.), *Reflections of Women in Antiquity* (New York, London and Paris, Gordon & Breach, 1981).

Dickens, Charles, *Our Mutual Friend*, edited with an introduction by Stephen Gill (Harmondsworth, Penguin, [1864–65] 1971).

Dirks, Nicholas, 'Colonial Histories and Native Informants: Biography of an Archive', in N. Dirks (ed.), *Colonialism and Culture* (Ann Arbor, University of Michigan Press, 1992).

Dodd, Valerie, *George Eliot. An Intellectual Life* (London, Macmillan, 1990).

Douglas, Lorimer, 'Black Slaves and English Liberty. A Re-examination of Racial Slavery in England', *Immigrants and Minorities*, 3:2 (1984).

Douglas, Sylvester, *Report of Cases Argued and Determined in the Court of the King's Bench, Volume 4 (1784–1785)* (London and Dublin, Sweet,

Stevens & Millikins, 1831).

Doyle, William, *The Parlement of Bordeaux and the End of the Old Regime, 1771–1790* (London and Tonbridge, Ernest Benn, 1974).

Draper, John William, *Human Physiology, Statistical and Dynamical; or, the Conditions and the Course of the Life of Man* (New York, Harper, [1856] 1868).

Draper, John William, *History of the Intellectual Development of Europe*, 2 vols (London, Bell Daldy, 1864).

Dublin Society, The, *The Art of Tanning and Currying Leather; With an Account of all the Different Processes Made Use of in Europe and Asia for Dying Leather Red and Yellow* (London, J. Nourse, 1774).

Dunscombe, W.K., 'Meningitis due to B. anthracis', *British Medical Journal* (30 January 1932).

Eagleton, Terry, *The Rape of Clarissa. Writing, Sexuality and Class Struggle in Samuel Richardson* (Oxford, Blackwell, 1982).

Earle, Rebecca, *Epistolary Selves. Letters and Letter Writers, 1600–1945* (Aldershot, Ashgate, 1999).

'Editorial. Language and History', *History Workshop Journal*, 10:2 (1980).

Ehrenberg, Victor, *The Greek State* (London, Methuen, [1960] 1969).

Eley, Geoff, 'Is All the World a Text?', in Terrence J. McDonald (ed.), *The Historical Turn in the Human Sciences* (Ann Arbor, University of Michigan Press, 1996).

Eliot, George, *Middlemarch* (Harmondsworth, Penguin, [1871–72] 1965).

Enchevarria, Roberto Gonzalez, *Myth and Archive. A Theory of Latin American Narrative* (Cambridge, Cambridge University Press, 1994).

European Commission, Environment Leather Project, *Deterioration of Vegetable Tanned Leather*, Protection and Conservation of the European Cultural Heritage, Research Report, 6 (Copenhagen, 1997).

Evans, Richard, *In Defence of History* (London, Granta, 1997).

Eyles, Leonora, *The Woman in the Little House* (London, Grant Richards, 1922).

Faller, L.B., *Turned to Account. The Forms and Functions of Criminal Biography in Late Seventeenth and Early Eighteenth Century England* (Cambridge, Cambridge University Press, 1987).

Farge, Arlette, *Le Goût de l'archive* (Paris, Editions du Seuil, 1989).

Farnie, D.A., *The English Cotton Industry and the World Market* (Oxford,

Clarendon Press, 1979).

Faubion, James D., *Michel Foucault. Aesthetics, Method and Epistemology. Essential Works of Foucault 1954–1984, Volume 2* (New York, The New Press, 1998).

Ferro, Marc, *The Use and Abuse of History, or, How the Past Is Taught* (London, Routledge, 1981).

Fifoot, Cecil, *Lord Mansfield* (Oxford, Clarendon Press, 1936).

Flint, Kate, '"The Mote Within the Eyes": Dust and Victorian Vision', in Juliet John and Alice Jenkins (eds), *Rethinking Victorian Culture* (London, Macmillan, 2000).

Foley, E. and E. Waugh, *Collecting Hooked Rugs* (New York, Century, 1927).

Forbes, John, Alexander Tweedie and John Conolly, *The Cyclopaedia of Practical Medicine*, 3 vols (London, Sherwood, 1833).

Foucault, Michel, *The Order of Things. An Archeology of the Human Sciences* (Tavistock, London, [1966] 1970)

Foucault, Michel, *The Archeology of Knowledge* (London, Tavistock, [1969], 1972).

Freeman, Mark, *Rewriting the Self. History, Memory, Narrative* (London, Routledge, 1993).

Freud, Sigmund, 'Jokes and their Relationship to the Unconscious', *Standard Edition of the Complete Psychological Works of Sigmund Freud*, 8 (London, Hogarth Press, [1905] 1960).

Freud, Sigmund, 'The Uncanny', in *Standard Edition of the Complete Psychological Works of Sigmund Freud*, 17 (London, Hogarth Press, [1919] 1955).

Freud, Sigmund, 'Beyond the Pleasure Principle', *Standard Edition of the Complete Psychological Works of Sigmund Freud*, 18 (London, Hogarth Press, [1920] 1950).

Freud, Sigmund, 'Humour', *Standard Edition of the Complete Psychological Works of Sigmund Freud*, 21 (London, Hogarth Press, [1927] 1961).

Frykstedt, M.C., '*Mary Barton* and the Reports of the Ministry to the Poor: A New Source', *Studia Neophilologica*, 52 (1980).

Fuller, John, *W.H. Auden. A Commentary* (London, Faber & Faber, 1998).

Gaskell, Elizabeth, *Mary Barton* (Harmondsworth, Penguin, [1848] 1970).

Gattrell, V.A.C., *The Hanging Tree. Execution and the English People, 1770–1868* (Oxford, Oxford University Press, 1994).

Gauldie, Enid, *Cruel Habitations. A History of Working Class Housing 1780–1918* (London, Allen & Unwin, 1974).

Giddens, Anthony, *Modernity and Self-Identity. Self and Society in the Late Modern Age* (Cambridge, Polity, 1991).

Gildea, Robert, *The Past in French History* (New Haven and London, Yale University Press, 1994).

Gisborne, Thomas, *An Inquiry into the Duties of Man in the Higher and Middle Classes of Society in Great Britain, Resulting from their respective Situations, Professions and Employments*, 2 vols (London, B. and J. White, 2nd edn, 1795).

Goff, Le, Jacques, *History and Memory* (New York, Columbia University Press, [1977] 1992).

Goodman, Deena, *The Republic of Letters. A Cultural History of the French Enlightenment* (Ithaca, Cornell University Press, 1994).

Gross, H. and H. Plate, 'Milzbrandbacillen-Meningistis' ('Meningitis due to Anthrax Bacilli'), *Klinische Wochenshcrift*, 19 (5 October 1940).

Guiraud, Jean-Michel, *La Vie intellectuelle et artistique á Marseilles á l'époque de Vichy et sous l'occupation, 1940–1944* (Marseille, CRDP, 1987).

Gurney, W.B., *The Trials of Jeremiah Brandreth* (London, Butterworth, 2 vols, 1817).

Haight, Gordon S. (ed.), *The George Eliot Letters. Volume V, 1869–1873* (London, Oxford University Press; New Haven, Yale University Press, 1956)

Hale, J.R., *The Evolution of British Historiography: From Bacon to Namier* (London, Macmillan, 1967).

Hall, W.D., *The Youth of Vichy France* (Oxford, Clarendon Press, 1981).

Hamant, Drouet, P. Chalnot and J. Simonin, 'Hyperacute Meningitis in Anthrax', *Bulletins et mémoires de la Société medicale des hopitaux de Paris*, 49 (23 January 1933).

Hands, Williams, *The Solicitor's Practice on the Crown Side of the Court of the King's Bench. With an Appendix Containing the Forms of the Proceeding* (London, J. Butterworth, 1803).

Hansard, T.C. (ed.), *The Parliamentary History of England, from the Earliest Period to the Year 1803, Volume XIX, comprising the period from ... January 1777 to ... December 1778* (London, T.C. Hansard, 1814).

Harrison, Barbara, *Not Only the 'Dangerous Trades': Women's Work and Health in Britain, 1880–1914* (London, Taylor & Francis, 1996).

Hawker-Smith, B., *Thrifty Rug Making. Including Surrey Stitch Rugs. With a Foreword by Lady Dowson* (Pitman, London, 1940).

Hawley, J.C., '*Mary Barton*: The View from Without', *Nineteenth Century Studies*, 3 (1989).

Herodotus, *The Histories* (Harmondsworth, Penguin, 1954).

Himmelfarb, Gertrude, *The Idea of Poverty. England in the Early Industrial Age* (London, Faber, 1984).

Hobsbawm, Eric, *Worlds of Labour. Further Studies in the History of Labour* (London, Weidenfeld & Nicolson, 1984).

Hoggart, Richard, *The Uses of Literacy* (Harmondsworth, Penguin, [1957] 1958).

Holdsworth, Clare, 'Dr John Thomas Arlidge and Victorian Occupational Medicine', *Medical History* 42:4 (1998).

Holdsworth, Sir William, *A History of the English Law*, 10 (London, Methuen, 16 vols, 1938).

Howells, Christina, *Derrida. Deconstruction from Phenomenology to Ethics* (Cambridge, Polity Press, 1999).

Hunter, Donald, *The Diseases of Occupations* (London, English Universities Press, 1955).

Hunter, Dard, *Papermaking. The History and Technique of an Ancient Craft*, 2nd edn (London, Pleiades Books, 1956).

Hunter, Paul J., *Before Novels. The Cultural Contexts of Eighteenth-century Fiction* (New York, Norton, 1990).

Impey, John, *The New Instructor Clericalis. Stating the Authority, Jurisdiction and Modern Practice of the Court of the King's Bench. With Directions for commencing and defending Actions, entering up Judgements, suing out Executors, and proceeding in Error* (London, W. Strahan & W. Woodfall, 1782).

Jackson, Mark, *New-born Child Murder. Women, Children and the Courts in Eighteenth-century England* (Manchester, Manchester University Press, 1996).

Johnson, Douglas, 'The Historian as Frenchman', *New Society* (7 August 1969).

Jordan, David P., *Transforming Paris. The Life and Labors of Baron Haussmann* (New York, Free Press, 1995).

Jordanova, Ludmilla, *History in Practice* (London, Arnold, 2000).

Kamuf, Peggy, 'Writing Like a Woman', in S. McConnell-Ginet *et al.* (eds),

Women and Language in Literature and Society (New York, Praeger, 1980).

Kaplan, Edward K. (ed.), *Mother Death. The Journal of Jules Michelet, 1815–1850* (Amherst, University of Massachusetts Press, 1984).

Kaplan, Steven Laurence, *Bread, Politics and Political Economy in the Reign of Louis XV* (The Hague, Martinus Nijhoff, 2 vols, 1976).

Kaplan, Steven Laurence, *Provisioning Paris. Merchants and Millers in the Grain and Flour Trade during the Eighteenth Century* (Ithaca and London, Cornell University Press, 1984).

Kauffman, Linda S., *Discourses of Desire. Gender, Genre and Epistolary Fiction* (Ithaca, Cornell University Press, 1986).

Kearns, Katherine, *Psychoanalysis, Historiography and Feminist Theory. The Search for Critical Method* (Cambridge, Cambridge University Press, 1997).

Kiple, Kenneth F., *The Cambridge World History of Human Disease* (Cambridge, Cambridge University Press, 1993).

Theresa Kitchel, Anna, *Quarry for 'Middlemarch'* (Berkeley, CA, University of California Press, 1950).

Kober, George M. and William C. Hanson, *Diseases of Occupation and Vocational Hygiene* (London, William Heinemann, [1916] 1918).

Lang, Cecil Y. (ed.) *The Letters of Matthew Arnold*, 3 vols (Charlottesville VA, University Press of Virginia, 1996).

Langlois, Claude and Charles Seignobos, *Introduction to the Study of History* (London, Duckworth, 1898).

Laplanche, Jean, *Life and Death in Psycho-analysis* (Baltimore, Johns Hopkins University Press, 1976).

Lawlor, Leonard, 'Memory Becomes Electra', *Review of Politics*, 60:4 (1998).

Lefebvre, Georges, *Etudes sur la Révolution Française* (Paris, Presses Universitaires de France, 1963).

Leith, H.J. Plender, *The Preservation of Leather Bookbindings* (London, Trustees of the British Museum, [1946] 1967).

Lemire, Beverley, *Fashion's Favourite: The Cotton Trade and the Consumer in Britain, 1660–1800* (Oxford, Oxford University Press, 1991).

Leslie, Esther, 'Dreams, Toys and Tales (a paper on Walter Benjamin first given at the conference Obscure Objects of Desire, UEA, 1997')', *Crafts*, 146 (1997).

Lévi-Strauss, Claude, *The Savage Mind* (London, Weidenfeld & Nicolson, 1966).

Levine, Philippa, *The Amateur and the Professional. Antiquaries, Historians and Archeologists in Victorian Britain, 1838–1886* (Cambridge, Cambridge University Press, 1986).

Levitt, Sarah, 'Clothing', in B. Rose (ed.), *The Lancashire Cotton Industry. A History Since 1700* (Preston, Lancashire County Books, 1996).

Lewes, G.H., 'The State of Historical Science in France', *British and Foreign Review; or, European Quarterly Journal*, 16 (1844).

Lewes, George Henry, *Sea-side Studies at Illfracombe, Tenby, the Scilly Isles and Jersey* (Edinburgh, Blackwood, 1858).

Liebs, E., 'Between *Gulliver* and *Alice*: Some Remarks on the Dialectic of GREAT and SMALL in Literature', *Phaedrus*, 13 (1988).

Lowe, Donald M., *History of Bourgeois Perception* (Brighton, Harvester, 1982).

McBride, David, *Some Account of a New Method of Tanning* (Dublin, Boulter Grierson, 1769).

McCalla, Arthur, 'Romantic Vicos: Vico and Providence in Michelet and Ballanche', *Historical Reflections/Reflexions Historiques*, 19 (1993).

McCarthy, Patrick J., *Matthew Arnold and the Three Classes* (New York, Columbia University Press, 1964).

McCormick, Kathleen, 'George Eliot's Earliest Prose: the Coventry *Herald* and the Coventry Fiction', *Victorian Periodicals Review*, 19:2 (1986).

McCowen, G.R. and H.B. Parker, 'Anthrax Meningitis', *Journal of the Royal Navy Medical Service*, 18 (October 1932).

Mackay, Carol, 'Melodrama and the Working Class', in Carol Hanbery MacKay (ed.), *Dramatic Dickens* (London, Macmillan, 1989).

McKeon, Michael, *The Origin of the English Novel, 1600–1740* (Baltimore, Johns Hopkins University Press, 1987).

McMillan, Margaret, *The Nursery School* (London, Dent, 1919).

Maier, C.S., 'Surfeit of Memory? Reflections on History, Memory and Denial', *History and Memory*, 5 (1993).

Malcolm, Janet, *In the Freud Archives* (London, Macmillan, [1983] 1997).

Mandelbaum, Maurice, 'The Presuppositions of Hayden White's *Metahistory*', *History and Theory*, 19 (1980).

Mandelbaum, Maurice, *Philosophy, History and the Sciences. Selected Critical Essays* (Baltimore and London, Johns Hopkins University Press,

1984).

Margolis, Nadia, 'The "Joan Phenomenon" and the French Right', in Bonnie Wheeler and Charles T. Wood (eds), *Fresh Verdicts on Joan of Arc* (New York, Garland, 1996).

Martin, Henri-Jean, *The History and the Power of Writing* (Chicago, Chicago University Press, [1994] 1998).

Marx, Karl, 'The Eighteenth Brumaire of Louis Bonaparte', *Pelican Marx Library. Political Writings, Volume 2. Surveys from Exile* (Harmondsworth, Penguin, [1869] [1858] 1973).

Marx, Karl, *Capital* (Harmondsworth, Penguin, [1867] 1976), 1.

Mason, Laura, *Singing the French Revolution. Popular Culture and Politics, 1787–1799* (Ithaca and London, Cornell University Press, 1996).

Mason, Michael, '*Middlemarch* and History', *Nineteenth Century Fiction*, 25 (1970–71).

Masson, J.M., *The Assault on Truth. Freud's Suppression of the Seduction Theory* (Harmondsworth, Penguin, 1985).

Mayhew, Henry, *Life and Labour of the London Poor*, 1 and parts of 2 and 3 (London, George Woodfall, 1851).

Mayhew, Henry, *London Labour and the London Poor*, 4 vols (New York, Dover Publications, [1861–62] 1968).

Mayhew, Henry, *The 'Morning Chronicle' Survey of Labour and the Poor*, 6 vols (Firle, Caliban, 1980–82).

Maza, Sarah, *Private Lives and Public Affairs. The Causes Celèbres of Prerevolutionary France* (Berkeley, Los Angeles and London, University of California Press, 1993).

Meiklejohn, A., *The Life, Work and Times of Charles Turner Thackrah, Surgeon and Apothecary of Leeds (1795–1833)* (Edinburgh and London, E & S Livingstone, 1957).

Miall, A., *Make Your Own Rugs*, (New York, Woman's Magazine Handbooks, 4, 1938).

Michelet, Jules, 'Rapport au Ministre de l'Instruction Publique sur les Bibliothèques et Archives des Départements du Sud-Ouest de la France', in *Oeuvres Complètes, Tome IV* (Paris, Flammarion, [1835] 1971).

Michelet, Jules, 'Preface de l'Histoire de France' [1869]; and 'Examen en des Remainments du texte de 1833 par Robert Casanova', *Oeuvres*

Complètes, Tome IV, (Paris, Flammarion, 1974).

Michelet, Jules, 'Jusqu'au 18 Brumaire' (1872–74), *Oeuvres Complètes, Tome XXI* (Paris, Flammarion, 1982).

Middleton, Bernard C., *The Restoration of Leather Bindings*, 3rd edn (British Library, Oak Knoll Press, 1998).

Miller, Nancy K., '"I"s in Drag. The Sex of Recollection', *The Eighteenth Century. Theory and Interpretation*, 22 (1981).

Millhauser, S., 'The Fascination of the Miniature', *Grand Street*, 2 (1983).

Milsom, S.F.C., 'The Nature of Blackstone's Achievement', *Oxford Journal of Legal Studies*, 1 (1981).

Ministry of Labour, *Report of the Committee of Inquiry on Anthrax* (London, HMSO, 1959).

Mitzman, Arthur, *Michelet, Historian. Rebirth and Romanticism in Nineteenth-Century France* (New Haven and London, Yale University Press, 1990).

Mink, Lewis O., 'Everyman His or Her Annalist', *Critical Inquiry*, 7:4 (1981).

Mitchell, B.R. and P. Deane, *Abstract of British Historical Statistics* (Cambridge, Cambridge University Press, 1962).

Mulherne, Francis, *The Moment of 'Scrutiny'* (London, Verso, [1979] 1981),

Moretti, Franco, *The Way of the World. The Bildungsroman in European Culture* (London, Verso, 1987).

Musgrave, P.W., 'Curriculum History: Past, Present and Future', *History of Education Review*, 17 (1988).

Neuberg, Victor E., *Chapbooks* (London, Woburn Press, 1976).

New, Peter, 'Chance, Providence and Destiny in George Eliot's Fiction', *Journal of the English Association*, 34:150 (1985).

Nord, Deborah E., *Walking the Streets. Women, Representation and the City* (Ithaca and London, Cornell University Press).

Norris, Christopher, *Deconstruction and the Interests of Theory* (London, Pinter, 1988).

Norris, Christopher, *Uncritical Theory. Postmodernism, Intellectuals and the Gulf War* (London, Lawrence & Wishart, 1992).

Oldham, James, *The Mansfield Manuscripts and the Growth of English Law in the Eighteenth Century*, 2 vols (Chapel Hill and London, University of North Carolina Press, 1992).

Oliver, Sir Thomas, *Occupations. From the Social, Hygienic and Medical Points of View* (Cambridge, Cambridge University Press, 1916).

Osborne, Thomas, 'The Ordinariness of the Archive', *History of the Human Sciences*, 12:2 (1999).

Ozouf, Jacques and Mona, 'Le Tour de la France par Deux Enfants. Le petit livre rouge de la République', in Pierre Nora, *Les Lieux de mémoire sous la dirction de Pierre Nora. I. La République* (Paris, Gallimard, 1984).

Palmer, Bryan D., *Descent into Discourse. The Reification of Language and the Writing of Social History* (Philadelphia, Temple University Press, 1990).

Parry, Leonard A., *The Risks and Dangers of Various Occupations and their Prevention* (London, Scott, Greenwood, 1900).

Patterson, Orlando, *Slavery and Social Death. A Comparative Study* (Cambridge MA, Harvard University Press, 1982).

Paull, Mrs, *The Romance of a Rag and Other Tales* (London, Kempster, 1876).

Paxton, Robert O., *Vichy France. Old Guard and New Order, 1940–1944* (New York, Knopf, 1972).

People's History, 'The People's History. Working Class Autobiographies from the British Library, Part I: 1729–1889; Part II: 1890–1920' (Brighton, Harvester Press Microform Publications and the British Library, 1986).

Phillips, M.L., *Hooked Rugs and How to Make Them* (New York, Macmillan, 1925).

Pinney, Thomas (ed.), *Essays of George Eliot* (New York, Columbia University Press, 1963).

Platt, K., 'Places of Experience and the Experience of Place', in L.S. Rouner (ed.) *The Longing for Home* (Notre Dame IN, University of Notre Dame Press, 1996).

Pomian, K., 'Les archives', in Pierre Nora, *Les Lieux de mémoire, sous la direction de Pierre Nora. III, Les France. 3. De l'archive à l'emblème* (Paris, Gallimard, 1992).

Ponder, Constant, *Report to the Worshipful Company of Leathersellers on the Incidence of Anthrax Amongst those engaged in Hide, Skin and Leather Industries* (London, Worshipful Company of Leathersellers, 1911).

Pratt, J.C. and V.A. Neufeldt (eds), *George Eliot's 'Middlemarch' Notebooks. A Transcription* (Berkeley, University of California Press, 1979).

Prest, J., *The Industrial Revolution in Coventry* (Oxford, Oxford University Press, 1960).

Rag Tax, *The Rag Tax. The Paper Makers' Grievance and How to Redress It, for Private Circulation* (London, privately printed, 1863).

Ramazzini, Bernardino, *A Treatise of the Diseases of Tradesmen* (London, Andrew Bell, 1705).

Rancière, Jacques, *The Names of History. On the Poetics of Knowledge* (Minneapolis, University of Minnesota Press, [1992] 1994).

Rapaport, Herman, 'Archive Trauma', *Diacritics*, 28:4 (1998).

Raven, J. and Naomi Tadmor (eds), *The Practice and Representation of Reading in England* (Cambridge, Cambridge University Press, 1996).

Rayner, J. L., *The Complete Newgate Calendar*, 5 vols (London, privately printed, 1826).

Reed, Ronald, *Ancient Skins, Parchments and Leathers* (London and New York, Seminar Press, 1972).

Reed, Ronald, *The Nature and Making of Parchment* (Leeds, Elmete Press, 1975).

Revell, James, *A Complete Guide to the Ornamental Leather Work* (London, privately printed, 1853).

Ricoeur, Paul, 'The Narrative Function', in John Thompson (ed.), *Hermeneutics and the Human Sciences* (Cambridge, Cambridge University Press, 1981).

Ricoeur, Paul, *Time and Narrative* (Chicago, Chicago University Press, 3 vols, [1983] 1984).

Riley, James C., *The Eighteenth-century Campaign to Avoid Disease* (New York, St Martin's Press, 1987).

Ripa, Cesare, *Baroque and Rococo Pictorial Imagery* (New York, Dover, [1758–60] 1971).

Roberts, Elizabeth, *A Woman's Place. An Oral History of Working-class Women 1890–1940* (Oxford, Blackwell, 1984).

Roberts, Matthew T. and Don Etherington, *Bookbinding and the Conservation of Books* (Washington, Library of Congress, 1982).

Robbins, Bruce, *The Servant's Hand. English Fiction from Below* (Durham and London, Duke University Press, [1986] 1993).

Roth, P.A., 'Narrative Explanation: The Case of History', *History and Theory*, 27 (1988).

Rousseau, Jean-Jacques, *Discourse on the Origin of Inequality* (Indianapolis, Hacket, [1755] 1992).

Rousseau, Jean-Jacques, *Two Essays on the Origin of Language. Jean-Jacques Rousseau and Johann Gottfried Herder* (Chicago, University of Chicago Press, [1781] 1966).

Rubinstein, David, *Victorian Homes* (Newton Abbott, David & Charles, 1974).

Samuel, Raphael, 'On the Methods of History Workshop. A Reply', *History Workshop Journal*, 9 (1980).

Samuel, Raphael, *Theatres of Memory. Volume 1: Past and Present in Contemporary Culture* (London, Verso, 1994).

Saxby, Mary, *Memoirs of a Female Vagrant, Written by Herself* (London, J. Burditt, 1806).

Scott, Sir Walter, '*Waverley*: A Postscript Which Should Have Been a Preface', *The Prefaces to the Waverley Novels*, ed. Mark A. Weinstein (Lincoln and London, University of Nebraska Press, [1814] 1978).

Sellars, Christopher C., *Hazards of the Job. From Industrial Disease to Environmental Health Science* (Chapel Hill and London, University of North Carolina Press, 1997).

Sewell, Mrs, *Our Father's Care. A Ballad* (London, Jarrold, 1861).

Shanahan, Robert H., Joseph R. Griffin and Alfred P. von Anersburg, 'Anthrax Meningitis. Report of a Case of Internal Anthrax with Recovery', *American Journal of Chemical Pathology*, 17 (1947).

Sharp, Granville, *A Representation of the Injustice and Dangerous Tendency of Tolerating Slavery; or of Admitting the Least Claim of Private Property in the Persons of Men, in England. In four parts* (London, Benjamin White, 1769).

Sharps, J.G., *Mrs Gaskell's Observation and Invention. A Study of Her Non-Biographic Works* (Fontwell, Linden, 1970).

Shipley Art Gallery, *Ragtime. Rugs and Wallhangings* (Shipley, Tyne and Wear Museums Service, 1988).

Smith, Bonnie, *The Gender of History. Men, Women and Historical Practice* (Cambridge, MA, Harvard University Press, 1998).

Smith, Goldwin, *The Study of History. A Lecture* (privately printed, 1859).

Snell, Keith, *Annals of the Labouring Poor. Social Change and Agrarian*

England, 1660–1900 (Cambridge, Cambridge University Press, 1985).

Snow, E.C., (Manager of the United Tanners' Federation), *Leather, Hides, Skins and Tanning Materials*, Resources of the Empire Series (London, Ernest Benn, 1924).

Society for the Encouragement of Arts, Manufactures and Commerce, *Report of the Committee on Leather for Bookbinding. With Four Appendices* (London, William Trounce, 1911).

'Special Feature: Language and History', *History Workshop Journal*, 27 (1989).

Spufford, Margaret, *The Great Reclothing of Rural England. Petty Chapmen and their Wares in Seventeenth-century England* (London, Hambledon, 1984).

Stafford, Andy, 'Barthes and Michelet: Biography and History', *Nottingham French Studies*, 36:1 (1997).

Standage, H. C., *The Leather Worker's Manual, being a compendium of practical recipes and working formulae for curriers, bootmakers, leather dressers &c* (London, Scott, Greenwood, 1900).

Steedman, Carolyn, 'Living Historically Now?', *Arena* (Australia), 97 (1991).

Steedman, Carolyn, *Past Tenses. Essays on Writing, Autobiography and History* (London, Rivers Oram, 1992).

Steedman, Carolyn, 'Inside, Outside, Other: Accounts of National Identity in the Nineteenth Century', *History of the Human Sciences*, 8 (1995).

Steedman, Carolyn, *Strange Dislocations. Childhood and the Idea of Human Interiority, 1780–1930* (Cambridge, MA, Harvard University Press, 1995).

Steedman, Carolyn, 'About Ends. Oh How the End is Different from an Ending', *History of the Human Sciences* 19:4 (1996).

Steedman, Carolyn, 'Raphael Samuel, 1934–1996', *Radical Philosophy*, 82 (1997).

Steedman, Carolyn, 'The Space of Memory: In an Archive', *History of the Human Sciences*, 11:4 (1998).

Steedman, Carolyn, 'State Sponsored Autobiography', in Becky Conekin, Frank Mort and Chris Waters (eds), *Moments of Modernity. Reconstructing Britain 1945–1964* (London, Rivers Oram, 1999).

Stewart, Susan, *On Longing. Narratives of the Miniature, the Gigantic, the Souvenir, the Collection* (Durham, NC, Duke University Press, 1993).

Syms, L.C., *Le tour de la France, par G. Bruno, ed. for school use by L.C. Syms* (New York, American Book Company, 1902).

Sucksmith, Harvey Peter, 'The Dust-Heaps in *Our Mutual Friend*', *Essays in Criticism*, 23 (1973).

Sutherland, John, 'Is Will Ladislaw Legitimate?', and 'What is Jo Sweeping?', in *Is Heathcliff a Murderer? Puzzles in Nineteenth-Century Fiction* (Oxford, Oxford University Press, 1996).

Taithe, Bertrand, *The Essential Mayhew. Representing and Communicating the Poor* (London, Rivers Oram, 1996).

Taylor, Charles, *Sources of the Self. The Making of the Modern Identity* (Cambridge, Cambridge University Press, 1989).

Taylor, John, *Elements of the Civil Law* (Cambridge, privately printed, 1767).

Temple Newsam House, *Country House Floors* (Leeds, Leeds City Art Galleries, 1987).

Thackrah, Charles Turner, *The Effects of Arts, Trades and Professions, and of Civic States and Habits of Living, on Health and Longevity: with Suggestions for the Removal of the Agents which Produce Disease and Shorten the Duration of Life*, 2nd edn (London, Longman, 1832).

Théorides, Jean, *Un grand médicin et biologiste. Casimir-Joseph Davaine (1812–1882). (Analecta medico-historica* [4]) (Oxford, Pergamon Press, 1968).

Thomas, Chantal, 'Barthes et Michelet. Homologie de travail, parallèle d'affection', *La Règle du jeu*, 15 (1995).

Thomas, Richard, *The Imperial Archive. Knowledge and the Fantasy of Empire* (London Verso, 1990).

Thompson, E.P., *The Making of the English Working Class* (Harmondsworth, Penguin, [1963] 1991).

Thompson, E.P., *Warwick University Ltd. Industry, Management and the Universities* (Harmondsworth, Penguin, 1970).

Thornton and Sons (Dewsbury) Ltd., R., *A Story of Woollen Rag Sales, 1860–1960* (London, Harley, 1960).

Tissot, Samuel Auguste, *De la Santé des gens des lettres* (Lausanne, Francois Graiset, [1766] 1768).

Tissot, S.A., *An Essay on Diseases Incidental to Literary and Sedentary Persons. With Proper Rules for Preventing their fatal Consequences and Instructions for their Care* (London, Edward & Charles Dilly, 1768).

Tissot, S.A., *A Treatise on the Diseases Incident to Literary and Sedentary*

Persons. Transcribed from the last French Edition. With Notes, by a Physician (London and Edinburgh, A. Donaldson, 1771).

Todorov, Tsven, *Littérature et la signification* (Paris, Larousse, Paris).

Uglow, Jenny, *Elizabeth Gaskell. A Habit of Stories* (London, Faber & Faber, 1993).

Vico, Giambattista, *The New Science of Giambattista Vico*, trans. Thomas Goddard Bergin and Max Harold Fisch (New York, Doubleday, [1744] 1961).

Viallaneix, Paul, 'Michelet: Le Magistère de l'Historien', *Le Histoire au XIXe siécle. Cahiers de l'Association internationale des études françaises*, 47 (1995).

Vincent, David, *Bread, Knowledge and Freedom. A Study of Nineteenth-century Working-class Autobiography* (London, Methuen, 1981).

Vovelle, Michel, 'La Marseillaise. La guerre ou la paix', in Pierre Nora, *Les Lieux de mémoire sous la direction de Pierre Nora. I. La République* (Paris, Gallimard, 1984).

Walker, K., 'Starting With Rag Rugs. The Aesthetics of Survival', in G. Elinor *et al.*, *Women and Craft* (London, Virago, 1987).

Watchel, N., 'Memory and History', *History and Anthropology*, 2 (1986).

Watson, Nicola, *Revolution and the Form of the British Novel, 1790–1825. Intercepted Letters, Interrupted Seductions* (Oxford, Clarendon Press, 1994).

Watt, Alexander, *The Art of Leather Manufacture, being a Practical Handbook* (London, Crosby Lockwood, 1885).

Watt, Ian, *The Rise of the Novel* (London, Chatto & Windus, 1957).

Webb, Sidney and Beatrice, *English Local Government. Volume 1. The Parish and the County* (London, Cass, [1906] 1963).

White, Hayden, *Metahistory. The Historical Imagination in Nineteenth-century Europe* (Baltimore and London, Johns Hopkins University Press, 1973).

White, Hayden, 'The Question of Narrative in Contemporary Historical Theory', *History and Theory*, 23 (1984).

White Hayden, '"Figuring the Nature of Times Decesed"', in *The Content of the Form. Narrative Discourse and Historical Representation* (Baltimore, Johns Hopkins University Press, 1987).

Williams, Raymond, *The Country and the City* (St Albans, Paladin, 1975).

Williams, Thomas Waller, *The Whole Law Relative to the Duty Office of a*

Justice of the Peace, 4 vols, (London, John Stockdale, 1812).

Wilson, Edmund, *To the Finland Station. A Study in the Writing and Acting of History* (New York, Doubleday, [1940] 1953).

Winnicott, D.W., 'The Capacity to Be Alone', in *The Maturational Process and the Facilitating Environment* (London, The Hogarth Press, [1958] 1965).

Winnicott, D.W., 'Transitional Objects and Transitional Phenomena', 'Playing: A Theoretical Statement', 'The Location of Cultural Experience', and 'The Place Where We Live' in *Playing and Reality* (Harmondsworth, Penguin, [1971] 1974).

Winnicott, D.W., *Playing and Reality* (Harmondsworth, Penguin, [1971] 1974).

Wolff, Janet, 'The Invisible *Flâneuse*: Women and the Literature of Modernity', in Andrew Benjamin (ed.), *The Problems of Modernity. Adorno and Benjamin* (London, Routledge, 1991).

Wright, Wilmer C., *De morbis artificum diatriba. Diseases of Workers. The Latin Text of 1713, revised, with translation and notes by Wilmer Cave Wright* (Chicago, University of Chicago Press, 1940).

Yerushalmi, Yosef Hayim, *Freud's Moses. Judaism Terminable and Interminable* (New York, Yale University Press, 1991).

Young, Arthur, *A Six Months Tour through the North of England*, 4 vols (London, W. Strahan, [1770] 1771).

Zouch, Henry, *Hints Respecting the Public Police, Published at the Request of the Court of Quarter Sessions held at Pontefract, April 24, 1786* (London, John Stockdale, 1786).

Index

Anderson, Benedict, 38, 147
anthrax, 23–5, 28–9, 161
'Archive Fever' (Derrida), 1–12,
    67–8, 146, 152
Arnold, Matthew, 105–6
Auden, W.H., 112, 134–5, 142, 145
autobiographical writing, 54–6,
    76, 147

Bachelard, Gaston, 79–81, 113,
    120–5
Bann, Stephen, 72, 76
Barthes, Roland, 27–8, 163
bastardy examinations, 46–7
Benjamin, Walter, 135
Berkhofer, Robert F., 146
biography, 149–50
Blackstone, William, 42
Blackwood, John, 95
Blount, George, 47
books, hazards associated with,
    22–4
bourgeois society, 91
brain fever, 21–2, 28
Brandreth, Jeremiah, 101–2
Burchell, Joseph, 50

Burn, Richard, 49
Burnett, Frances Hodgson,
    125–7
Burnett, John, 121
Burney, Fanny, 29–30
Burnouf, Eugène, 10, 42, 49
Burton, Antoinette, 2–3, 5
Butler, John, 47
byssinosis, 20

Carlyle, Thomas, 101–2
Carr, David, 143–4, 149
carte-postale concept, 151
Catacombs of Paris, 162
cerebritis, 22
Clifton, Sir Gervase, 43–4, 47
Cobb, Richard, 72–3, 81
common law, 42
Const, Francis, 50
Corbin, Alain, 117–18
cotton industry, 129–31
county record offices, 28
Coventry, 89–90, 97, 100
Coventry Herald, 100–1, 103
Crowell, Ivan, 132
Cumberland, Sarah, 43–5

Cyclopaedia of Practical Medicine, 20

Davaine, Casimir, 24
Derrida, Jacques, 1–6, 10–12, 31, 39–40, 44, 67, 83, 146, 151–2
Dewald, Carolyn, 94
diachronicity, 152
Dickens, Charles, 78, 115, 157–63, 167
Douglas, Lorimer, 52
Draper, George William, 163–4
dust, 20–7, 152, 157–64
   dual meaning of verb, 160–1
   philosophy of, 165–6

Eagleton, Terry, 74
Edzard, Christine, 78
Eliot, George, 89–108
Evans, Mary Ann, 89, 100, 103, 108
   see also Eliot, George
Eyles, Leonora, 116–17

Ferguson, Adam, 103
Fielding, Henry, 150–1
Fifoot, Cecil, 49
Flint, Kate, 161
Forbes, John, 20–2
Foucault, Michel, 2, 66–7
French Revolution, 40, 101, 161–2
Freud, Sigmund, 2–12 *passim*, 67–8, 76, 160, 165

Gaskell, Elizabeth, 112–14, 122–7, 133–6
Gauldie, Enid, 121

Gill, Stephen, 157
Gisborne, Thomas, 44
Grand Ordinance Criminelle, 41
Guizot, François Pierre, 103
Gurney, W.B., 102

Hegel, Georg Wilhelm Friedrich, 103
heritage industry, 78–9
Herodotus, 92–4, 108
historical novels, 89–91
history as an academic subject, 66–7
Hoggart, Richard, 114–17, 129, 132
Holyday, Samuel, 46
Howe, Charlotte, 51–7

identity, 76–7
Io, abduction of, 93–4

James, Henry, 89
Johnson, Douglas, 72
Judaism, 3–4, 7, 9
justices of the peace, 42–5

Koch, Robert, 24

Lancashire, 129, 132
Langlois, Claude, 148
Laplanche, Jean, 77
law, 42
   see also Poor Laws and poor relief
Le Goff, Jacques, 66
leather and leather-working, 23–6
Lefebvre, Georges, 72

Lemire, Beverly, 132
Leslie, Esther, 135
letters as historical documents,
    74–5
Lévi-Strauss, Claude, 123
Lewes, George Henry, 89, 94,
    103–4
'linguistic turn' in historical
    studies, 143, 145
littleness, theories of, 123–4
London Society for the
    Encouragement of Honest
    and Industrious Servants, 48
Lowe, Donald, 91

McMillan, Margaret, 118–19
Mal d'archive (Derrida) see
    'Archive Fever'
Manchester, 129
Mandelbaum, Maurice, 153
Mansfield, Lord, 48–53
Manton, Mary, 46, 48
Maria Theresa of Austria, 69
Marseillaise, the, 161–2
Marx, Karl, 157
Mary Barton, 112–15, 121–4,
    128–36
Mason, Michael, 93–4
Mayhew, Henry, 47, 115–16,
    119–20, 124, 132, 158–61,
    166, 168
Maza, Sarah, 56
meningitis, 21–2, 28–9
metonymy, 124–5
Michelet, Jules, 17, 26–9, 38–40,
    42, 69–72, 81, 103–4, 150–2,
    161–4, 167

micro-history, 79
Middlemarch, 89–108
migraine, 27
Millar, James, 103
Mink, Louis, 143–4, 147, 149
Mitzman, Arthur, 71
Mnemosyne myth, 66
'molecular' vision, 79
Moretti, Franco, 147, 166–7
Mulhern, Francis, 106

Napoleonic criminal codes, 41
National Archives of France, 69
Neufeldt, V.A., 101–2
The Newgate Calendar, 54
Norris, Cristopher, 152–3

object-relations theory, 82, 135
occupational disease, 19–21
Oldham, 129
Oliver, Thomas, 21
Our Mutual Friend, 115, 157–9,
    162, 167–8
overcrowding, 121
overseers of the poor, 49

Page, Henry, 43
paper-making, 19–20, 23, 130–1,
    157, 165
Paris, 162–3
parliamentary franchise, 97–8, 105
Parry, Leonard, 21
Pasteur, Louis, 24
Pentridge Rising, 101–2
'The People's History', 54
Peter the Great, 69
petty sessions, 45

Poe, Edgar Allan, 151
Poor Laws and poor relief, 41–2,
    48–9, 52–3
potential space, 82–3
Pratt, J.C., 101–2
Prentice, Archibald, 101
psycho-analysis, 3–9, 77
Public Record Office, 28–9, 69

quarter sessions, 45

Rancière, Jacques, 146, 151
Ranke, Leopold von, 11–12
Rayner, Pierre, 24
revisionist history, 8
Ricoeur, Paul, 144–5, 149
Robbins, Bruce, 55
Roberts, Elizabeth, 132
Roman Law, 42
Romola, 104
Rubinstein, David, 118

Samuel, Raphael, 78–9
Savoy, House of, 69
Saxby, Mary, 54–5
'scientific' history, 9–10
Scott, Walter, 90–1
second-hand clothes trade, 132
Seignobos, Charles, 148
settlement cases, 49–54
Smith, Adam, 103
Smith, Bonnie, 10
Snell, Keith, 45
social history, 3, 70, 103, 150–1
Spectator, 94

statute law, 42
Stewart, Susan, 123–4
Stoler, Ann Laura, 4
Sutherland, John, 99

Thackrah, Charles, 20, 22–4
Thompson, Edward, 98, 101–2,
    106–7
Thrale, Hester, 29–31
time-consciousness, 144
Times, The, 100, 131
topoanalysis, 79, 120
trades unions, 21

Vico, Giambattista, 26, 69–70,
    103–4, 107

Ward, Philip, 43–4, 150
Warwickshire, 89–90
waste, principle of, 166–7
Waverley, 90–1
Wells, Elizabeth, 47
White, Hayden, 11, 143–4, 149,
    153
Wilkinson, John, 47
Wilson, Edmund, 70, 72
Winnicott, D.W., 81–2
working-class consciousness, 98,
    102–5

Yerushalmi, Yosef Hayim, 3–4,
    9
Young, Arthur, 129

zymotic theory, 161